The life of Mendelssohn

Musical lives

Each book in this series describes the life
and music of a major composer, revealing
the private as well as the public figure. While
the main thread is biographical, the music
appears as an integral part of the narrative,
each volume thus presenting an organic view
of the composer, the music and the circumstances in which the music was written.

Published titles

The life of Mendelssohn

PETER MERCER-TAYLOR

CAMBRIDGE
UNIVERSITY PRESS

PUBLISHED BY THE PRESS SYNDICATE OF THE UNIVERSITY OF CAMBRIDGE
The Pitt Building, Trumpington Street, Cambridge, United Kingdom

CAMBRIDGE UNIVERSITY PRESS
The Edinburgh Building, Cambridge CB2 2RU, UK   www.cup.cam.ac.uk
40 West 20th Street, New York, NY 10011–4211, USA   www.cup.org
10 Stamford Road, Oakleigh, Melbourne 3166, Australia
Ruiz de Alarcón 13, 28014, Madrid, Spain

First published 2000

Printed in the United Kingdom at the University Press, Cambridge

Typeset in FF Quadraat 9.75/14 pt, in QuarkXPress™ [SE]

A catalogue record for this book is available from the British Library

Library of Congress cataloguing in publication data
Mercer-Taylor, Peter Jameson.
The life of Mendelssohn / Peter Mercer-Taylor.
    p.   cm. – (Musical lives)
Includes bibliographical references (p.) and index.
ISBN 0 521 63025 8 (hardback); 0 521 63972 7 (paperback)
1. Mendelssohn-Bartholdy, Felix, 1809–1847. 2. Composers – Germany – Biography.
I. Title. II. Series.
ML410.M5 M66 2000
780'.92–dc21
[B]   99-058441
ISBN 0 521 63025 8   hardback
ISBN 0 521 63972 7   paperback

CONTENTS

ILLUSTRATIONS

18 Mendelssohn on his deathbed, drawn by his friend Eduard
    Bendemann 206

Sources

Grateful acknowledgement is made for the use of illustrations from the
following sources:

Bildarchiv Preussischer Kulturbesitz, Berlin (1, 5); Staatsbibliothek zu
Berlin – Preußischer Kulturbesitz, Musikabteilung mit Mendelssohn-
Archiv (2, 4, 8, 10, 11, 13, 18); Landesbildstelle, Berlin (3); Rare Book,
Manuscript, & Special Collections Library, Duke University (9);
Stadtgeschichtliches Museum, Leipzig (12); The Mansell Collection,
Time-Life Syndication (14); Bodleian Library, University of Oxford (16)

ACKNOWLEDGEMENTS

Much of my own thinking about Felix Mendelssohn and his music took shape in the course of conversations with Joseph Kerman, Anthony Newcomb and Stephen Rumph, and it is to them that my first thanks go. Like all Mendelssohn scholars of the last two decades, I owe an immeasurable debt to the work of R. Larry Todd, whose exhaustive acquaintance with the documentary material surrounding Mendelssohn's life has underpinned an immense body of scholarship as distinguished by its thoughtfulness and grace as by its methodological rigour. The work of a rising generation of scholars – Greg Vitercik, John Michael Cooper, Marian Wilson Kimber and Steven Lindeman deserve special mention – has also been an inspiration and model.

Work on this project was furthered by the generous financial support of the Valparaiso University Committee on Creative Work and Research. Among my many colleagues at Valparaiso University who have contributed to the completion of this book, I must first name Colleen Seguin, a tireless and insightful editor without whose meticulous attention to the first draft the whole would have turned out much the worse. Mark Schwehn has remained, throughout, a mentor in the richest sense of the term. My task was made easier in countless ways by the efforts of the Interlibrary Loan and Reference staffs at Valparaiso University's Moellering Library, particularly Susan Wanat. Thanks to Penny Souster at Cambridge University Press for her support of the project at every stage along the way, and to Ann Lewis, as searching and diligent an editor as one could hope for.

I am grateful to my children, David, Katie and Andrew, for keeping it all in perspective. Greater still is my debt to my wife, Beth, without whose manifold shows of support this project would have been unthinkable.

1 Beginnings

What a history! – A fugitive from Egypt and Palestine, here I am and find help, love, fostering in you people. With real rapture I think of these origins of mine and this whole nexus of destiny, through which the oldest memories of the human race stand side by side with the latest developments.

Rahel Varnhagen on her deathbed, 1833[1]

Towards the end of the Gregorian Calendar's year 1811, a young Jewish couple, Lea and Abraham Mendelssohn, left the city of Hamburg with their three children and a sizeable sum of money. They fled in disguise at night, knowing that, had the French authorities seen fit to detain them and had recognised Abraham for who he was, the whole destiny of their growing family might be thrown into question. Their oldest child, Fanny, was seven at the time, the youngest, Rebecka, only a few months. Between these was the two-year-old Felix.

Abraham, like many Hamburg bankers and business people, had made a small fortune underwriting the traffic of contraband through the port city, defying the trade blockade through which Napoleon had sought, since 1806, to cripple the English economy. In 1811, with the terrifying results of increased French military presence attending the arrival of Marshal Louis Davôust, many came to sense that the rewards no longer outweighed the risks. Luckier than many, the Mendelssohns escaped without incident. Their arrival in Berlin signalled the beginning of a happy, prosperous period for the family that would not end until the deaths of the two oldest children – Fanny and Felix – within a few months of each other in 1847.

The sketchy familial records of the flight from Hamburg leave no indication how much Fanny – much less Felix – understood about the dangers of the trip they were undertaking. But the whole passage must have been surrounded with a sense of grand adventure similar to that surrounding the trip that their paternal grandfather, Moses, had made to Berlin almost seventy years before. His circumstances, however, could not have been more different. The fourteen-year-old Moses made the eighty-mile trip from his hometown of Dessau on foot, with few prospects and, as the story goes, only a single gold ducat to his name. His intelligence and passion for learning were his sole resources. Abraham's family, by contrast, arrived with considerable means, seeking a stable economic and social environment within which to further their financial prosperity, to educate their children, and to enjoy a fuller civic integration than even their fortunate forebears had. Where Moses had headed straight to Berlin's Jewish ghetto – the only conceivable destination for an impoverished Jew – Abraham and his family moved within a few years into one of the city's finest residences. For Moses, Berlin was a city of strangers, with the exception of the teacher he had followed there. By 1811, members of Abraham and Lea's families had been established and respected figures in the community for decades. Within two years of their arrival, Abraham had become a member of Berlin's town council (though not its first Jewish member; David Friedländer had enjoyed that distinction); the Mendelssohn home, around the figure of the gifted, superbly educated Lea, became a regular meeting place for Prussia's leading intellectual and cultural figures. In Lea and Abraham's harrowing flight from Hamburg to Berlin – from a position of fear and instability to one of security and prosperity, from a fast-paced port city to Prussia's conservative heart – we may perceive an encapsulation of their families' generation-spanning quest, along with countless German Jews, for self-actualisation and social acceptance. For Abraham's family, this quest had begun with Moses' decision, in October 1743, to set out for the Prussian capital.

The driving cliché of Felix Mendelssohn biographies since his own lifetime has been his life's almost total lack of conflict or adversity. He was born into circumstances as comfortable as almost any German citizen, and in such circumstances he remained for his entire life. But if Felix's life story in no way represents a struggle with adversity, it is no less crucial to recognise in it the consequences of such a struggle, one that had gone on for two generations.

It is impossible to gauge the accuracy of the quotation at the beginning of this chapter. These words were ostensibly pronounced by Rahel Varnhagen – the pole-star of Berlin salon culture at its height, who was considered by many intellectuals and dignitaries 'the greatest woman on earth' – on her deathbed.[2] They were recorded after her death by Rahel's husband, Karl August Varnhagen von Ense (a Christian by birth). But however literally authentic these words may be, they ascribe to Rahel a psychological point of arrival that affirms a *telos* of happy, unproblematic assimilation. The familiar story of the life of Felix's grandfather, Moses, doubtless contains elements of mythology, most of its known details not committed to paper until after his death (his own humility was no help in the matter: 'My biographical data', he wrote by way of preface to the scantiest of autobiographical sketches, 'have actually always seemed so unimportant to me that I never bothered to keep a record of them'[3]). But Moses' life story remains one of the most important biographical narratives of the Jewish emancipation, and in this sense a critical point of reference for understanding the motivations, desires and fears that shaped the Mendelssohn family's experience throughout the beginning of the nineteenth century. Crucial to an understanding of the exuberance with which Felix's parents embraced the cultural and intellectual possibilities inherent in their financial advantages was the knowledge that these advantages were hard fought, and unthinkable a few decades before.

★

On Elul 12, 5489 – the day the Christians called 6 September 1729 – Felix's grandfather, Moses Dessau, was born in the town from which he would take his name, a town whose population of 9,500 included around 150 Jewish families. His mother, Sarah Bela Rahel, was the daughter of one of Dessau's most distinguished Jewish families, claiming among her ancestors the famous – indeed, semi-legendary – Saul Wahl, said to have ruled as King of Poland for a single night. Moses' father, Menahem Mendel, was a minor official in the Synagogue. By the end of his career, he had risen to the position of teacher and scribe, which brought with it a good deal more respect than money. It was from Menahem that Moses received his earliest education and, we may assume, his life-long passion for the written word. After he had mastered the basics of Hebrew script, Moses' education was entrusted to the Beth Hamidrash, the school whose field of enquiry was limited to the Talmud and its commentaries. As a foil to the dry arcana of these studies, Moses was drawn by his own passion and curiosity to the Bible. Reports of his prodigious capacity for memorising lengthy passages of the Hebrew Scripture would reverberate, two generations later, through the preternatural feats of musical memorisation ascribed to his grandchildren, Fanny and Felix.

Around the age of thirteen, Moses came across a work which proved pivotal to the development of his young mind, Moses Maimonides' *More Nevukhhim*, the *Guide of the Perplexed*. Completed in 1190, this challenging volume – intended, as its author indicates, for 'thinkers whose studies have brought them into collision with religion'[4] – confronted openly the difficulties of reconciling reason and faith. A ban set forth in 1305 had forbidden the reading of this book by anyone under the age of twenty-five. While Moses consumed Maimonides' text voraciously, this transgression was not without its consequences. It was at about this time that he contracted a severe illness, probably a tubercular infection, which resulted in lifelong spinal curvature. 'Maimon', he would later recall, 'weakened my body but invigorated my soul'.

Moses was soon hit with a second blow: his teacher, R. David

Fränkel, had been summoned to Berlin to serve as Chief Rabbi. A strict disciplinarian and a scholar of legendary energy – his students recalled that he often arose at midnight to work on his path-breaking commentary on the Jerusalem Talmud – Fränkel was admired and beloved by his students, in whose well-being he took the keenest interest. As sad as the departure of his teacher might be in itself, Moses also had practical matters to consider: having recently undergone his bar-mitzvah, he was expected to begin earning a living. Without trade, skill or family money, the most likely course ahead was the life of a pedlar. With this depressing prospect in view, Moses set about persuading his family to allow him to follow Fränkel to Berlin to continue his studies. After lengthy negotiations – some reports say four months' worth – they agreed.

In the autumn of 1743, as we have seen, the young Moses arrived in Berlin. He probably paid his *Liebzahl*, the 'body tax' required of all Jews crossing a frontier or entering a city, and received his paper *Passierscheine* ('pass') authorising his presence in the city. From here, he sought out the squalid blocks that were home to the great bulk of the city's Jewish population. Though not the gated, physically isolated ghetto that Jews had occupied prior to their expulsion in 1572, the new Jewish settlement – a region between the Spree and the Neue Friedrichstrasse which actually overlapped with the parishes of several Christian churches – was still crowded and disease-ridden.[5]

Fränkel did all he could to sustain the boy; he found dwelling for Moses in an attic room of a merchant, Hayyim Bamberg, and paid him what little he could to copy his own scholarly work. Apart from the free weekly meals that certain charitable Jewish families offered students, Moses' diet for each week of the next several years, so the story goes, consisted of a single loaf of bread, which he would notch into daily portions at the beginning of the week.

Through these years, Moses continued his religious studies with Fränkel with unchecked enthusiasm. But the same hunger for knowledge that had led him to the Bible in earlier years drove him, through his student days in Berlin, towards vast realms of European secular

1 The Mühlendamm, Berlin, viewed from the Molkenmarkt, with Veitel Heine Ephraim's Palais on the right: steel engraving by Finden after a drawing by Stock

culture – literature, philosophy, science and mathematics – far beyond those permitted by local Jewish authorities. If the physical lines circumscribing the Jews' permissible places of residence were drawn from without, the religious, intellectual and cultural lines that separated the beleaguered Jewish community from the Christian world were drawn, and drawn firmly, from within. At stake was the community's very self-definition. Nonetheless, in private hours in his garret, Moses sailed far beyond the intellectual horizon of the ghetto, taking up a dual residency, as it were, in his Jewish surroundings and in the European intellectual tradition that was, for most Jews, a closed book.

At this time, Germany's Jewish children were, by and large, taught only Yiddish, rarely the native tongue of the surrounding city. This was the first frontier into which Moses set forth: having picked up a bit of German from Rabbi Fränkel, he worked his tireless way through a tome of Protestant historical theology, Gustav Reinbeck's *Betrachtungen über die Augsburgische Confession*, which had happened to fall into his hands. Though he had soon mastered the language and begun to reap the rich rewards of his labour, he was not ignorant of the attendant risks. He was helpless to intervene when a boy three years younger than himself, whom Moses had been tutoring, was caught by the Jewish authorities with a German book he had been fetching for Moses. The younger boy was ejected from the city.

Word spread around the Jewish community of the brilliant young scholar, whose physical infirmity – his hunched back and the stammer he had had since youth – only added to his fascination. A number of gifted, sympathetic allies soon fell across his path. He found a tutor in logic, geometry and medieval Jewish philosophy (Maimonides was still an important presence) in the philosopher/ mathematician Israel Samoscz, recently driven out of Poland for his progressive religious ideas. Abraham Kisch, the well-educated product of a wealthy Prague family, gave him his first lessons in Latin. Around his seventeenth year, Moses attracted the attention of another young man, six years his senior, who was to prove pivotal not only in his education, but in drawing Mendelssohn into the mainstream of Berlin's cultural affairs. Aron Salomon Gumpertz – an aspiring student of the Humanities who would end up in medical school at the University of Frankfurt-an-der-Oder – was the scion of a wealthy Jewish Berlin family. He not only opened to Moses the French and English languages, but made available to him works by the leading philosophers of the time, Leibniz and Wolff, and discreetly invited Moses into a group of philosophically minded masters and pupils at a Gentile public school.

In his twenty-first year, Mendelssohn was offered a position as tutor to the children of the wealthy Jewish silk manufacturer Isaac Bernhard, a post which allowed him to reap a modicum of financial stability from his intellectual achievements. An equally important benefit of Mendelssohn's new position was the fact that, as an employee of a *Schutzjude*, he was relieved of the constant fear of expulsion from the city. He would not receive his own *Schutzbrief* (letter of protection) until 1763. (In supporting Mendelssohn's appeal for protection, the Marquis d'Argens – who had come to know and admire Mendelssohn – wrote to King Friedrich: 'A philosopher who is a bad Catholic hereby begs a philosopher who is a bad Protestant to grant a favour to a philosopher who is a bad Jew. There's too much philosophy involved in all of this for reason not to side with my request.'[6]) And the granting of Mendelssohn's own *Schutzbrief* was itself only a limited victory. In a charter of 1750, Friedrich had placed restrictions on, among other things, the lot of many *Schutzjuden*, distinguishing a class of 'irregular' protected Jews who did not pass their privilege on to their children. This was the class Mendelssohn joined in 1763, his children remaining unprotected until 1787, the year after his – and, more to the point, Friedrich's – death.

Four years after Mendelssohn took the post of tutor in the Bernhard home, as the children outgrew the need for his services, Isaac Bernhard was sufficiently impressed by the young man to entrust to him the post of book-keeper and correspondent in the family silk factory. This institution was to provide Mendelssohn with financial stability for the rest of his life. He became the factory's manager upon Bernhard's retirement, entering into a full partnership, after Bernhard's death, with his widow. Though Mendelssohn occasionally lamented the stifling drudgery of his business affairs – 'A good book-keeper', he wrote in 1758, '. . . should be given a medal for divesting himself of his mind, wit, and all emotion, turning himself into a clod so as to keep his books in order'[7] – he was well aware that his lot might have been immeasurably worse.

By the time Mendelssohn took up this post, his friend and former tutor, Gumpertz, had become secretary to the Marquis d'Argent, whose influence, as a close associate of Friedrich the Great, on Mendelssohn's behalf we have already seen. Under Gumpertz's guidance, Mendelssohn found himself moving in Berlin's highest intellectual and cultural circles, through which his reputation spread quickly. It was during this time that he made what was perhaps his closest lifelong friendship, with critic and playwright Gotthold Ephraim Lessing. Lessing's early comedy, *The Jews*, had just appeared, its brilliant and morally upstanding protagonist probably based on Gumpertz himself. Years later, Lessing would immortalise his friend Mendelssohn, too, in the title character of his play, *Nathan the Wise*, an articulate, powerful dramatic plea for religious toleration.

In 1755, Lessing edited and published Mendelssohn's *Philosophical Conversations* (*Philosophische Gespräche*), a dialogue between two friends on various philosophical matters. Later that year came Mendelssohn's contribution to the newly formed discipline of aesthetics, *Letters on the Sentiments* (*Briefe über die Empfindungen*), whose 'language of the heart' critics praised at once. Though both of these works were published anonymously, and Mendelssohn's footing in the German language was not yet sure enough to move without Lessing's close editorial guidance, the *Letters on the Sentiments* earned its author a solid position in German letters. In the years that followed, Mendelssohn, Lessing and publisher Friedrich Nicolai became important critical proponents of German literature, denouncing the pervasive French dominance that found its wellspring in the royal court itself. In their journal *Literaturbriefe*, Mendelssohn even went so far as to publish a Germanophilic critique of a volume of Friedrich the Great's own collected verse, *Poésies diverses*. In his successful defence against the inevitable trouble that followed – a denouncement by Johann Gottlieb Heinrich von Justi, a founder of German political science, prompted a brief ban of the *Literaturbriefe* – Mendelssohn is said to have written, with characteristic deftness and tact, that 'Writing poetry is like bowling, in that whoever bowls, whether king or peasant, must have the pinboy tell him his score'.

In 1762, with his fame spreading quickly and his financial circumstances relatively secure, the thirty-two-year-old Mendelssohn met the woman he would fall in love with and marry. Fromet Gugenheim, the daughter of a Hamburg merchant whose once-prosperous family had fallen on hard times, was a friend of both Gumpertz's fiancée and one of the Bernhard daughters. Initially shocked by Moses' ugliness, Fromet is said to have been won over by an encounter which, though impossible to document, is emblematic of the sensitivity and prodigious cleverness ascribed to Mendelssohn in the many stories around which his semi-mythical persona was crystallising. Sensing her repulsion at his physical appearance, the story goes, Mendelssohn turned the conversation to the question of whether marriage partners were fore-ordained in heaven:

> When I was born, my future wife was also named, but at the same time it was said, Alas! she will have a dreadful humpback. O God, I said then, a deformed girl will become embittered and unhappy, whereas she should be beautiful. Dear Lord, give me the humpback, and let the maiden be well made and agreeable![8]

Fromet embraced Mendelssohn, and the engagement was soon announced.

The pair were married that June, and appear to have enjoyed an agreeable life together. The Bernhards insisted on underwriting the decoration of the couple's new house on Spandau Street, in which the Mendelssohns would spend the entirety of their married life. Of eight children, six survived to adulthood, including three daughters – Brendel (later Dorothea), Recha, and Henriette – and three sons – Joseph, Abraham and Nathan.

The Mendelssohns' house soon came to be known for regular evening gatherings that formed a nexus of the city's intellectual activities. Berlin's most distinguished citizenry could be found side by side with impoverished students or travellers eager for a look at the famous 'Jew of Berlin'. Though Moses, contemporaries recall, often said little at these gatherings, his contributions were judicious and compassionate when they came.

Mendelssohn's international reputation was secured once and for all with the 1767 publication of his *Phaidon or On Immortality, in three dialogues*. Moving from a partial translation of Plato's *Phaedo* into Mendelssohn's own meditations, *Phaidon* captivated its initial audience both through its considerable literary beauty and its effort to reconstitute traditional religious certainties through the very philosophical language whose stark rationality had threatened to bankrupt them. *Phaidon* became one of the most widely read books of its time, soon translated into every major European language. Proclaimed the 'German Socrates', Mendelssohn secured at a stroke a reputation as one of the leading philosophical minds of his generation.

Throughout this time, Mendelssohn had struggled to distance his intellectual life from his religious one. Though it was perhaps inevitable that his religion should ultimately be brought into a public forum, the transition might have been a smoother one. The catalyst for this transition came in the person of Johann Caspar Lavater, the young Zürich deacon known both as a tireless Christian proselytiser and as the inventor of the science of phrenology. Lavater had admired Moses for years, having visited the Mendelssohns' home for the first time in 1763. Six years later, he dedicated his German translation of Charles Bonnet's *Palingénésie philosophique* – an apologia for the revelatory foundations of Christian dogma – to Mendelssohn, proclaiming that Moses should either embrace Christianity or publicly refute it.

Mendelssohn published a quiet, dignified response, assuring his Christian interlocutor that he would have abandoned Judaism long before if he were not fully convinced of its truth. At the same time he adumbrated the underpinnings of an argument for religious tolerance that would strongly inform his later writings, claiming that the religious laws of Judaism, though strictly binding for the Jew, did not apply to others, and that the essential doctrines of his faith were demonstrably universal in their validity:

> Why should I convert a Confucius or a Solon? As he does not belong to the Congregation of Jacob, my religious laws do not apply to him; and on doctrines, we should soon come to an understanding. Do I think there is a chance of his being saved? I certainly believe that he who leads mankind on to virtue in this world cannot be damned in the next.[9]

Lavater replied with contrition, and further exchanges between the two authors were conciliatory. But the controversy left in its wake a flurry of pamphlets and editorials on the issue of Judaism which placed Mendelssohn, clearly the moral victor, at centre stage.

The strain of the whole experience proved too much for Mendelssohn's frail, nervous constitution. Writing and reading now brought on blackouts and fits of dizziness. Over the seven years that followed, Mendelssohn withdrew from public affairs almost entirely, reading and producing little. His grandson, Felix, inherited Moses' constitution, and was suffering similar complaints at an even younger age. Had Felix responded as Moses did – and he contemplated similar measures – his life would almost certainly have been a good deal longer.

Upon re-entry into public life, Mendelssohn seems to have recognised that, for better or worse, his position in Europe's public affairs brought with it an obligation to play his part in bettering the lot of the Jewish people, a task he pursued diligently for the remainder of his life. He soon proved himself, among other things, an articulate and effective intercessor on behalf of Jewish communities throughout Europe threatened with persecution or expulsion. An important

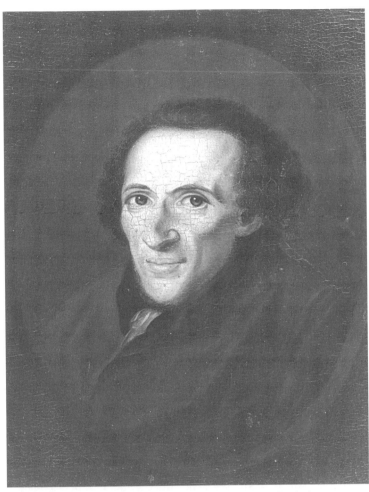

2 Moses Mendelssohn, 1786: oil on wood by Johann Christoph Frisch

testament to the heightened profile – largely due to Mendelssohn's influence – of the Jewish plight in public discourse was the appearance of Christian Wilhelm Dohm's *Upon the Civil Amelioration of the Jews* in 1781. This work seems to have been composed in response to Mendelssohn's request that Dohm, a twenty-nine-year-old Christian admirer of Mendelssohn, intercede with Louis XVI on behalf of the bitterly oppressed Jews of Alsace.

Mendelssohn's own publications also displayed a new commitment to improving the lot of European Jewry. His 1778 condensation of the *Hoshen hamishpat*, the *Ritual Laws of the Jews*, helped to establish a new spirit of judicious mutual understanding between Jewish communities and the German authorities who monitored them. To the consternation of Jewish elders across the German-speaking world, Mendelssohn also undertook a new German translation of the Hebrew scriptures, completing – with a handful of assistants – the Pentateuch, Ecclesiastes, the Psalms and the Song of Solomon (the last only discovered among his papers after his death). The importance of the publication of Mendelssohn's Pentateuch to the generations that followed is inestimable, particularly in the role it played in bringing the German language into everyday Jewish life.

In 1783 Mendelssohn completed his most important philosophical work, *Jerusalem, or On Religious Power and Judaism*, a sustained explication of his decision to remain Jewish despite the apparent allure of Christianity on the one hand, and of atheistic rationality on the other. Immanuel Kant, whose *Critique of Pure Reason* had signalled the twilight of enlightenment philosophy, pronounced *Jerusalem* 'irrefutable', observing that Mendelssohn had 'demonstrated the necessity of unlimited freedom of conscience for every religion with such thoroughness and lucidity that, on our side, the Church too will have to consider how to sort out whatever can burden and press the conscience, which in the end must tend to unite man in respect of the essential points of religion'.

Jerusalem was to be the last major work Mendelssohn completed. He caught a chill on the last day of 1785, and died four days later of an apoplexy of the brain, mourned by the Jewish and gentile community alike. His intelligence, graciousness and dignity had abolished the perception of Jews as dishonest and uneducable by their very nature, prejudices on which the entire political and economic subjugation of European Jewry was based. At the same time, he had demonstrated to Jews themselves not only the feasibility of full engagement with the Christian world, but that assimilation into Christian society was not predicated on the dilution, much less the rejection, of one's faith.

The political ramifications of Mendelssohn's pleas for religious tolerance were immense, though more discernible outside of his native Prussia than within. The enlightened Emperor Joseph II was almost certainly influenced heavily by Dohm's *Upon the Civil Amelioration of the Jews* in his decision to issue the 'Toleranzpatent' of 1782, which brought about the gradual lifting of laws oppressing the Jews. Shortly after Mendelssohn's death, the French Count Honoré de Mirabeau expressed his deep respect for his life and work in the book, *Sur Moses Mendelssohn et sur la réforme politique des Juifs*. Mirabeau would prove instrumental in obtaining for the Jews the civil liberties which the French Revolution accomplished for the Christian populace, assured through a formal declaration by the French National Assembly on 27 September 1791. 'It is fortunate for us', Moses had once remarked, 'that no one can insist on the rights of man without at the same time espousing our own rights'.[10]

★

In the course of his life, Moses Mendelssohn had neither sought nor attained more than a modest living. But he had created for his children an environment in which it was possible for them to seek degrees of both financial empowerment and social status which Moses himself could hardly have dreamed of in his own youth. By the time of Fromet's death in 1812, she had watched her children take their places among the more affluent members of northern Europe's emerging middle class, while making inroads into Paris's and Berlin's most influential intellectual and cultural circles. Fromet and Moses had provided their children with the most thorough education their means could afford, including exposure to philosophy, literature, religion and mathematics, Moses himself playing an active role in the education of the two oldest, Brendel and Joseph. While the intelligence and prudence of the sons wrought tremendous financial gains in banking, it was the daughters of the family who succeeded in carrying on the spirit of their father's quiet conquest of the European cultural world, as members of a generation that radically redefined the possibilities of the female intellectual life. The heady vitality of the turn-of-the-century salon culture in which Moses' daughters immersed themselves would flow directly – if in more measured supply – into the childhood home of their nephew, Felix.

If Moses exercised a forward-looking even-handedness in his approach to his daughters' education, the same could not be said of his attitude towards their marriages. As tradition dictated, he had arranged marriages for two of his daughters, Brendel and Recha, though both would abandon these relationships; Henriette never married.

As if pressing to an extreme her father's struggle for tolerance and heightened freedoms for his co-religionists, Brendel's refusal to be governed by tradition extended to almost every aspect of her social, intellectual and religious life. Emblematic was her rejection of the very name her parents had given her in exchange for the more romantic 'Dorothea'. In spite of a physical plainness – 'There was nothing about Dorothea to entice one to sensuality', her friend Henrietta Herz reported – her forthright manner and staggering erudition won her friends among Berlin's intellectual elite. Soon after her marriage to the young banker, Simon Veit, in 1783, the twenty-year-old Dorothea took up her parents' practice of holding regular evening gatherings at her home, involving a loose and expanding circle of literary and intellectual acquaintances. About the same time, two of Dorothea's closest friends, Rahel Levin (later Varnhagen) and Henrietta Herz, also established salons. As the century neared its close, it was in the houses of these three young Jewish women that Berlin's most elevated conversations were carried out among philosophers, theologians and literati as diverse as Friedrich Schleiermacher, Johann Gottlieb Fichte, Friedrich and Wilhelm Schlegel, and Alexander and Wilhelm Humboldt (the last pair had been frequent visitors at Moses and Fromet's house, and would be well known in Abraham's).

It was the dubious charms of the younger Schlegel brother, Friedrich, that would finally draw Dorothea out of this tight-knit community – indeed, out of the fabric of her own family. By the time Dorothea and Friedrich met in 1789, it was patently clear that her husband Simon, though a gracious personality and a stalwart provider, was in no way equal to his wife in intellect or adventurousness. In the course of the decade that followed, members of their circle became aware that Dorothea had discovered both intellectual and physical satiety in the gifted, if undisciplined, Friedrich. When the situation was finally made known to Simon Veit, he not only agreed to free Dorothea from a marriage that must have come to seem burdensome to both of them, but granted her custody of their two sons, providing a modicum of financial support for their upkeep. Perhaps as a result of the general censure – the arrangement raised eyebrows even among their most liberal-minded friends – Dorothea and Friedrich left, yet unmarried, for Jena, where Friedrich had obtained a position as lecturer.

Through the years that followed, which appear to have been some of the happiest of her life, Dorothea established another thriving salon. While Friedrich's output remained erratic, Dorothea herself turned her hand with considerable success to literature and literary criticism. In answer to Friedrich's *Lucinde*, an uneven and shockingly immodest novelistic testament to their relationship, Dorothea produced her own novel, *Florentin* (a projected second volume was never published). This book received considerably greater acclaim from contemporary readers than Friedrich's work, and led to a string of translations, historical narratives and critical articles through which Dorothea sought to stabilise the family's always precarious financial situation.

If her family had been scandalised from the start by her union with Schlegel, they were dealt a second blow with Dorothea's decision to convert – as thousands of Jews did in the first years of the century – to Protestantism, thus removing a technical obstacle to her second marriage. Dorothea was the first member of her immediate family, though she would not be the last, to turn away from the injunction her father had set forth in *Jerusalem*: 'As long as we cannot demonstrate any authentic liberation from the Law, all our sophistries cannot free us from the strict obedience which we owe to the Law'. Her Protestant wedding to Schlegel took place in Paris, shortly after the couple's move there in 1804.

Dorothea and Friedrich's home soon came to house one of Paris's most celebrated salons, but the family's apparent contentment through the years that followed proved fragile. In 1808, the couple converted to Catholicism, leaving Paris for Cologne, then Cologne for Vienna, where Friedrich had secured a minor court position. Though Dorothea continued attending salons in Vienna, the humiliations of the Napoleonic Wars had dampened spirits in the city, and Friedrich and Dorothea's own best days seemed to be behind them. One source of solace for Dorothea through these years was watching her two sons establish considerable reputations in the art world, consolidating at the same time the family's total commitment to their new faith. As a member of the so-called 'Nazarenes' in Rome, Philipp came to be known as one of Germany's most important painters of New Testament imagery. After the 1829 death of Friedrich – who by then had become corpulent and, by many accounts, shiftless – Dorothea moved to Frankfurt to spend her last decade with Philipp. In the final years of her life, she would see a great deal of her nephew, Felix – who admired her – and the Frankfurt woman he married; Dorothea was the only member of Felix's family to attend his wedding in 1837. She died two years later, on 3 August 1839.

If it is possible to view Dorothea's turbulent life, particularly in retrospect, as a glamorous expression of a gifted, Romantic imagination, more glamorous still was the career of her younger sister, Henriette. Henriette, too, came to intellectual maturity in the Berlin salons, finding a lifelong friend and confidante in the brilliant Rahel Levin. Like her father, Henriette's first employment was as a tutor to the children of a wealthy Jewish family, an offer which took her to Vienna in 1799. She spent the first decade of the nineteenth century in Paris, where she took up residence with her brother, Abraham, who was working in a Jewish banking house called Fould's. In spare rooms of the Foulds' mansion, Henriette set up a school for girls, hosting, too, her own highly successful evening salon. As one might expect, conversation frequently consisted of delicate negotiations between French and German political perspectives, in which Henriette needed every ounce of the tact she had inherited from her father. Varnhagen von Ense, the diplomat who would later become Rahel Levin's husband, recalled fondly the attractions of this institution in 1810, describing its gracious leader in terms reminiscent of those through which many described her father:

> Although plain and slightly deformed, she was nevertheless attractive in appearance, at once gentle, firm, modest, and confident in her whole nature. She had a quick intelligence, wide knowledge, clear judgement, the most refined courtesy, and the choicest tact.
>
> She was well acquainted with the literature of Germany, France, and England, also to some extent of Italy, and spoke French and English like a native. Such qualities could not lack a noble circle of acquaintances, which, however, she sought to limit as much as possible, on account of the duties of her school. As long as Madame de Staël dared to remain in Paris, she came very often to Fräulein Mendelssohn's; so did Benjamin Constant. I first saw Madame de Constant at her house. Madame Fould, who occupied the house in front of the garden, sometimes took her guest to visit her pleasant neighbours. Spontini sat there with us for whole evenings in the moonlight meditating on new laurels to be added to those just won by his 'Vestale' . . .[11]

As distinguished a figure as Henriette had become by her thirty-sixth year, she could hardly have anticipated the opportunity that was to draw her away from this existence. In 1812, she accepted an offer to undertake the education of Fanny Sébastiani, the only daughter of the widowed Count Horace Sébastiani, a celebrated former general who had served under Napoleon, and would go on to become a marshal. Henriette would hold the post until Fanny's marriage thirteen years later.

Despite the splendour of her new lifestyle – she and Fanny scraped by, with the help of four servants, in the hotel next to the emperor's, with second-floor rooms overlooking the Champs Elysées – Henriette's move into the highest circles of the French establishment placed her in a slightly awkward position in her family. As we have seen, pressure from French forces during the occupation had forced Abraham, the sibling to whom Henriette had long been closest, out of Hamburg only a few months before she assumed this post. Years after Napoleon's defeat, Henriette actually found herself a close neighbour of Louis Davôust, under whose reign of terror Abraham and his family had fled. Henriette's peculiar drive to defend him encapsulates touchingly the paradoxes of her situation (calling to mind, perhaps, Hannah Arendt's famous remark on the 'banality of evil'):

> Marshal Davôust, his wife, who is the real organisational head of the house, and their children are with us every day. When he first heard my name, he asked General S., who happened to be with us, whether I had any relations at Hamburg, as he had known very worthy and well-respected people of the same name in that place . . . I cannot understand the political life of this man when I see him at home and with his children. He is as good a father as Abraham . . . I can explain the atrocities committed at Hamburg under his government only in one way. He seems to be very dull and ignorant. He is without influence in his own house, and I suppose was the same as commander: some miscreant acted in his place.

After Fanny's marriage to the Duke of Choiseul-Praslin, Henriette moved to Berlin, where she lived very comfortably on the 3,000 franc annuity offered as a pension by Sébastiani. She died there in 1831, not living long enough to witness the unhappy end met by her pupil in 1847. In one of the nineteenth century's most sensational news stories, Fanny was brutally murdered by her husband, who committed suicide in prison days before his trial.

Shortly after accepting the post in the Sébastiani household, Henriette – who had bitterly chastised Dorothea for her 1804 conversion – herself embraced the Catholic faith, a decision made easier by the recent death of her mother. Surely her father himself would have found it difficult to resist the simple word of thanks with which

Henriette began her last will and testament: 'As in these words I speak for the last time to my dear relations, I hereby thank them for all the aid and friendship they have shown me during my life, and especially for having in every way tolerated the exercise of my religion, and never having shown any hatred towards it'.

★

In 1803, Friedrich von Gentz remarked that 'The women are, . . . among the Jews, one hundred per cent better than the men'.[12] Though this pronouncement is doubtless extreme, it is not difficult to imagine that the more mundane professional paths chosen by Fromet and Moses' sons may have precluded their full development towards the intellectual vigour and sheer personal charisma of their sisters. Joseph, the oldest, was the only one of the boys old enough to receive tutoring from his father, though Moses was never convinced of his potential as a scholar. Despite a lifelong interest in the sciences, the great bulk of Joseph's energies were poured into the establishment and operation of a banking business, one which thrived under his leadership and remained in operation under the Mendelssohn name until the Second World War. The youngest son, Nathan, made a professional pursuit of his own early interest in the emerging fields of physics and mechanics, becoming a well-respected engineer and founding member of Berlin's Polytechnic Society.

At the age of twenty, the middle son, Abraham, took his first steps down the path his older brother had chosen, moving to Paris in 1797 to take up a junior position at the banking house of Fould's. Though the move took him away from his family – at least until Henriette's arrival four years later – Abraham found in urban, post-Revolutionary France a teeming environment in which he as a young Jew could enjoy, perhaps more fully than anywhere else in Europe, the freedoms promised by his father's legacy.

As pleased as Abraham was to share these happy surroundings with his sister in the first years of the new century, Henriette appears to have been instrumental in bringing into play the forces that would ultimately lead to his departure from Paris. She had become a close friend of Lea Solomon, a member of one of the wealthiest and most distinguished Jewish families in Europe. Lea's father was a Prussian court jeweller; her maternal grandfather, Daniel Itzig, was not only one of the richest men in Berlin but, as financial advisor to Friedrich II, one of the most influential. It soon occurred to Henriette that this charming, educated woman would make a fine sister-in-law.

If Henriette and Abraham's family had gained entry into Germany's cultural mainstream through their father's intellectual achievements, Lea's family took a more established route. The 'court Jew' had been an accepted part of aristocratic life since the Middle Ages. Though the rights of even the most well-placed Jews remained limited and their position precarious, Jews were depended upon for the provision of ready capital, the acquisition of choice imported goods, or the execution of more delicate international missions, playing the role of trusted diplomats and advisors. Emblematic of both the potential glories and the potential dangers of such a lifestyle was the career of Joseph Süss Oppenheimer in the early decades of the eighteenth century, who would form the subject of the anti-Semitic Nazi film, *Jud Süss*. As Minister of Finance to the Duke of Württemberg, Oppenheimer proved visionary in the financial consolidation and administrative reorganisation of the court. But he made enemies along the way, and found himself utterly unprotected after the duke's death. In 1738 he was convicted of accepting bribes and summarily hanged. Happier were the increasingly common instances in which ties with a particular court were passed on for generations within a single family, an obvious aid to financial security and expansion. The Rothschilds were only the most famous family from the mid-eighteenth century to expand their interests into an international financial empire. In 1791, the Prussian court's decision to make Daniel Itzig Prussia's first Jewish citizen – with a patent of naturalisation whose rights extended to his family and his descendants – marked the beginning of a move from tolerance to acceptance, though it would be over twenty years before the same right was extended to Prussia's Jewry in general.

It is perhaps to Abraham's credit that he chose to propose to a woman whose education and intellectual subtlety more than rivalled his own. Lea's family spared no expense in the education of their children. By her early twenties, she drew and played the piano superbly, had mastered English, French and Italian, and had even taken to reading Homer in the original Greek. We catch a glimpse of the thoughtful, occasionally poetic imagination of a remarkable twenty-two-year-old in this 1799 letter to a friend who had turned the topic to romantic matters:

> You ask for my opinion about the constancy of a man's love-sickness. That is rather a puzzling question for me who have no routine whatever in the affairs of the heart. The violent, changeable character of men gives little opportunity for edifying or consolatory observations upon this subject, and for one Werther and one Pölchau there exist a hundred thousand fickle ones who call the fire of the moment passion. Of that sacred and everlasting flame they see only the reflection, which, growing weaker and weaker, leaves them but the name of a feeling, the true signification of which remains to them a mystery.

Lea's feelings on the subject of men's constancy did not prevent her from taking a serious interest in the young Abraham Mendelssohn, whom she married in 1804. In answer to his future mother-in-law's refusal to allow her daughter to marry 'a mere clerk', Abraham reluctantly agreed to quit Paris for Hamburg, the free Hanseatic city that was Germany's largest port town. Here, with the benefit of Lea's considerable dowry, it was possible for Abraham to enter into a full partnership with his brother, Joseph. The family remained in Hamburg for seven years, the thriving family business supported for most of these, as we have seen, by the trade of illegal British goods under the French blockade. The couple spent this happy period lodged in what Lea describes as 'a pretty little cottage with a balcony!!! situated on the Elbe close to the Neumühlen'. These years witnessed the births of their first three children, Fanny, on 14 November 1805; Felix, on 3 February 1809; and Rebecka, on 11 April 1811. As harrowing as their flight from Hamburg must have been, it was indeed satisfying to return as prosperous, accomplished young adults to the town in which Abraham and Lea had both been raised, a beautiful, growing family in tow and a substantial amount of capital with which to secure their future.

2 The prodigy

As on the day that lent you to the world
The sun and planets stood in salutation,
Forthwith you flourished on and ever onward
According to the law effective when you started.
You must be so; you cannot flee your selfhood.
Thus have the sibyls and the prophets stated,
And neither time nor force will ever alter
Intrinsic form, evolving as it lives.

Johann Wolfgang von Goethe, 'Primal Orphic Words' (1820)[1]

The Mendelssohns could hardly be said to have escaped Napoleon's grasp with the move to Berlin. Rather, they exchanged a city whose chosen form of resistance was covert and economic for a Prussia – for six years a vassal state to France – poised on the brink of an all-out war of liberation against French forces whose hold on Europe was becoming increasingly tenuous. In October of 1806, King Friedrich Wilhelm III's ill-advised decision to go to war with France had been met with a crushing defeat at the Battle of Jena. The 1807 Peace of Tilsit had given France all of Prussia's territories west of the Elbe, and exacted a heavy toll of money and men for the continuation of Napoleon's campaigns.

Napoleon's influence on the political and social structures of Prussia was by no means unsalutary, at least from a liberal standpoint. The French occupation had occasioned the implementation of an array of reforms, some of which had been in process for years, others

3 Napoleon's triumphal 1806 entry through Berlin's Brandenburg Gate: anonymous engraving

dictated by Napoleon himself. Restrictions associated with 'estates' – social divisions determined by birth – were lifted. Nobility thus gained access to middle-class careers, while peasants and bourgeoisie now had the right to purchase property from the nobility. Serfdom was abolished, though nobility still enjoyed the power of civil jurisdiction over their former serfs and the power to police their own lands. Wilhelm von Humboldt spearheaded widespread educational reforms, including the establishment of secondary schools – *Gymnasia* – and the University of Berlin, which opened its doors in 1810.

In keeping with the spirit of reform – and following closely the French lead – Chancellor Hardenberg issued a decree on 11 March 1812, declaring that 'Jews and their families currently residing in our States and in possession of general privileges, patents of naturalisation, letters of protection, and concessions are considered inhabitants and citizens of Prussia'.[2] The decades that followed witnessed a major influx of Jews from their insulated communities in ghettos and small towns to urban centres; between 1816 and 1849, the number of Jews in Berlin rose from 3,373 to 9,595.[3]

However promising all of this reform was on paper, its impact on Prussia's social environment – on the condition of its Jews in particular – was ambiguous to say the least. Indeed, popular resistance to Napoleon's occupation expressed itself in a groundswell of retrenchment against many of the reforms associated with the French Revolution. Johann Gottlieb Fichte's *Reden an die deutsche Nation* ('Addresses to the German Nation'), delivered in the amphitheatre of the Berlin Academy in the winter of 1807–8, helped bring a new nationalistic spirit into focus. One important aspect of this rising fervour was the consolidation of Germany's Christian identity. Organisations like the Christlich-deutsche Tischgesellschaft (German-Christian Assembly), founded in 1811, attracted some of Berlin's most important intellectual figures, including Fichte himself, Friedrich Karl von Savigny and Clemens Brentano (who once likened Jews to 'flies, the last traces of the Egyptian plague'). Symptomatic of this anti-Semitic undercurrent was the presence of such tales as 'The Jew in the Thornbush' among those anthologised in the course of the Grimm brothers' effort – which began about this time – to bring German folklore and folk narratives to the centre of the popular consciousness. This instructive tale involves the torture and eventual hanging of a goateed Jew.

In the years after Napoleon's defeat, and the subsequent settlements reached at the Congress of Vienna (1814–15), many of the reforms of the war years rapidly lost momentum. By 1820, Friedrich Wilhelm III had dismissed most key political reformers from office. Though it would not attain the severity of Metternich's hold on Austria, a period of political retrenchment began in the north, mirrored in a general decline of the Enlightenment-charged spirit of tolerance that had peaked two decades earlier.

If Fichte's *Reden* constituted a launching point – at least symbolically – for the German people's self-conscious quest for their own identity, one Berlin family who accepted this mission as conscientiously as any was the Jewish Mendelssohns. The venues through which the Mendelssohns sought with all their resources to render themselves *echt* German citizens – Germany's language, its literary and artistic history, its convivial societies, its religion – followed to the letter Fichte's recipe for cultural nationhood.

Flush with the financial success of his Hamburg venture, Abraham was in an excellent position to offer aid in the struggle against Napoleon, and took this opportunity soon after their arrival in Berlin. In 1813, this former francophile put tens of thousands of thaler towards the equipment of volunteer soldiers, also funding a military hospital in Prague. By the end of the war, the Mendelssohn bank had become one of the half-dozen largest banks in the city, and Abraham's patriotism was acknowledged with a position on Berlin's city council.

Despite Abraham's rapid ascent to financial and social prominence, the notion of 'assimilation' is of only limited use in describing the trajectory of the Mendelssohns' ascent in Berlin's cultural and intellectual activities. The daily life of the family was orientated to a remarkable extent around a tightly circumscribed domestic space, a space which enabled them to remain at arm's length from the cut and thrust of the city's activities. Until Felix's brief stint at the university, their children did not attend public schools, educated instead by a brilliant array of private tutors. Lea ventured out into society infrequently, and Abraham retired from banking in 1821, at the age of forty-five, to dedicate his time fully to his family. The mansion and ten-acre estate at 3 Leipzigerstrasse which the family would purchase in 1825 served as an imposing physical expression of their overriding concern with establishing a secure, isolated domestic environment within which Abraham and Lea could conduct what they appear to have taken as their principal life's work: the proper rearing of their children.

This they executed in superlative fashion. Not only did the children benefit from tutors who were themselves figures of remarkable accomplishment, but the Mendelssohn house – both 3 Leipzigerstrasse and their previous dwelling at 7 Neue Promenade in the Spandauer Vorstadt – hosted an endless stream of Berlin's luminaries, and became a regular attraction for distinguished visitors to the city. In Sarah Rothenberg's words, 'the Mendelssohns maintained their privacy, and Europe came to their living room'.[4] Julius Schubring, who came to know the family well through these years, recalled their household around 1825, observing that their considerable financial resources

> were employed neither to maintain a vain system of ostentation nor of luxurious living, but, on the contrary, to promote every possible development of intellectual resources and keep up a truly refined tone. The parents and their four children – their happiness then unclouded by any untoward event – were harmoniously united to each other by unusual warmth of affection and congeniality of character, and produced a most pleasing impression on everyone who entered their house. Their existence was a domestic one, inasmuch as they felt little inclination to go out, being most partial, after the labours of the day, to spending the evening in familiar intercourse with one another. It was seldom, however, that they were

found quite alone; they either had a number of young people who were on a friendly footing with them, or else their circle was filled up with another class of visitors. But it was seldom that there was what is called a regular party. Whoever felt so inclined went, and whoever took a pleasure in going was welcome. Science, art, and literature were equally represented . . . Celebrated and uncelebrated people, travellers of all kinds, and especially musicians, though not to the exclusion of other artists, found their efforts judiciously appreciated. The conversation was always animated and spirited.[5]

By this point the Mendelssohns were utterly estranged from the majority of European Jewry, who continued to live and work in Jewish communities. As strongly as Felix's grandfather, Moses, had advocated for German literacy among the Jews, he would likely have been mortified to discover that his gifted grandson could not number Hebrew among the generous handful of languages he had in his grasp by his late teens. Fichte had proclaimed in the Reden, 'men are formed by language far more than language is formed by men'; the Germans, not the Jews, were the Mendelssohns' chosen people.

Through their first years in Berlin, it fell to Abraham and Lea – as it fell to every Jewish family of their social standing and aspirations – to consider converting to Christianity. Two of Abraham's sisters, Dorothea and Henriette, had been baptised, as had several members of Lea's extended family. The immediate catalyst for the Mendelssohns' conversion seems to have been Lea's brother, Jacob Bartholdy, who had been baptised into Protestantism in 1805. Widely viewed as somewhat eccentric, Jacob enjoyed respectable successes as a diplomat, a historian, and a patron of the arts. His 'Casa Bartholdy' in Rome – where he was appointed Prussia's consul general in 1815 – attracted an important group of German painters, the 'Nazarenes', whose ranks, as we have seen, included Abraham's nephews Philipp and Johannes Veit. On the occasion of his own conversion, Jacob had adopted the Christian name, Bartholdy, taken from the former owner of one of his properties on the River Spree. He encouraged Abraham and Lea to take this name as well.

Jacob's arguments for conversion could not properly be called pro-
selytising. The crux of his logic lay not in recognising Christianity as a
'true' revealed religion, but in reducing Judaism to a form of cultural
deviance whose vaguely sadistic passage from generation to generation must be interrogated and defended by its practitioners:

> You may remain faithful to an oppressed, persecuted religion, you
> may leave it to your children as a prospect of life-long martyrdom, as
> long as you believe it to be absolute truth. But when you have ceased
> to believe that, it is barbarism.[6]

On 21 March 1816, Abraham and Lea quietly had their children baptised into Protestantism in the Jerusalemkirche. The parents were
themselves baptised during a trip to Frankfurt in October 1822. They
also appended the name Bartholdy to their own – 'a Christian
Mendelssohn is an impossibility', Abraham wrote – a decision that
was met with no great joy among the children; in an 1829 letter to
Felix, Fanny characterised 'Bartholdy' as 'this name that we all
dislike'.[7] But from 1823 onward, Felix habitually signed himself, in
correspondence and music compositions, 'Felix M. B.', 'Felix
Mendelssohn Bartholdy', or some combination of these names and
initials.

Abraham's letters from around the time of Fanny's confirmation –
during which he was in Paris, having been sent to represent Berlin in
the settlement of French war reparations – reveal a thoughtful, sober
effort to guide his daughter through a process he and Lea had obviously undertaken with the most serious consideration. The rational-
istic tones of his argument for conversion are highly evocative of his
own father's pleas for religious tolerance, rooted in the conviction
that all religions are united in their basic doctrinal assumptions.
'There is – whatever religion one chooses – only one God', he wrote,
'one virtue, one truth, one happiness. You will find all of this, if you
follow the voice of your heart; live so that it be ever in harmony with the
voice of your reason.'

At the same time, where Moses' insistence on the duty owed by the

Jew to the Jewish law was finally based on genetic considerations, Abraham sees the roots of his own Judaism as purely cultural. His Kantian vision of 'the divine instinct in us and in our conscience' to which the individual is ultimately responsible enables Abraham to accord religious practices the somewhat derisive title of 'human ordinances'. He even appears to hold out to his daughter the possibility – a theologically dubious one, from a Christian standpoint – of recognising in Jesus not an incarnation of the divine, but a human being worthy of respect chiefly as the executor of an exemplary life:

> The outward form of religion . . . is historical, and changeable like all human ordinances. Some thousands of years ago the Jewish form was the reigning one, then the heathen form, and now it is the Christian. We, your mother and I, were born and brought up by our parents as Jews, and without being obliged to change the form of our religion have been able to follow the divine instinct in us and in our conscience. We have educated you and your brothers and sisters in the Christian faith, because it is the creed of most civilised people, and contains nothing that can lead you away from what is good, and much that guides you to love, obedience, tolerance, and resignation, even if it offered nothing but the example of its founder, understood by so few, and followed by still fewer.
>
> By pronouncing your confession of faith, you have fulfilled the claims of society on you, and obtained the name of a Christian. Now be what your duty as a human being demands of you, true, faithful, good . . .

*

If Moses Mendelssohn would likely have been troubled at the course of his grandchildren's religious upbringing, the same could certainly not be said for the manner in which their education was undertaken. Abraham and Lea spared no effort or expense in surrounding their children, from the earliest age, with gifted educators in an array of fields.

Abraham and Lea themselves gave their children their first structured exposure to literature, the fine arts, arithmetic and French. In

1819, philologist Karl Wilhelm Ludwig Heyse was brought on as *Hauslehrer* – a position approximating Moses' in the silk merchant's house – to instruct the children in general subjects and classical languages. Professor Johann Gottlob Samuel Rösel educated the children in painting, landscape art in particular, a pastime for which Felix displayed no small talent and which he would continue to enjoy for the rest of his life. By his late teens, Felix had largely mastered French and English, and was producing competent German translations from texts in Greek, Latin and Italian. By the same time, he proved an accomplished gymnast, swimmer, horseman, dancer and chess player.

Music was a central component of the children's education from the start. Fanny and Felix received their first piano lessons from Lea, herself a sensitive and polished musician. During an 1816 family trip to Paris, they had the opportunity to take lessons with the celebrated Marie Bigot, whom Haydn and Beethoven had both applauded for her interpretations of their music, and violin lessons from Pierre Baillot. Back in Berlin, their prodigious development at the keyboard was soon entrusted to the supervision of Ludwig Berger, a well-respected virtuoso who had studied with Clementi and Cramer. Carl Wilhelm Henning gave them lessons in violin, an instrument on which Felix could soon boast respectable competence (Ferdinand Hiller, who would become one of Mendelssohn's closest friends in adulthood, was astonished at the teen-aged Felix's ability to sightread a violin sonata by Aloys Schmitt 'very cleverly and well, though the brilliant passages were naturally somewhat sketchy'[8]). On 28 October 1818, the nine-year-old Felix made what appears to have been his public debut, playing the piano in a trio for two horns and piano by Joseph Wölfl.

Needless to say, all of this was achieved through a regimen of almost incredible strictness. By his tenth year, Felix was rising at five each morning and looking forward to a day almost every moment of which was purposeful. In a letter of 22 March 1820, he offers a slice of life:

I have six hours of Latin a week: two for Caesar, two for Ovid, one for grammar, and one for exercises . . .

In mathematics I am reading the 5th book of Euclid, which seems to be much more difficult than everything else I have described.

In addition, with Fanni I have two hours of history, two of arithmetic, one of geography, and one of German speaking. – The violin progresses well – I have two lessons a week and am playing etudes by Kreutzer. – Also on Monday and Tuesday I go to the Singakademie where I hear beautiful things . . . My work schedule is so organised, that I prepare tasks in the evening that I have received in the morning.[9]

The figure who contributed more than anyone to the formation of Felix's musical identity through these years was Carl Friedrich Zelter, the director of the distinguished Singakademie Felix names in his letter, whom the Mendelssohns hired in 1819 to instruct Fanny and Felix in composition. But for an injury sustained in his youth, the rough-hewn, rough-spoken Zelter would have followed in his father's footsteps to become a stonemason. Despite counting Hegel, Schiller and Goethe among his friends, Zelter continued until his death to cultivate a coarseness in his personal manner which verged, on many occasions, on tastelessness (in one characteristic story, a nervous young girl presenting her voice for his examination was moved to tears by his encouragement: 'Sing away, I can bear as much as anybody else').

Zelter's method of instruction in composition was situated within a pedagogical legacy traceable more or less directly to J. S. Bach. Zelter had received his primary grounding in composition from Christian Friedrich Carl Fasch, founder of the Singakademie, and from Johann Philipp Kirnberger. While employed at the court of Frederick the Great, Fasch and Kirnberger had both worked closely with Carl Philipp Emanuel Bach, who had been trained by his father, Johann Sebastian. Kirnberger had, himself, had lessons from J. S. Bach, as well, and claimed to set forth, in his treatise *Die Kunst des reinen Satzes* (1774–9), a compositional method based closely on J. S. Bach's own.

The natural upshot of all of this was a course of study rooted firmly in the contrapuntal practices of the mid-eighteenth century. Felix's systematic progress from around September 1819 to May 1820 is laid out in a bound manuscript, now at the Bodleian Library in Oxford, in which we find first exercises in thoroughbass (a form of harmonic shorthand that flourished in the Baroque and early Classical periods), chorale, invertible counterpoint, canon and fugue.

If Felix's composition lessons encouraged him to keep his musical imagination planted in the eighteenth century, these roots were planted more deeply still through his participation, along with Fanny, in the Singakademie. This organisation – which had been under Zelter's direction since Fasch's death in 1800 – had ardently promoted briefer examples of Bach's still little-known choral music from the time of its founding in 1791. By the time Felix and Fanny joined, the Singakademie's library (whose core holdings had been donated by Lea's aunt, Sara Levy) had also become one of Europe's most important collections of J. S. Bach's manuscript material.

It was thus under Zelter's guidance that one of the over-arching convictions of Mendelssohn's musical career crystallised: the sense that his primary obligation was to the music of the past. Though he would find his own voice – indeed, a compositional language of startling originality – within only a few years, his entire compositional outlook remained conditioned by the standards and, to a large extent, the practices of his distinguished German forebears. At the same time, his professional work as a conductor and pianist would be bent largely towards preserving and reviving the most significant work of Germany's musical past, that is, towards laying the groundwork of the classical music canon as we know it today.

*

Even in light of the hyper-inflated rigour of Felix's education, the quality and sheer number of his early compositions almost defies belief. By his fifteenth birthday, his oeuvre included a set of twelve string *sinfonie*, four concertos (for violin, piano, violin and piano, and two pianos), a violin sonata, three piano quartets, several small piano sonatas, four musical works for the stage (three Singspiels and a comic opera), and an array of songs and choral pieces.

Early in Mendelssohn's development as a composer, Abraham and Lea instituted a series of Sunday musical gatherings, assembling not only friends and invited guests, but musicians from the royal chapel and singers from the opera. Felix and Fanny frequently performed at the keyboard, though Felix also conducted and took turns at the violin. Most valuable, though, was the opportunity for the Mendelssohn children to hear their works performed and appreciated almost as soon as they were completed. These gatherings soon came to be well known among Berlin's cultural elite, and it was in this environment that Felix made countless important personal contacts (we will have more to say about this in the next chapter).

Even the first fruits of Felix's labours – the first six string *sinfonie*, the G-minor Piano Sonata, and the Singspiel, *Die Beiden Pädagogen*, were all completed in 1821 – are works of astonishing polish. The early string *sinfonie* plant their stylistic feet firmly in the north German style of the mid-eighteenth century, rife with extended passages in which Carl Philipp Emanuel Bach – Felix's most direct model – would have found nothing out of the ordinary. The textures are spare and pervasively contrapuntal, though, importantly, not as spare in performance as they appear on the page. In keeping with mid-eighteenth-century practice, Mendelssohn apparently fleshed out the harmonic framework from the keyboard: 'Felix played in discreet accompaniment', critic and friend A. B. Marx recalled, 'and mostly or entirely as thoroughbass, [taking] the place of the winds'.[10]

The material of these pieces often feels insufficiently memorable to warrant the working out it receives. Though Marx had to admit his 'admiration for his skill in the movement', he was compelled to tell the young composer, about one of the *sinfonie*, 'that there was nothing underneath it, that I had found no content to match the movement's proficiency'. Nonetheless, those seeking here early signs of Mendelssohn's mature style can certainly find them. The first movement of the first *Sinfonia* closes with a fast, noisy unison passage –

slightly off-kilter in rhythm and harmonic direction alike – that bespeaks an early taste for the gestural language that would come to dramatic fruition in the development section of the 1825 Octet's first movement. Similarly, the appearance of chorale-like material in the deeply haunting second movement of the Sixth Symphony anticipates the use of chorales in many later instrumental movements: the scherzo of the 1840 symphony-cantata, *Lobgesang*, for instance, or the finale of the Second Piano Trio in C minor of 1845.

Mendelssohn's approach to matters of form is symptomatic of the archaising spirit that pervades these works; we find among the first handful of string *sinfonie* nothing like full-fledged Classical 'sonata form', the structural practice that held sway in instrumental composition from the last decades of the eighteenth century onward. The first movements of Haydn, Mozart and Beethoven's mature symphonies, and most other multi-movement instrumental genres, were all shaped through the same basic structural design: in the 'exposition', a home key is established but soon abandoned, arrival at a contrasting key being firmly anchored through some sort of thematic event (usually – though less often Haydn's work – a contrasting 'second subject'); a 'development' section follows, marked by harmonic and often thematic wandering; this gives way to the 'recapitulation', which recalls most or all of the exposition's material but remains in the home key throughout. Mendelssohn's first string *sinfonie* rely on a basic tonal departure–return scheme in a 'pre-sonata-form' condition, moving from a first key to a second one, but rarely articulating this motion in any noteworthy way.[11] Where the whole structure of the Classical sonata-form movement depends on a variety of textures – well-differentiated thematic material, filler material, coda material, and so forth – the outer movements of Mendelssohn's early *sinfonie* tend to follow the Baroque practice of sticking to a single texture and emotional affect throughout.

Mendelssohn's first efforts to come to terms with the language of the Viennese 'Classical' style were not without mis-steps. In one early stab at sonata form – the first movement of the G-minor Piano Sonata

4 The twelve-year-old Felix at the keyboard, drawn by his future brother-in-law,
Wilhelm Hensel

– the result is so schematic as to defeat the dramatic purpose altogether. The second key area of the movement is established not with a new subject, nor with a Haydnesque rethinking of the first subject, but with an almost exact duplication of the first subject, simply transposed to B♭ (the closing material of the exposition is based, too, on the transitional material that had followed the first subject). If this scheme results in a conspicuously stiff exposition, it leads to near-disaster in the recapitulation. Mendelssohn brings back the material of the second key area in its entirety, now in the tonic, heedless of the fact that this means two nearly identical iterations of the first subject in the same key. Happily, the charming main material of this movement is sufficiently light on its feet to bear repetition, an early suggestion of the mercurial, featherweight textures that would so distinguish many of the works of Mendelssohn's first maturity.

Mendelssohn makes a much closer approach to Mozart in his music for the stage. His second such effort, *Die Beiden Pädagogen*, was a one-act Singspiel first performed in the Mendelssohn home in April 1821. Its libretto – adapted by family friend Johann Ludwig Casper from Eugène Scribe's *Les deux Précepteurs* – concerns love, intrigue and contemporary pedagogical debates (handled in a spirit of safely circumscribed irreverence). Even the work's overture seems to hail from different terrain than the string *sinfonie*, its jubilant soft–loud opening gambit a worthy sidekick to the *Figaro* overture. The second vocal number is a shapely, dramatically propulsive trio that would not feel too out of place in *Così fan tutte*. Most impressive, however, is the extended 'Quartet and Chorus', No. 10, in which the social distinction between the peasants and the main characters is played out in the same breed of metrical layering – the simultaneous sounding of a chorus in one metre and a quartet in another – that we find, in three layers, at the ball in the first-act finale of *Don Giovanni*. Moments of this kind speak not only to the contrapuntal achievements of the young composer, who had just turned twelve, but to his sheer ambitiousness, driven as he is not only to recapture the style of his cherished

Mozart, but to try his own hand at one of Mozart's most inspired technical achievements.

Through these remarkable years and beyond, Felix's closest friend and musical confidante was his older sister, Fanny. As universally applauded as Felix was, many found even greater praise for his sister's achievement. Their close friend Eduard Devrient recalled that Mendelssohn's playing, though 'extraordinarily dextrous and possessed of great musical assurance', still 'did not equal that of his older sister Fanny'. Hiller compares the impression made by the pair at an 1822 musical matinée: 'Felix played one of his quartets – in C minor, if I recollect right; but I was most struck by his sister Fanny's performance of Hummel's *Rondeau brillant* in A, which she played in a truly masterly style'. Family friend Julius Schubring, too, recalls that Fanny was 'long [Felix's] equal in composition and pianoforte-playing'. At the same time, the two enjoyed a relationship of the most profound mutual respect and affection. 'I have always been his only musical adviser', Fanny wrote of her thirteen-year-old brother, 'and he never writes down a thought before submitting it to my judgement. For instance, I have known his operas by heart before a note was written.'

Even as early as Felix's tenth year, however, it was clear that he was expected – indeed, encouraged – to outpace his sister. Though it is rarely productive to gauge the decisions of previous centuries against the political climate of our own, the family's faltering support of its oldest child through her mid-teens forms one of music history's most heartbreaking stories of squandered potential. In an 1820 letter from Paris, Fanny's father offered this sage advice:

> Music will perhaps become his [Felix's] profession, while for you it
> can and should only be an ornament, never the root of your being and
> doing. We may therefore pardon him some ambition and desire to be
> acknowledged in a pursuit which appears very important to him,
> because he feels a vocation for it, while it does you credit that you
> have always shown yourself good and sensible in these matters; and
> your very joy at the praise he earns proves that you might, in his place,

have merited equal approval. Remain true to these sentiments and to this line of conduct; they are feminine, and only what is truly feminine is an ornament to your sex.

However well intentioned Abraham's respect in his discussions of 'the weighty duties of a woman', Fanny seems to have been unsettlingly slow to take as her own the job description itself. 'You must become more steady and collected', her father charged the recalcitrant twenty-three-year-old, 'and prepare more earnestly and eagerly for your real calling, the only calling of a young woman – I mean the state of a housewife'. With her marriage to painter Wilhelm Hensel the following year, Fanny effectively turned her back on any serious possibility of life as a professional musician.

A defining point of divergence between the artistic experiences of the two came in 1821, when Zelter decided to facilitate the twelve-year-old Felix's entry – and Felix's alone – into one of the most important relationships of his young life. In October, Zelter, Felix and Zelter's daughter, Doris, left Berlin for a two-week visit with Johann Wolfgang von Goethe. On 6 November, Felix gave a report of their first meeting:

> Now listen everybody, all of you! Today is Tuesday. Sunday, the Sun of Weimar, Goethe, arrived. In the morning we went to church, where half of the 100th Psalm by Handel was performed . . . Afterwards I wrote the short letter dated the 4th and went to the Elephant [a hotel in Leipzig], where I drew Lukas Cranach's house. Two hours later Professor Zelter came. Goethe is here, the old gentleman is here! In a flash we were at the bottom of the steps – in Goethe's house. He was in the garden, and was just coming around a hedge; isn't that odd, dear Father, just the way it happened when you met him? He is very friendly, but I don't think any of his portraits look at all like him. He then inspected his interesting collection of fossils, which his son organised, and kept saying: Hm, hm, I am quite pleased; afterwards I walked around the garden with him and Prof. Zelter for another half hour. Then we sat down to eat. One would think he was fifty years old, not seventy-three. After dinner Fräulein Ulrike, Goethe's wife's

sister, requested a kiss, and I did likewise. Every morning I receive a kiss from the author of *Faust* and of *Werther*, and every afternoon two kisses from Goethe, friend and father. Fancy that!! . . . In the afternoon I played for Goethe for over two hours, in part fugues by Bach, and in part I improvised. In the evening they played whist, and Prof. Zelter, who played at first, said to me: Whist means that you should keep your mouth shut. Strong language! In the evening we all ate together, even Goethe, who usually never eats at night.

Over the fourteen days that followed, Felix and Goethe appear to have developed a remarkable rapport, indeed as close a friendship as can be imagined between two whose ages were separated by sixty years. Felix wrote home on 10 November:

I play far more here than I do at home, seldom for less than four hours, often for six and sometimes as many as eight hours. Every afternoon Goethe opens his Streicher and says: 'I haven't heard you yet today, play something for me'. He sits down beside me and when I've finished (I improvise most of the time), I ask him for a kiss or else give him one. You cannot imagine how kind and gracious he is . . . I don't find him imposing in build, he's no taller than father. But his bearing, language, name – those things are imposing.

★

The trip to Weimar was only the first in a series of journeys that punctuated Felix's early teens. The next came the following year, in July 1822, as the family set off together on an ambitious trip of some three months to Switzerland. Such ventures, particularly for a family of six, were inherently so costly that the whole enterprise smacked of uncharacteristic ostentation. But for a number of reasons, this seemed a good time to get out of Berlin for a while, despite Lea's lifelong antipathy to travel. The previous year, in July of 1821, she had given birth to her fifth child, who was stillborn. Abraham, tired of the struggles of daily life in a professional sphere which had never come to feel like his native climate, had also recently decided to leave banking.

At the same time, exposure to the famous scenery of Switzerland was itself an important component of the children's aesthetic education. The first years of the century had witnessed an explosion in scenic travel literature. The region of the Alps the family explored through these weeks – though they did not get as far as Italy – would soon be immortalised in one of the genre's landmarks, William Brockendon's *Illustrations of the Passes of the Alps by which Italy communicates with France, Switzerland, and Germany*, published in twelve parts between 1827 and 1828 (including 109 engravings prepared in the course of around sixty trips through the Alps). Felix makes a somewhat surly acknowledgement of his own self-conscious participation in the popular aestheticisation of landscape in a 22 August letter to Zelter: 'So, we are now in Interlaken, right in the middle of Switzerland, whose beauty cannot be expressed in words, as every guidebook in the world has already stated'. The children's education in the visual arts centred almost entirely on landscape and, to a lesser extent, architecture (as a result, Felix's finely nuanced landscapes were balanced out, in his visual oeuvre, by amateurish, cartoon-like people). Lea's Swiss letters were singled out for praise by her sister-in-law, Henriette, precisely for their keenly developed sense for landscape as an aestheticised subject, in which the real and the ideal are inextricably folded into one another:

> [Y]our letters are a true (not panorama but) diorama – a much more perfect work of art – showing us everything in the greatest possible exactness, and with all the changes of light and shade as the varying daylight produces them. We have a diorama at Paris just now, and one of the pictures represents the Sarnenthal, with a lake, and glaciers in the distance. I almost fancied, dear Lea, I saw you on the bank of the lake, and the others on the surrounding mountains.

For Felix, just as important as visual impressions were auditory ones; his letters from this trip – particularly those to Zelter – reveal an acute awareness of his sonic surroundings, and a fascination with capturing these highlights, too, in prose. In a 19 July letter from

Frankfurt, he reports in detail on the sound of a pistol shot fired in the mountains: 'The shot had barely sounded when an echo came back from the closest cliff, and then about five seconds later there was a second distant echo, which sounded like rolling thunder'. More elaborate is his recollection of yodelling, an account in which we can discern the imaginative mingling of music, natural sounds, visual splendour and national identity that would so strongly inform much of his orchestral music in the coming years:

> Certainly this kind of singing sounds harsh and unpleasant when it is heard near-by or in a room. But it sounds beautiful when you hear it with mingling or answering echoes, in the valleys or on the mountains or in the woods, and there, such shouting and yelling seems truly to express the enthusiasm of the Swiss people for their country. And when one stands on a crest early in the morning, with a clear sky overhead, and hears the singing accompanied, now loudly, now softly, by the jingling of cowbells from the pastures below, then it sounds lovely; indeed, it fits perfectly into the picture of a Swiss landscape as I had imagined it.

The trip was rich in personal contacts, as well. In Kassel, a letter of introduction from Zelter secured them an audience with composer Louis Spohr. In Frankfurt, they paid a visit to pianist Aloys Schmitt, who had previously tutored Mendelssohn in Berlin. It was during this visit that Felix made his first acquaintance with Schmitt's pupil, Ferdinand Hiller, one of his closest friends in adulthood. On the return trip, the entire family had the opportunity to meet Goethe, who received them warmly, and happily (if somewhat patronisingly) pronounced Fanny 'as gifted as her brother'.

The C-minor Piano Quartet completed in the course of this journey – like the two that followed over the next three years (opp. 1, 2 and 3) – gave evidence of a new maturity in Mendelssohn's compositional development, particularly in his full engagement with the formal practices of Mozart and Beethoven. His writing for strings proved as confidently idiomatic as that for piano, though the generous deployment of pianistic virtuosity in these three works offers a distinctive point of contact with the concerto, another genre in which Mendelssohn was heavily involved through these years (in a diary entry from his 1824 visit to Berlin, Ignaz Moscheles actually recalls being shown Felix's 'Concerto in C minor', probably referring to the First Piano Quartet).

Even as the ambitiousness and imaginative force of each work increased, Mendelssohn's pace did not slow. In addition to the piano quartets, he produced sonatas for viola and clarinet, and an impressive sextet for the improbable combination of violin, two violas, cello, bass and piano. The increasingly substantial string *sinfonie* – all twelve of which were completed by 1823 – balance deftly a new fascination with the incorporation of strict fugue and often remarkable touches of originality in instrumental colour. The series culminated, in March of 1824, in Felix's first symphony for full orchestra, op. 11. Notwithstanding the somewhat gratuitous fugue in the middle of the fourth movement, this fiery piece bears no trace of a student's stiffness (it attests, too, to a more than passing acquaintance with Mozart's G-minor Symphony, K. 440, particularly in the second subject of its first movement and the first subject of its last). Even more ambitious are the double piano concertos of 1823 and 1824, which display a conversance with Beethoven's, Dussek's and Field's work in the genre.[12] The slow movements of these remarkable works show Felix already heavily invested in the lyrical language that would find its fullest expression in the *Songs Without Words*.

It was thus with a seasoned composer that Abraham set off for Paris in 1825, one of his chief aims being to hear Luigi Cherubini – the imposing director of the Paris Conservatory – pass judgement on the young Felix's chances of succeeding as a professional musician. Abraham and Lea had never been altogether pleased at the thought of a musician in the family. Egged on by his brother-in-law, Jacob – ironically, given Jacob's own ardent support of the arts – Abraham frequently proved 'doubtful about [Felix's] profession, dissatisfied with the career of an artist whose success must always remain uncertain'.[13] In 1824, Moscheles found Felix's parents inexplicably 'concerned about Felix's future, and . . . unsure whether he has sufficient talent'. Persuaded as he was that Felix's prodigious gifts rivalled Mozart's, Moscheles could only remark dryly that Abraham and Lea were 'quite different from the usual parents of child prodigies that I have come across so often'. Indeed, this backdrop may help to account for Mendelssohn's over-arching concern – in composition and performance alike – with keeping the rigorous discipline underpinning his craft close to the surface. Music was never an exercise in self-indulgence, but a respectable, learned practice.

Happily, Cherubini's decision was affirmative, as Mendelssohn cheerfully (but without evident surprise) reports in a letter of 6 April. After hearing Felix's F-minor Piano Quartet, the characteristically tight-lipped Cherubini 'came up to me smiling and nodded to me. Then he told the others: "Ce garçon est riche, il fera bien; il fait même déjà bien".' Cherubini was hardly the only celebrity with whom Mendelssohn came into contact on the trip. Paris at this time boasted the world's largest collection of piano virtuosi, who figured heavily among the musicians Mendelssohn met or re-established ties with: Hummel, Moscheles, Rode, Kalkbrenner, Baillot, Liszt and Kreutzer, as well as Rossini and Meyerbeer.

Though his family had understandably imagined that Felix would be delighted to be brought to such surroundings, the reality was rather different. Indeed, Felix's letters from this sojourn offer our first good hard look at a side of his character which not even his most sympathetic contemporary chroniclers could gloss over: Felix could be astonishingly critical. Ferdinand Hiller, who rarely tires of reminding us of Felix's innate modesty, remarked of the boy at about this time, 'his opinions on art and artists . . . were full of the vivacity natural to his age, and had in them something – what shall I call it? – over-ripe and almost dogmatic'. A. B. Marx had been the recipient (not for the last time) of what seems to have been a characteristic Mendelssohnian commentary on an early choral work; in response to Marx's untutored effort at learned counterpoint, Felix was finally moved to cry: 'That –

that can't be! That isn't right! That [indicating the fugue] is no music at all!'

Felix doubtless came by this tendency honestly. His father was only too aware of his own disinclination to gentleness, writing in 1819, 'I do not often bestow praise, but I do so the more conscientiously when there is a cause for it'. We have already caught glimpses of Zelter's capacity for gruffness, which he certainly did not spare in Mendelssohn's case; he was famously vigilant in guarding Felix against any inclination towards arrogance or pride. Julius Schubring also recalls Felix's piano instructor, Berger, as 'not very liberal of his praise'.

Nonetheless, family members back home were disconcerted at the ferocity of which Felix proved himself capable. To an uninspired fugue by composer Sigismund Ritter von Neukomm, who had been extremely kind to his young visitor, Felix wrote to his family, 'He ought to be called Altkomm instead of Neukomm'. The same letter that reports Cherubini's favourable pronouncement on Felix's F-minor Quartet includes the youth's own assessment of his older colleague: '[Cherubini] is dried up and wizened. The other day I heard one of his masses at the royal chapel, and it was as droll as he is peevish, i.e., beyond all measure.' The Parisian public comes under fire as well; Felix is expansive indeed on the subject of the city's famous musical *soirées*:

> [W]hen music is being played the ladies tell each other fairy tales, or jump from one chair to the next as if they were playing musical chairs. Right in the middle, it occurs to an old man in a corner to call out: *charmant*, and his two somewhat pretty daughters repeated: *charmant*, whereupon all the young men in the salon called out: *délicieux!*, and the joys of music are savoured . . . Now am I unjustified in finding these soirées awful?

The only effect of Fanny's chastening – 'My son, your letters consist of nothing but criticism' – was a reminder that not even she was secure from his scorn. Indeed, the tone of Felix's response seems almost cruel in light of Fanny's inevitable frustration at not having been able to make the trip herself: 'Do think a little, I beg of you! Are you in Paris, or am I? So I really ought to know better than you.'

To put such tendencies in the most charitable possible light, Mendelssohn is here beginning to explore an aspect of his musical persona utterly inseparable from his creative life. He was not simply an artist, but a critic, an arbiter of taste and quality. This instinct – which would shape his entire career – constituted perhaps the most important legacy of the Mendelssohns' several generations of involvement in Berlin's salon culture. The same faith in the contrapuntal practices of J. S. Bach that shaped Mendelssohn's compositional identity found voice at once in his early efforts to sort through the musical world around him. If the alphorn had enchanted him in the course of his 1822 trip to Switzerland, he had found the singing of the local girls incomprehensible, bewildered by the presence of a semi-improvised voice – by whom 'everything is spoiled' – at the top of their characteristic four-part texture: 'For this girl never sings a melody; she produces certain high notes – I believe just at her discretion – and thus, at times, horrible fifths turn up'.

His refusal to acknowledge the possibility of musical practices outside the circumscribed conventions in which he himself was educated – what we might almost term a confusion of conservatism for literacy – extends just as confidently to the realm of contemporary composition. In his remarks on a symphony of Wilhelm von Boguslawski, a young composer with whom he was in correspondence, Mendelssohn proves baffled by the more progressive tendencies of the first movement's development section: 'The conclusion does not please me at all, on account of the modulation into A♭ major and A♭ minor in a piece in G major!'[14]

Needless to say, the sixteen-year-old Felix had better-than-average cause to be confident in his own abilities and his own opinion. His skills at the keyboard placed him in company with all but the greatest virtuosi in Paris, and the compositions of his early adolescence had been staggering in both their volume and consistently high quality. But just as the family's new residence at 3 Leipzigerstrasse – into which they moved in 1825, shortly after Felix and Abraham's return from Paris – far outpaced in splendour their former dwelling, Mendelssohn was soon to take his own great leap forward into complete artistic maturity. It is only by comparison with the incredible achievements of his first year in this house that the original, finely wrought products of his early teens come to feel like the work of a student.

3 First maturity

Here's a marvellous convenient place for our rehearsal. This green
plot shall be our stage, this hawthorn-brake our tiring-house.

William Shakespeare, *A Midsummer Night's Dream*, III.i

In the autumn of 1820, as Henriette Mendelssohn prepared her
brother, Abraham, for his return to Berlin after an extended stay in
Paris, she sent with him a note to his wife. In tones that must have been
bittersweet for both author and recipient, this missive makes it clear
that Abraham had still developed no more than a grudging attachment to Berlin:

> Now you have your dear, noble husband home again, and quite as you
> must wish him, with a slight tinge of ill-humour against the France
> of today. Whether this will raise Berlin in his estimation I do not
> know; anyhow, he never forgets that his happiness has both bloomed
> and ripened into the most beautiful fruit there; and for such fruit he
> readily forgoes some of a more substantial kind which does not grow
> in your climate.[1]

Five years later, when Abraham returned to Paris to place Felix on trial
before Cherubini, another important aim of the visit was to escort
Henriette back to Berlin. Her obligations as governess to Fanny
Sébastiani had concluded, as we have seen, with Fanny's marriage the
previous autumn. Just weeks before setting off on this trip, Abraham

had purchased the palatial Berlin property through which he at last expressed, as Lea put it, 'serious intentions of settling here definitely'. It was in these magnificent buildings at 3 Leipzigerstrasse, and the several acres of land behind them, that he invited Henriette to live out her days, surrounded by Abraham's family and a close-knit group of friends. It was not so much that Abraham had finally discovered a personal fondness for the city. Rather the city had yielded to Abraham a space within which he and his family could live in happy seclusion, open to the elements they found most attractive, secure from the rest.

The property was situated near the Potsdam Gate, in a part of Berlin still only thinly settled. Enclaves of this sort were growing increasingly scarce in the city. Berlin's development into a major urban centre in the course of the seventeenth and eighteenth centuries had been shaped by the visions of a series of Hohenzollern rulers for whom practical and aesthetically informed urban planning served as a most important venue to political prestige. The early nineteenth century brought a shift in direction. With a growing population, slackened governmental control over rents and housing prices, and rapidly increasing industrialisation, the city began to take on the look of a modern urban environment. What little greenery that existed was disappearing from this town which was, in the words of contemporary author Fanny Lewald (who would attend several of the Mendelssohns' Sunday musicales), 'surrounded by sandy desert without trees or shrubbery, as far as the eye can see'.[2]

An immediate and lasting part of the property's appeal was the fertility of the soil around 3 Leipzigerstrasse, where 'fruits of a more substantial kind' had indeed taken root: lime, chestnut, elm and beech trees were a physical legacy of a more enlightened age in the city's history, during which, under Frederick the Great's rule, the Mendelssohn's plot of land had been part of the Thiergarten. Even in the throes of the extensive restoration process necessary to make the dilapidated buildings inhabitable, Lea's descriptions of the grounds breathe an air of disbelief that such a world could exist in Berlin. 'A whole row of rooms', she wrote to her cousin, Henriette Pereira, 'opens on to a garden, which is itself surrounded by other gardens, and that is why one doesn't hear any carriages or see anyone, and why there is no dust'. These gardens were backed by a large meadow and – to make the idyllic picture complete – 'a small farm where a farmer makes his living from twelve cows, providing us with fresh milk and butter'.

Their first years in this house appear to have been the Mendelssohn family's happiest hour. They counted among their regular guests some of Berlin's most distinguished cultural and intellectual lights: the philosopher Hegel, the botanist and geologist Alexander von Humboldt, orientalist Friedrich Rosen, poet Ludwig Robert, legal scholars Ludwig Heydemann and Eduard Gans, and philologist Gustav Droysen. Heinrich Heine was a regular guest, as well, though the Mendelssohns were never totally at ease with his blasé cynicism, and were hardly alone in resenting his famous 1826 pronouncement that 'the baptismal certificate is the entrance ticket to European culture'. 'I don't like him at all', Fanny wrote in 1829, though recognising him still as 'a poet, a true poet'.[3]

In their lavish new accommodations, the Sunday *musicales* took on an even greater prestige than before, bringing to Fanny and Felix's new works a star-studded and attentive audience. As Paul Heyse – the son of the children's tutor, later a celebrated novelist – recalled: 'The hall was like a shrine, in which an enthusiastic congregation absorbed every tone with the utmost attention'.[4] If Heine's poetry would inspire some of Felix's most impressive songs, the poet was hardly alone among the acquaintances and friends of these years who would bear significantly on the young composer's professional and artistic development, and through whom Felix quickly outgrew the insular tendencies of Zelter's tutelage. In A. B. Marx – the editor of the *Berliner allgemeine musikalische Zeitung* (for whom neither Zelter nor Abraham could find a kind word) – Felix found an ear bent as sympathetically and intelligently as his own towards Beethoven. Marx appears to have had a shaping hand in Felix's breakthrough work, the overture to *A Midsummer Night's Dream*, op. 21, and in the development of

Mendelssohn's attitude towards descriptive music in general. Actor/singer Eduard Devrient, at least according to his own account, was almost single-handedly responsible for pushing Felix to revive Bach's St Matthew Passion in 1829, an event that, as we shall see, brought the young conductor his first real taste of international acclaim. It fell to Felix's closest friend, Karl Klingemann, to provide the libretto for his first publicly performed Singspiel, Die Hochzeit des Camacho. Theologian Julius Schubring, a student of Schleiermacher, would go on to compile the texts of Mendelssohn's two completed oratorios. A frequent guest, too, was Ferdinand David, the violinist who would become Felix's Concertmaster in later years in Leipzig.

Felix answered this great leap forward in domestic luxury with a composition that marked a similar advance in his own artistic development, a creative pivot of such significance that it bears dwelling on at some length. On 25 October 1825, he completed the first draft of the Octet for four violins, two violas and two cellos, dedicated to his close friend, violinist Eduard Rietz. The work constituted not only Felix's first unqualified masterpiece, but one of the nineteenth century's greatest chamber works. The ensemble itself was apparently unprecedented in the consequential history of chamber music. Ludwig Spohr – whom Felix had met for the second time the previous year – had produced the first of his double string quartets in 1823. But even if Mendelssohn had become aware of Spohr's highly experimental works, they bear little conceptual resemblance to Mendelssohn's Octet; Spohr writes for two string quartets conversing as more or less discrete ensembles, 'the full eight-voice complement', as Spohr himself puts it, 'reserved for only the climactic moments of the composition'.[5] Mendelssohn's Octet sets in with all eight parts at once, fully seven independent lines in its opening bars. The string Sinfonie had afforded Mendelssohn the opportunity, through various divisions of parts, for extensive five- and six-part counterpoint, going briefly as far as eight in the Andante of Sinfonie 9. But sustained contrapuntal writing in eight parts constituted a tour de force in and of itself, and a worthy culmination of Mendelssohn's whole contrapuntal education.

The Octet carries the weight of its technical challenges lightly, however, parting ways with Mendelssohn's earlier work most significantly in the sparkling originality of its melodic material. In keeping with the sheer enormity of the piece is a soaring first subject that covers a range of over three octaves in its first eight bars (the registrally expansive opening subject of Mozart's C-major String Quintet may have served as an inspiration). Employing the double-period construction with which Haydn often plumped up the first-subject material of his later symphonies, Mendelssohn sets out his opening subject, departs from it, then returns to it, still in the home key of E♭, before getting on with the structure-defining modulation to B♭. This enormous anchor of harmonic stability is counterbalanced by a second subject of exceptional harmonic instability, stated first in the (expected) key of B♭, then straying off into a G-major restatement. The joyous material that closes the exposition (in B♭), like comparably situated material in so many of Mozart's sonata-form movements, offers some of the movement's most inspired ideas. This broad, richly worked exposition established a *modus operandi* Mendelssohn would sustain for most of his career.

It is the Octet's buoyant finale that embodies most fully the spirit pervading Mendelssohn's whole environment during these joyful months. The first subject is an eight-part fugue, whose unbroken string of quavers (presto, ¢) is set forth first by the cello at the bottom of its range. Though it is impossible to take seriously this sputtering *basso profundo* – any more than one can take seriously the cello/bass subject of the trio of Beethoven's C-minor Symphony that must have been its inspiration – the fugue unfolds in a contrapuntal scheme as ambitious as any in the piece up to this point, which is saying a great deal. Such an opening mirrors touchingly the balance between brilliant erudition and unbridled, youthful laughter that so defined the community that Felix and Eduard Rietz, the dedicatee of the piece, shared. With the increasingly close entries of the final three voices, telescoping to stretto, an image of the impatience of youth rises before us, the exuberant young genius stumbling over himself in his race towards a full eight-part texture.

The third movement represents Felix's first extended, thoroughgoing effort at the fleet-footed scherzo texture for which he would soon become famous. The movement, by Felix's own account, was inspired by the *Walpurgisnacht* Dream in Goethe's *Faust*. Fanny explains:

> the whole piece is to be played staccato and *pianissimo*, the tremulandos coming in now and then, the trills passing away with the quickness of lightning; everything new and strange, and at the same time most insinuating and pleasing, one feels so near the world of spirits, carried away in the air, half inclined to snatch up a broomstick and follow the aerial procession. At the end the first violin takes flight with a feather-like lightness and – all has vanished.

Though Felix would not make this particular association public, this scherzo offers the first important sign of one of the most distinctive creative impulses of his late teens: the increasingly purposeful exploration of connections between music and other cultural forms. Most of the major compositions of the next three years – the *Midsummer Night's Dream* overture (after Shakespeare), *Die Hochzeit des Camacho* (a Singspiel based on Cervantes), the *Calm Sea, Prosperous Voyage* overture (after two poems of Goethe), the music for Berlin's 1828 *Dürerfest* – show a composer bent on examining various permutations, we might say, of the idea of *learned* music. Fully capable, by this time, of tossing off music that communicated his technically sound musical training, the next great challenge was to create music that would reflect more broadly the richness and diversity of his education, to discover musical inroads into contemporary processes of cultural formation and reclamation through which figures as diverse as Shakespeare, Dürer, Cervantes and Goethe were emerging as foci of the German cultural consciousness.

Mendelssohn discovered one of the most important such inroads of his career the summer following the composition of the Octet. In this case, he would not keep the source of his inspiration private.

★

Sebastian Hensel describes the summer of 1826 as 'perhaps the happiest time in the life of Abraham Mendelssohn'. The same could probably be said for the lives of the younger members of the household, who, Hensel relates, 'led a fantastic, dreamlike life . . . like one uninterrupted festival day, full of poetry, music, merry games, ingenious practical jokes, disguises and representations'. One frequent source of entertainment for this happy group was the staging of scenes, acts, even entire productions of whatever plays had caught their collective fancy. By 1826, their literary horizons – long defined by Goethe, Schiller and the beloved Jean Paul – had extended to the work of William Shakespeare. The husband of Felix's aunt Dorothea, Friedrich Schlegel, had generated beautiful German translations of seventeen of these plays between 1797 and 1810, which were just then being reissued. At some point in the course of these blissful summer months, Felix hit on the idea that would rapidly develop into the greatest success of his young life, an overture to Shakespeare's *A Midsummer Night's Dream*.

Performances of opera overtures as independent concert pieces had become a standard (and occasionally lamented) part of European concert life. Though Mendelssohn's notion of an entirely self-contained overture – an overture, as it were, to an opera that does not exist – appears to have been quite an original stroke, this move is not unlike the process through which the mid-eighteenth-century symphony made its break from the opera *sinfonie*. Indeed, the *Midsummer Night's Dream* overture's debts to contemporary operatic overtures – Spohr's *Jessonda* and Weber's *Oberon* in particular – have often been noted (Mendelssohn was involved in a performance of the *Oberon* overture at the time of its composition). But Mendelssohn's new conception called forth a degree of descriptive detail only hinted at in the great bulk of operatic overtures. It called forth, too, a cornucopia of imaginative material that has remained startlingly fresh as its most direct models have fallen into obscurity.

Four painstakingly orchestrated opening chords – which grow denser by delicate degrees – seem to depict the gradual accumulation of massy substance from thin air, not so much opposing themselves to the silence that precedes and divides them as materialising magically from that silence. The elfin music that follows clearly finds its prototype in the scherzo of the Octet, but achieves a more sheer translucence. Much earthier music is to follow, not least the mimetic brayings of the transfigured Bottom. The second subject was taken by Marx – who evidently played a crucial role in the conceptual genesis of the piece – to portray 'the wanderings of the young pairs of lovers'. Suavely chromatic as this subject may be, it could justly be charged with the lack of rhythmic imagination from which a great many of Mendelssohn's second subjects would suffer. The overture's structure is even more expansive than the Octet's first movement, and even richer in melodic material. In what would soon become a standard device for Mendelssohn, the exposition's material is curtailed in the recapitulation, so that the first subject is followed almost immediately by the second (before the Octet's publication a few years later, Mendelssohn drastically trimmed the recapitulation of its first movement along the same lines).

The fact that so many of Felix's most ambitious early works bear descriptive titles or programmes has tended to place critical conversation about these pieces into broader conversations about the unfolding of programme music in the early nineteenth century. Appropriate as this may be, Mendelssohn's own early programmatic works obviously took root in their own distinctive psychological terrain, and it is tempting to turn a speculative eye towards the motivations, apart from the abstract unfolding of compositional problem-solving, that may have underpinned these works. Though Felix here moves well beyond the retrogressive studiousness of many of his student works, we may still discern an innate distrust of unbridled expressivity. Composition, it appears, is never something so self-indulgent as emotional outpouring, but a precisely crafted response to the cultural artefacts among which Mendelssohn's education situated him. By seeking out programmes through which to 'explain' the most experimental reaches of his increasingly individual compositional voice, Mendelssohn essentially reinscribes the notion of 'faithfulness' on to even his most original utterances. However novel the *Midsummer Night's Dream* overture may be, Mendelssohn invites us to view its creation as an act comparable to Schlegel's translation of the play, a translation of Shakespeare's drama into Mendelssohn's own native tongue. A. B. Marx's complaint against an early version of the work – 'I could perceive no *Midsummer Night's Dream* in it' – points to the fundamental question Mendelssohn invites us to ask of such a piece: how accurately was this translation carried out? How faithful to its original? This principle comes fully into focus in Lobe's recollections of his conversations with Mendelssohn on the subject of this overture, in which Mendelssohn explains to an understandably bewildered Lobe why he considers the overture not a work of genius, but a stroke of luck:

> [W]hat I call luck here is the idea for the subject of this overture,
> which had the ability to provide me with musical ideas and forms that
> could appeal to the general public. What I was able to do as a
> composer, I was able to do before then. But I had never had a similar
> subject before my imagination. That was an inspiration, and a lucky
> one.[6]

Mendelssohn's success on this count was clear enough. Ludwig Rellstab's assessment was echoed by most of the works' commentators: 'a fantastic, intellectual work that allows Shakespeare's romantic play to shimmer through in a happy tone painting'.[7]

★

On 11 November 1826, Ignaz Moscheles' touring schedule brought him again to Berlin, where he at once paid a visit to the Mendelssohns to check on the progress of the two young prodigies he had heard two years before. He listened with delight to Fanny and Felix's rendition, at the keyboard, of the *Midsummer Night's Dream* overture, Felix offering, too, his intensely Beethovenian E-major Piano Sonata and several other works. Moscheles's records the event in his diary:

> This great genius, who is still so young, has made rapid progress since we were last together. This progress has, alas, been acknowledged by only very few outsiders, in addition to his teachers Zelter and Louis Berger. Like others before him, this prophet will have to seek glory in foreign lands.

To the cosmopolitan, London-based Moscheles, Berlin seemed a provincial backwater. Its opera culture was robust enough, and the Singakademie served its rather limited purpose admirably, but this was, in Moscheles' view, hardly a worthy canvas for the life's work of an artist of Mendelssohn's calibre. Just as importantly, it was by no means clear that the city's musical public – many of whom had been exposed to Mendelssohn's work in the Sunday musicales – were sufficiently perceptive, or temperamentally equipped, to appreciate the genius they had in their midst. Whether Moscheles' final pronouncement was correct was an issue the Mendelssohns would confront a few years later, when they sent Felix on a three-year quest for fairer pastures, if, indeed, there were any out there. A matter of more immediate importance was for the young genius who had been educated and nurtured within their walls to take his first firm steps into the public sphere, to see if this hothouse flower could survive transplantation into the out-of-doors.

Very encouraging indeed was the enthusiastic reception accorded the *Midsummer Night's Dream* overture at a Stettin concert on 20 February 1827. Carl Loewe, the concert organiser, also joined the composer in Mendelssohn's Double Piano Concerto in A♭. As imposing a profile as these two works cut, they were dwarfed by the item that made up the second half of the programme (which Mendelssohn's biographer Eric Werner describes as 'one of the most remarkable concerts in the history of musical performance'): the northern European première of Beethoven's Ninth Symphony, in which Mendelssohn played first violin.

Gratified as he was at his reception in Stettin, Mendelssohn had no time to rest on his laurels. Immediately upon returning home, he threw himself into preparations for a performance that might, if it came off, prove a much more significant professional victory than this concert. The director of the Schauspielhaus, Count Karl Friedrich von Brühl, and its musical director, Gaspare Luigi Spontini, had at last agreed to a production of Mendelssohn's comic opera, *Die Hochzeit des Camacho*. The première took place, after considerable complications, on 29 April.

Camacho had been completed nearly two years before, in August 1825. The libretto was the work of Karl Klingemann, based on episodes from Cervantes' *Don Quixote*, which had recently appeared in a German translation by Ludwig Tieck (who had also taken over the series of Shakespeare translations begun by Schlegel). Spontini proved insultingly patronising in an early discussion with Felix on the subject of the score, and appears to have decided early on to make the production as frustrating and humiliating as possible for the eighteen-year-old in whom he may already have discerned a serious competitor. Never known for his gregariousness, Spontini had been brought to Berlin by Friedrich Wilhelm III in 1820, and had grown increasingly spiteful with the years. To Spontini's terrific frustration, the most significant operatic event of his tenure in the city had been the revelatory 1821 première of Weber's *Der Freischütz*. In Mendelssohn's case, he took no chances. Preparations were fraught with complications and delays, culminating in a scene between a frustrated Abraham and Spontini – heretofore a frequent visitor at 3 Leipzigerstrasse – which marked the end of whatever cautious amicability had existed between them.

As helpful as Felix's perceived victimisation was in rallying sympathy for the composer in the wake of the event itself, *Camacho*'s tepid reception reflected only too accurately the piece's worth. The audience at the première (which took place not in the main hall of the Schauspielhaus, but in the smaller chamber theatre) included many friends and acquaintances, but not even they could muster a persuasive show of enthusiasm. Applause after the first act was vigorous enough, but it became apparent as the second act wore on that Mendelssohn was not making the sort of effect to which he had grown accustomed in more intimate surroundings. The composer fled, despondent, into the night before the final curtain. Illnesses among the cast and further complications prevented a projected second performance from taking place, and Mendelssohn chose not to press the issue. A repeat performance never occurred, and apart from incidental music Mendelssohn never put before the public another work for the stage.

The magnitude of this failure, from the young composer's perspective, must be measured not against his existing achievements, much less those to come, but against his hopes. As a boy of twelve, he had witnessed the triumphant première of *Der Freischütz*, an experience not soon forgotten. Though he would hardly dare hope for a similar reception – no German operatic composer has duplicated it – this impression no doubt lingered still as an ideal in the back of his mind. His own work neither deserved nor received comparable welcome, and Mendelssohn must himself have been only too aware that he had outgrown this music by the time of its first performance.

Despite occasional flashes of originality, particularly in the work's superb orchestration, *Camacho* suffers as much from a dearth of memorable melodies as from Klingemann's somewhat underdeveloped sense of dramatic pacing. Eduard Devrient, a member of the original cast, remarked that it suffered even by comparison with Mendelssohn's earlier private efforts in the genre. The vigorously Weberesque overture struggles to get airborne, and even within its relatively short span begins to feel stiff and unmotivated. The curtain goes up on a love duet – 'Happy days of youth, made lovelier by love!' – which typifies the dramaturgical miscalculations to which Mendelssohn and his inexperienced librettist frequently fall prey. Totally absent are the complex interpersonal dynamics that animate and shape Figaro and Susanna's opening duet under Mozart and Da Ponte's expert hands. Here we find only blissful assertions of faithfulness between the two lovers, Quiteria and Basilio, mingled with vague intimations that trouble is brewing for the couple; as it happens, Quiteria's father intends her not for Basilio, but for Camacho. The moment is engaging as a display of intimacy, and might have made perfect sense to the private audience to which Mendelssohn was accustomed, an audience joined through bonds of friendship. But a broader public cannot at once feel itself a part of this intimate moment. The genius of the crowd scene that opens *Der Freischütz* lies in the fact that it gives the *Volk* assembled in the theatre an on-stage community with which to identify, thus a sense of immediate attachment to the protagonist who springs from their ranks. (Indeed, *Der Freischütz*, in an early draft, had begun with an encounter between Agathe and the Hermit, which was wisely deleted as dramatically untenable. That the Hermit's Act III entrance becomes, by this deletion, a pitifully unsupported *Deus ex machina* was a flaw even the work's first critics found difficult to forgive.)

★

Mendelssohn decided to nurse his stung ego by once more putting some distance between himself and his hometown, this time with a walking tour through the Harz Mountains, Franconia, Bavaria, Baden and the Rhineland in the company of Gustav Magnus and Albert Heydemann (Eduard Rietz was with the party as far as Thuringia). By September, he was able to look back on the heart-breaking events of April with cool resolve – indeed, with what proved to be unwarranted optimism:

> people expect something special from me, and much more than was achieved in *Die Hochzeit des Camacho* . . . I have blazed a path for myself in instrumental music . . . but in other areas I have yet to. I know that I shall also be able to do so in the genre of opera . . .

The recuperation process did not, of course, require Felix to put his work behind him altogether. One of the most joyful letters of the journey comes from his Baden hotel, where acquaintances and strangers alike had cajoled him into a number of impromptu performances: 'I opened the piano, and after the first few notes there were thirty or forty people there in the room, French, English,

Strasburgers, cosmopolitans . . . applauding very liberally. . .' This was still the environment in which Mendelssohn felt most at home, conjuring an aura of warm *Gemüthlichkeit* even among complete strangers.

In Frankfurt he met once more with Ferdinand Hiller, who did not recognise him at first: 'His [Felix's] figure had become broad and full, and there was a general air of smartness about him, with none of that careless ease which he sometimes adopted later in life'. Among the many musicians with whom Mendelssohn came into contact in this city – including also pianists Henri Herz and Ferdinand Ries – a figure of particular interest for Mendelssohn was Johann Nepomuk Schelble. The founder and director of Frankfurt's Caecilienverein, Schelble was emerging as one of Germany's most forceful advocates of Handel, J. S. Bach and, within a few years, Felix Mendelssohn. Apart from Zelter, Schelble represented Mendelssohn's most important model in the realm of historical choral music performance. Two years later, Mendelssohn's own first unqualified public triumph – the revival of Bach's *St Matthew Passion* – seemed to mark his own first resolute step down a similar professional path.

Another highlight of the journey for Felix was his September meeting in Heidelberg with Justus Thibaut. Mendelssohn was well acquainted with Thibaut's idiosyncratic but widely read book, *Reinheit der Tonkunst* ('Purity in Music') which had appeared two years earlier, and soon fell into a relationship of the deepest mutual respect: 'there is but one Thibaut', he wrote, 'but he is worth six. What a man!' Though he was surprised at Thibaut's essentially instinctive way of dealing with music – scarcely rivalling Mendelssohn in his historical knowledge, much less analytical skill – Mendelssohn traced his own interest in sixteenth- and seventeenth-century Italian choral music (whose 'purity' was the subject of Thibaut's book) to these conversations. On his return to Berlin he took up the composition of sacred music with greater enthusiasm than ever before, much of it decidedly Catholic in stylistic hue. It is difficult to escape the sense that, in his life as both a composer and, soon, a conductor, Mendelssohn was beating a hasty retreat from the heady, high-stakes environment of opera into the more familiar, more secure terrain of choral music.

★

Mendelssohn soon became a busy young man on his return to Berlin. He had secured a position at the university in May with a metrical translation of Terence's Latin comedy, *The Woman of Andros*, and began his studies in October (he had already begun signing his name 'Felix, stud. phil.' over the summer). There he attended Hegel's lectures on aesthetics, Carl Ritter's on geography, and those of legal historian and family friend Eduard Gans on the history of political freedom.

Hardly had his studies begun than he suffered a private blow as serious, in its way, as the public humiliation of the *Camacho* affair, and Karl Klingemann was once more involved. Klingemann had been called to London as attaché to the Hanoverian delegation, an appointment that would remove him from Berlin indefinitely. His departure was heart-breaking to the young circle of friends. 'Our Sundays', Fanny wrote to him two days before Christmas, 'are no longer so fairy-like: the true spirit of fun and pleasure is gone, and you know best who carried it away! It is a pity!'

Notwithstanding Fanny's closing gambit here, Klingemann's departure seems not to have been the only source of unrest at 3 Leipzigerstrasse. Tensions that may have been at work for years within the household were growing less and less easy to conceal, and there is a sense that the patina of magic that had surrounded life at 3 Leipzigerstrasse was growing difficult to sustain. Though there is no evidence of a full-blown falling out, and the two remained close for their entire lives, Felix's correspondence with Fanny from about this time includes occasionally heated exchanges that point to serious points of stress beneath the surface. In September, for instance, in response to the news that Fanny had been sorting among his belongings, Felix offered the chilling warning:

> You must get a rap on the knuckles . . . are you the inquisition? Do you spy on me? Is the string, on which I flutter, long, but unbreakable? You were in my room? Prying into my things? . . . Take care, fair flower, take care . . .!

5 Fanny in 1829, affectionately rendered by Wilhelm Hensel

Regardless of the sources of this particular disagreement, tension was perhaps inevitable in a household of four children which revolved, increasingly, around a single one of them. The ascent of Felix's star proved particularly tough on the younger pair of siblings. Rebecka – an excellent singer, though she would largely give up music in her married life – would later reflect on her teenage years:

My older brother and sister stole my reputation as an artist. In any
other family I would have been highly regarded as a musician and
perhaps been leader of a group. Next to Felix and Fanny, I could not
aspire to any recognition.

Less happy still was the youngest of the family, Paul, whose adolescence was the most difficult the house had suffered through. Writing
in 1830, Felix reflected on life around 1827 (in a portion of the letter
Paul chose to suppress in his own edition of Mendelssohn's travel
letters), happy to report that:

> all of the little discords we may have had with one another from time
> to time three years ago – since the morning when we were quarrelling
> so awfully and I threw you off the chair, whereupon you scratched
> me, whereupon I told on you, whereupon you couldn't stand me,
> whereupon I became very angry (I think you will remember) – have
> completely disappeared, and probably forever.

To make matters worse, Felix's creative development had taken a
strange and, to some, troubling course. In the eighteen months following the *Midsummer Night's Dream* overture, he composed no new
orchestral music. The intermittently bristly A-minor Quartet he completed in October of 1827, together with two recent piano sonatas,
exhibited more fully than any works yet the influence of late
Beethoven, a development about which Abraham was openly dis-
traught ('He was then in a constant state of irritation', Felix recalled of
these months, 'incessantly abusing Beethoven and all visionaries; and
this . . . made me sometimes very unamiable'). Most distressing to Lea
was the fact that the thirst for contrapuntal challenge which had
created the Octet had lately converged with Felix's blossoming interest in older forms of vocal polyphony. The often archaising offspring
of this union – the *Te Deum* for double chorus, the *Tu es Petrus* for five-
voice chorus and orchestra, and the first of a series of Bach-inspired
chorale cantatas, *Christe, du Lamm Gottes* – Lea described to
Klingemann as 'stillborn children', lamenting in December 1827, 'he
now composes only the type of pieces that nobody may see and that

can hardly be performed'. Though several of these remarkably accomplished works – whose culminating *tour de force* was the sixteen-voice *Hora est* completed in December 1828 – were indeed performed, enjoyed and acclaimed through these years, none went into print in Mendelssohn's lifetime. And they were certainly not geared to place Felix on the cutting edge of European musical life, where Lea was justifiably convinced he belonged. The family breathed a collective sigh of relief at the appearance, in May 1828, of a new concert overture, *Calm Sea, Prosperous Voyage*, which was a more than worthy successor to *Midsummer Night's Dream*, if a slim notch below it in melodic richness and sheer charisma.

History has been kinder to the A-minor Quartet than Mendelssohn's family seems to have been. 'The tendency of this piece', Hiller recalled, 'had not been appreciated in his own circle, and he had a feeling of isolation in consequence'. By the time of his magisterial 1959 biography, Eric Werner was able to offer this rather more encouraging assessment, and was hardly the first to single the work out for this sort of praise: 'had Mendelssohn been able to maintain the level of this quartet, his name would stand in close proximity to that of a Mozart or Beethoven!' (Needless to say, Werner's was a simpler age than our own in matters of critical analysis, an age in which assessments of this kind could be – and in this case were – based on two simple measures: the prevalence of unifying devices and a piece's harmonic resemblance to Wagner's *Tristan und Isolde*.) This quartet does indeed outpace even Beethoven, in all but his most extreme musings, in its degree of dissonance, and one can well imagine why its frequent intimations of something like inner torment would make Abraham 'rack [his] brains to discover the composer's thoughts'.[8]

The piece sets off cheerfully enough, however, from an A-major introduction that concludes with an incipit, 'Ist es wahr?', of Mendelssohn's own amorous Lied, 'Frage'. At the end of the finale, following a brief reprise of a subject from the slow movement, this introduction returns, now terminating with the closing lines of the Lied. This was hardly the first time Mendelssohn had attempted this

sort of cyclic design (the Octet, a most conspicuous example, had featured a reprise of scherzo material in the finale), but it is the most
thoroughgoing, and thoroughly steeped in Beethoven's precedents.
'That is one of my principles', Mendelssohn had written the previous
year. 'The relation of all four or three or two or one movements of a
sonata to each other and their respective parts.'[9]

The influence of Beethoven was nowhere more evident, though,
than in Mendelssohn's increasingly ambitious piano sonatas of this
period. The lyrical opening of the E-major Sonata of 1826, the first that
Mendelssohn would put into print, occupies the same sonic world as
Beethoven's late sonatas, especially in a lyrical opening subject evocative of Beethoven's opp. 101 and 110. Here, too, material from the first
movement is recalled in the last (the immediate model in this case
being perhaps Beethoven's op. 101). The Sonata in B♭, completed on 31
May 1827, bears unmistakable resemblances in melody, structure and
tonal planning to Beethoven's B♭ 'Hammerklavier' Sonata, which
Mendelssohn had performed in Stettin the previous February. In this
case, as in the Octet, it is the Scherzo that returns in the finale, though
Weber's influence edges out Beethoven's through the bulk of this brilliant movement.

A compositional agenda more distinctly Mendelssohn's own is set
forth in the Sieben Characterstücke ('Seven Character Pieces') op. 7.
These seven little works gave the public their first hard look at the stylistic eclecticism – deeply informed by a frankly historicistic sensibility – that would be a sticking point for Mendelssohn's critics
throughout his career. Rarely does Mendelssohn offer so clear a look
at the compositional programme that so bewildered Franz Brendel,
for example, in his 1845 assessment of Mendelssohn's career.
Mendelssohn, Brendel argued,

> did not take Beethoven's last period – where a composer dedicated to
> the new ideal would have found the point of departure for further
> development – as his starting point, nor, in general, did he follow any
> one specific master; rather, he tended to take the entire past,

Sebastian Bach and Mozart, as his prerequisite, and not so much in order to seize upon a specific task or to set out straightaway in an entirely modern direction.

The first of the seven pieces is a dense, contrapuntal web that makes no apology for its debt to Bach. The jolly fugue that makes up the third movement takes the language of Handel as its point of departure; the fifth is firmly rooted in the abstruse fugal style that so pervades Beethoven's late works. Distinctively Mendelssohn's own is the closing piece, 'Leicht und luftig', which taps into the same fleet-footed vein that generated the fairy music of the *Midsummer Night's Dream* overture and the Scherzo of the Octet. Needless to say, all is authorised, in this early salvo, by the rubric of the 'character piece', a designation that places these daring evocations of the past safely in musical quotation marks.

With his overture on the subject, Mendelssohn was not the first composer to turn his attention to Goethe's poetic diptych, 'Meeresstille' and 'Glückliche Fahrt' ('Calm Sea' and 'Prosperous Voyage'); Beethoven had set the pair as a cantata in 1822. Two years later, A. B. Marx – who was just then beginning to travel in Mendelssohn's circle – produced a lengthy review of Beethoven's work in the *Berliner allgemeine musikalische Zeitung*, a journal he had just founded. Beethoven's whole conception was flawed, in Marx's estimation, by his choice of the choral medium – 'Anyone who truly experiences the poem can do so only in complete isolation'. Mendelssohn's 1828 overture, completed sometime in late spring, fared more prosperously, being hailed in Marx's contemporaneous monograph, *Über Malerei in der Tonkunst*, as bringing to perfection the union of words and music called for by Beethoven's Ninth Symphony.

The work is conceived, as Fanny puts it, not as an overture with introduction, but as 'two separate tableaux'; thus, though the adagio 'Meerestille' is closely related thematically to the molto allegro e vivace 'Glückliche Fahrt', the former arrives at a full stop on the tonic chord, suggesting formal closure and complete stasis rather than forward motion. The opening idea of the allegro subject bears a suspicious structural resemblance to Cherubino's 'Non so più' aria (a rather different image of unbridled forward motion), though it is based – as is practically every idea in the piece – on the four-note descending motif set out by the basses in the first bars of the adagio. The whole culminates in a coda organised around a jubilant fanfare for three trumpets, evidently hailing the vessel's safe arrival at port, that 'adds a connotation', as Lawrence Kramer puts it, 'of mercantile adventure, the modern (that is, capitalist) heroism of voyaging for wealth'.[10]

This conclusion seems a highly significant one. Mendelssohn here sets forth as his musical point of arrival the musical language of public, communal celebration: his next symphony, the 'Reformation', would arrive at a similar conclusion with its closing chorale, mingled with intimations of vocal fugue; the 'Scottish' Symphony, as we shall see much later, turns to the language of the commemorative *Festgesang* in the coda of its finale. There is a strong sense that such musical narratives figure substantively in Mendelssohn's broader pursuit of alternatives to the conceptualisation of music as unchecked personal self-expression (we have touched on this issue, from a different angle, with respect to his programme music in general); the *telos* of these works is in the celebration of the collective utterance, not in introspection. As choral music – music for use by an amateur public in a convivial setting – was threatening to edge out instrumental concert music in Mendelssohn's compositional programme, even his instrumental music seems to move towards valorising the moment of collective music-making as its logical goal.

★

At the same time that this overture was taking shape, Mendelssohn completed a work much more directly tied to his emerging interest in public musical life: a large cantata (*Grosse Festmusik*) for the Berlin Academy of Fine Arts festival commemorating the three-hundredth anniversary of Albrecht Dürer's death on 18 April. Though at first reluctant to accept the commission, Mendelssohn found himself more wildly acclaimed on this occasion than ever before. Fanny, who recognised in the event a reversal in Mendelssohn's troubled artistic fortunes, describes his reception at the dinner that evening, and the happy impact the whole affair had had on her brother:

> I cannot tell you how Felix was honoured and courted by people of distinction, known and unknown; but one thing I must add, that towards the end of the meal Zelter and Schadow took him by the hand, and the latter made a speech to him and solemnly proclaimed him an honorary member of the Artists' Association, of which he received the diploma. At the same time his health was proposed and enthusiastically cheered. Yesterday the whole day was taken up by visits of congratulation. But what rejoices me most is that he himself is so pleased with this day, and shows himself more susceptible than hitherto of the honours he received. I assure you he is more excellent and more amiable from day to day . . .

Festivals commemorating great figures or events in German history were emerging as an increasingly important forum for the dissemination of popular nationalistic sentiment. They found their roots in the massive French festivals of the Revolutionary years, though the German article tended to be more pointed in its historical dimension. Through celebrations 'commemorating the noble dead', in the words of Prussian propagandist E. M. Arndt, 'history enters life and life itself becomes part of history'. It is hardly surprising that Protestant Germany perceived in the sixteenth century what Arthur Groos describes as 'a principal locus for contemporary discourse about "German-ness", a cultural unity projected backward onto the period of the Reformation'.[11] Commemorations of Luther, Dürer and Hans Sachs constituted a focal point in the crystallisation of Prussian national identity. Mendelssohn was to become a regular contributor to events of this kind.

The entry of history into public life was nowhere clearer than in the work of the man who designed the sets for the *Dürerfest*, Karl Friedrich Schinkel, whose career reflected a set of priorities not at all unlike

6 Karl Friedrich Schinkel's perspective drawing of his 1818 design for the new Singakademie

those taking shape in Mendelssohn's mind. Though principally an architect, Schinkel's portfolio also included monuments to Queen Luise, General Scharnhorst, and Frederick the Great. At the time of the *Dürerfest*, one of Schinkel's most ambitious projects – the new public museum – was under way, a work, as one recent history puts it, in which 'Schinkel could indulge . . . freely in his belief that architecture should educate and improve the public by awakening its members to their own identity and to that of the historical culture to which they belong'. Mendelssohn was a regular patron of Schinkel's Schauspielhaus in the Gendarmenmarkt, where *Camacho* had been performed. Schinkel had been responsible, too, for the initial design of the Singakademie's new accommodations, which had enabled them to move out of the Academy of Science. The public spaces he was called on to create thus defined the trajectory of Prussia's cultural revitalisation, spaces facilitating and, as it were, authorising the popular celebration of drama, music and the fine arts. Schinkel's neoclassical architectural language – consolidated during his two-year visit to Italy – points to the state's eagerness to allow Prussian cultural life to crystallise around the appropriation of whatever past models seemed most relevant, drawing, as the architect himself put it, on the 'great vast store of forms that had already come into being, deposited in the world over many millennia of development among very different peoples'.

If this event left Mendelssohn feeling as warmly as he ever had towards the Berlin public, his finest hour arrived a few months later, with the Singakademie's 11 March 1829 revival of Bach's *St Matthew Passion* under Mendelssohn's baton. Mendelssohn had begun rehearsing parts of the work privately two years earlier. It was evidently Eduard Devrient who determined that a full performance should be undertaken, and Devrient who proved sufficiently tenacious with the sceptical Zelter to obtain his approval of the project.

Though the work had not been performed since Bach's lifetime, Mendelssohn can hardly be said to have single-handedly rescued Bach from obscurity (as much ink has been spilled debunking this myth as putting it in place). The influence of Bach's keyboard music on composers throughout the late eighteenth and early nineteenth centuries – Mozart and Beethoven not least among them – is well documented. Lea's family took for granted the centrality of Bach's work to the keyboard repertory (her famous observation at Fanny's birth – 'She has Bach-fugue fingers' – reveals a great deal about Lea's own musical outlook, quite apart from its interest as prophecy). At the centre of Bach fandom in Berlin was Mendelssohn's great aunt, Sara Levy, a former student of Sebastian's son, Wilhelm Friedemann Bach. Manuscripts from Levy's personal library constituted a large fraction of the Singakademie's holdings, and as a harpsichordist, she had spearheaded a recrudescence of interest in Bach's concertos in the Berlin of Mendelssohn's youth.

Bach's choral music was another matter. Despite piecemeal signs of popular interest – most importantly renditions of motets and other smaller works by Berlin's Singakademie and Frankfurt's Caecilienverein – Bach's choral music had fallen into almost total neglect. By the late 1820s, the need for a reconsideration of Bach's larger choral music had become apparent in many quarters across northern Germany. In a letter of April 1828, Fanny cited Schlesinger's impending decision to publish the St Matthew Passion (an event in which A. B. Marx played no small part) and Schelble's direction of a portion of the B-minor Mass in Frankfurt, concluding, 'The movement is general, the same wind is rustling in all the branches, there is no shutting one's ears to it'.

The score of the work from which Mendelssohn conducted the St Matthew Passion was a copy of a score prepared by Zelter from Bach's original performing parts, which then belonged to the Singakademie. Mendelssohn made numerous cuts, doing away with many arias and chorales, and picking his way meticulously through the recitatives. Though the performance may not have been historically accurate by modern standards, the audience at the première (which sold out in a matter of hours) certainly felt that they had received the genuine article, and it came as a revelation. After a second performance,

Mendelssohn wrote to Klingemann, 'There was a crowd and a noise the like of which I have never experienced at a concert of sacred music'. As astonishing as the rediscovery of Bach may have been, just as surprising was a glimpse of the amazing conductor whose own enthusiasm had brought the whole to life. By the time of the performance itself, word had spread through the city of this youngster who conducted and accompanied each rehearsal with passion, with thoughtful precision, and entirely from memory. At a stroke, Mendelssohn had become one of the leading figures in the historical performance movement, indeed, one of Germany's most celebrated conductors. Goethe responded to Zelter's reports on the occasion, 'It is as if I heard the roaring of the sea from afar'. Berlin did not get to enjoy the young star for long, however; by the third performance of the work, Felix had left town.

4 The Grand Tour

[T]he horse moved blamelessly along, at an equal step with the
humble pedestrian, so that the father, from the pulpit of the saddle,
could send down innumerable rules of life and jurisprudence. But
how could Walt listen to them? He saw only within and without the
bright morning fields of youthful life, or the landscapes on both
sides of the road; or, more distant, the shaded flower-garden of love,
and the high, cloudless mount of the muses, and at last the towers
and columns of smoke rising from the outspread city.

Jean-Paul, Flegeljahre[1]

On 10 April 1829, flush with the success of the St Matthew Passion performance, Mendelssohn set out on his great Bildungsreise. Though
these three years of travel would be rich in professional accomplish-
ments, the primary aim of the trip was to settle on a locale in which he
might undertake his life's work. Spring and summer were spent in
England and Scotland. Fanny's October wedding (which, as it happened, he missed) and the December celebration of his parents' silver
wedding anniversary occasioned a return to Berlin before the most
substantial portion of the journey, which began in May 1830.
Travelling through Weimar, Munich and Vienna, he arrived at last in
Rome, where he spent the winter. After heading as far south as
Naples, Mendelssohn returned through northern Italy, Germany and
Switzerland to spend the sad second winter of his journey in Paris. A
brief return to England during the spring concert season of 1832

7 Europe in 1815

reaffirmed the mutual fondness he and the London public had discovered on his initial visit. The journey closed with his June arrival in Berlin.

Constructing a narrative of this period is one of the biographer's happiest tasks, as Felix himself emerges as his own greatest chronicler: articulate, thorough, insightful, touching and very funny. The letters through which he sought to sustain intimate bonds with family and friends at home afford not only a detailed – often day-by-day – account, but clear and frank insights on his developing artistic sensibility. The first major collection of his correspondence published were letters from Italy and Switzerland, a volume that (though far from complete) ran to well over 300 pages. Though these letters were intended to be passed through the hands of the entire circle, even copied for distribution to distant friends and family, Mendelssohn's letters outline distinctly the personal dynamics operating within the tightly knit household. It is often to Rebecka, perhaps his closest personal confidante, that he addresses his most intimate remarks concerning the light-hearted flirtations, real and contemplated, so essential to the social life of the young cavalier he was becoming. He provides Fanny with regular reports on his progress on the many compositional projects he was kicking around at any given moment. Paul receives occasional mumblings on the bewildering intricacies of European currencies. Lengthy letters to Zelter record his musical impressions in amazing detail, peppered with actual musical quotations (his notebook of musical jottings was just as essential to him as the sketchbook that was his constant companion). To his father he dutifully reports on the plans, hopes, negotiations and achievements shaping his life as a young professional.

★

Rebecka and Abraham accompanied Felix as far as Hamburg: Mendelssohn set off across the Channel on Saturday 18 April. Thanks to fog, engine trouble and heavy boat traffic at the mouth of the Thames, he did not set foot on dry London ground until Tuesday (as Klingemann, who greeted him on his arrival, recalled, 'he is on better terms with the sea as a musician than as an individual or a stomach'). 'Picture me', Mendelssohn wrote of the voyage,

> dragging myself around from one fainting fit to the next, from early Sunday to Monday night, disgusted with myself and everything else, cursing the steamer, England, and especially my own *Meeresstille*, and scolding the steward as hard as I could.[2]

Mendelssohn's initial bewilderment at the monstrous, incredibly diverse urban expanse of London – 'It is fearful! It is maddening!' – is understandable. At the beginning of the century, London had over a million inhabitants, roughly twice as many as Paris. The city had swollen to over two-and-a-half million by mid-century. The young man's hold on sanity was not as tenuous, however, as his early letters suggested. Within days of his arrival, he had ensconced himself comfortably in a close-knit circle of (mostly German) friends who would be his constant companions through his entire stay in London: Karl Klingemann, of course, with whom Mendelssohn would tour Scotland in the summer; Friedrich Rosen, the orientalist whose younger sister would later become Klingemann's wife; attorney Ludwig von Mühlenfels, driven out of Berlin by legal troubles almost a decade before, though he would return there before Felix himself. Most touching of all – and certainly most significant from a professional standpoint – was the devoted attention of Ignaz Moscheles and his wife, Charlotte, long-time celebrities of the city whose tours and introductions soon left Mendelssohn feeling entirely at home. It was largely through Moscheles' efforts that Mendelssohn found himself travelling in circles that included London's brightest musical lights: Sir George Smart, John Baptist Cramer, Muzio Clementi and Sir Thomas Attwood, among others. By the first of May, Felix was able to write: 'I'm feeling very well, by the way, life here suits me wonderfully. I find the city and its streets altogether beautiful'.

Mendelssohn immediately awoke to a thriving, diverse concert life shaped largely by convictions comfortingly similar to his own. The 'Concerts of Antient Music', which admitted no work less than twenty years old, had kept Handel and a number of Baroque contemporaries (though not Bach) constantly before the public since the eighteenth century. While London had also been attracting Europe's leading virtuosos since the 1790s, and virtuoso-driven concerts of fashionable 'modern' music were as popular as ever in the late 1820s, there were important counter-forces at the heart of the city's musical life. The Philharmonic Society, created in its current form in 1813, had been founded with an eye towards the promotion of 'Classical music'. Offering concerts centred on the instrumental works of Beethoven, Mozart and Haydn, the founders initially banned soloists altogether, considering virtuosity an empty distraction from an appreciation for the genuine art of composition (Mozart and Beethoven's concertos were essentially unknown). 'The orchestra is outstanding', Mendelssohn gushed, 'full of fire and strength, and the basses and violins in particular play quite splendidly'. Nowhere was Mendelssohn's innate artistic sympathy with the orchestra's founders clearer than in his own refusal – later reiterated in Paris – to perform in public until a composition of his had been performed by the Society.

Relatively inexperienced as he was in the complex and often thankless business of self-promotion, Mendelssohn's initial encounters with London's musical powers-that-be were not without discouraging missteps. A series of misunderstandings – blended with what Mendelssohn perceived to be an element of intrigue on the part of the Philharmonic Society's director, Sir George Smart – made it seem for a time as though he would not find his way on to the Society's play list at all before the end of the season. At Moscheles' prompting, Smart had paid a visit to Berlin's 3 Leipzigerstrasse during an 1825 tour of the continent (a tour that had also involved meetings with Beethoven and Weber). As impressed as he had been with Fanny and Felix – 'I strongly recommended young Mendelssohn to visit England' – Smart displayed no initial interest in promoting him when he arrived. Appearing in public had not been the initial aim of the trip, and Mendelssohn had denied, early on, that he even planned on the attempt. This soon emerged, though, as his chief goal.

Happily, these early tribulations were soon put behind him, a chance encounter with more conciliatory members of the Society leading to an immediate opportunity. When Mendelssohn at last did succeed in setting his C-minor Symphony before the orchestra, with its somewhat conservative minuet replaced by an arrangement of the scherzo from the Octet, his reputation was made at a stroke. The first rehearsal – 'one of the happiest moments within my recollection' – took place before an audience of around two hundred. Orchestra and audience alike were taken totally by surprise by 'this small fellow with the stick' (the conductor's baton was still a novelty, though Spohr had appeared with one), and the euphoric composer 'had to shake at least

8 Mendelssohn as dandy in 1829: oil painting by James Warren Childe

two hundred different hands'. After the piece's 25 May performance –
'The success was greater than I could ever have dreamed' –
Mendelssohn found himself one of the most discussed, most sought-
after musical figures in the city.

Not only was the C-minor Symphony itself hailed as a work of
genius, the scherzo tumultuously encored, but its composer offered

the English a model of the gentleman musician: cultivated, well spoken and genuinely modest. His command of the language was at least serviceable, his slight lisp rendering spotty syntax more charming still. Just as importantly, he was a man of independent means, unsullied by the debasing – in the eyes of the elite – influences of the increasing professionalism that distinguished London musical life from the teens onward. 'Father wonders all the time', Fanny wrote in June, 'why you still haven't accepted any money';[3] Mendelssohn did well to follow his own instincts in the matter. The Athenaeum's 22 July notice of Mendelssohn's last appearance (of 13 July) reads as much like a letter of introduction as a concert review:

> A most extraordinary man, whose name we have not hitherto presented to our readers, and whose appearance here was one of the grand features of the concert. We allude to M. Mendelssohn a pianoforte player of almost transcendent talent, which becomes more admirable when something of the man was known. He is very young, independent in station, his father being an opulent banker in Leipsic [sic]; and with a thirst and love of music nearly unparalleled, his modesty blinds him to the success with which he has cultivated it . . . As a performer, his abilities are first-rate. In the act of playing he is lost to everything besides the instrument before him. His memory is represented as being the most wonderful of his faculties.[4]

By the time of this review, Mendelssohn had appeared in four concerts. Five days after his first appearance, he made his English debut at the keyboard, performing Carl Maria von Weber's Konzertstück. The selection of this piece – whose 1821 première Mendelssohn had probably witnessed, though it was still unknown in England at the time of his arrival – was savvy in several respects. The Konzertstück was ferociously demanding from a technical standpoint, and Mendelssohn rendered this dazzling display of pianistic virtuosity transcendent by performing the work from memory, a highly exceptional practice at the time. Just as importantly, Mendelssohn was effectively asserting his affiliation with the distinguished German musicians who had preceded him in the conquest of the English musical imagination, a line extending from Handel, through Haydn, to Spohr and Weber. This, too, was a letter of introduction, as it were, a communication from a common friend to say that this unfamiliar newcomer was to be welcomed. The reception of the work doubtless brought with it a sense of vindication, on Mendelssohn's part, on behalf of the older composer. Weber – whom, as Mendelssohn wrote, the English had 'really treated . . . shamefully' – had died in George Smart's house during preparations for the 1826 première of *Oberon*. (The German iron merchant, Heinke, in whose house at 103 Great Portland Street Mendelssohn lodged during this visit, was the one who had picked the lock to Weber's bedroom where his body was discovered.[5])

At a 24 June concert, the *Midsummer Night's Dream* overture was performed under Felix's direction, to thunderous acclaim. A *Harmonicon* critic found the work 'sparkling with genius and rich in effect . . . the musician has studied the poet, has entered into his thoughts, and even caught some of his imagination'. This concert also found Mendelssohn at the keyboard for Beethoven's 'Emperor' Concerto (whose slipshod handling by the orchestra drove its soloist nearly to distraction). By the beginning of July, he had marshalled enough enthusiasm and goodwill to undertake personally the organisation of the concert that would mark his final appearance for the year, a brilliant extravaganza for the benefit of Silesian flood victims. Though its 13 July date was exceptionally late in the season, the roster was so crowded with celebrities that vocal solos had to be banned, the brightest operatic luminaries of the city allowed to appear only in ensembles. Along with a repetition, by popular demand, of the *Midsummer Night's Dream* overture, this concert included Mendelssohn's E-major Double Concerto, performed with Moscheles. By this point, it was not clear which of the two benefited the most by association with the other.

What *was* clear is that whatever doubts had lurked in the hearts of Mendelssohn's parents – even in his own – as to his prospects for success as a professional musician had been put to rest once and for all. Surrounded by some of the best friends he would ever have, celebrated in London as only a handful of musicians had ever been celebrated, Mendelssohn's fate had been sealed in the course of a few weeks. Though he would never settle there, Mendelssohn would return to London almost yearly.

In sizing up Mendelssohn's experience in London, particularly the seemingly inexplicable fact that he never seriously considered settling down there, we must bear in mind that English society was far from universally pleasing to him. His closest friends were a circle of German expatriates. As profound as his contentment may have been in their company, this was only an oasis in the midst of a society whose general aspect held little appeal; his social existence in London was grounded, to a great extent, in the same drive towards self-satisfied insularity that underpinned life at 3 Leipzigerstrasse. A letter of 9 May to A. B. Marx offers a glimpse of his familiar capacity for scorn: 'they worship Beethoven and edit him, they worship Mozart and are bored with it, they worship Haydn and rush him to death. Music is a thing of fashion and is pursued as such.' Though this letter was written at the height of his frustrating pursuit of an entree into the society he was describing, he would still be characterising London musicians as 'miserable dross' in late October (though, as we shall see, he had other things to be grumpy about by that time). At a deeper level, Mendelssohn never quite made his peace with the 'cold-bloodedness of London society and people', that is, the pervasive sense of human alienation that was part and parcel of life in a city of that size: 'one becomes almost cold and indifferent to other people there, when there is a fire alarm only looking out the window to see where the flames are, then falling calmly back to sleep if they aren't too close'.

★

On 22 July, Mendelssohn and Klingemann set off by coach for Edinburgh. Mendelssohn had never been so far from nature for so long, and was overwhelmed with the Scottish landscape from the moment of his arrival: 'God is so kind in Edinburgh'. Soon after their arrival, they visited Holyrood Palace, and the desecrated chapel in which Mary had been crowned Queen of Scotland. It was there, as

Mendelssohn reported, 'that I found the beginning of my Scottish Symphony'; he would not find the end until 1842.

The pair set out on 31 July for a day-long journey to visit Sir Walter Scott at Abbotsford. They found Scott distracted by preparations for his own imminent departure, 'stared at him like fools', and were rewarded for their troubles with 'one half-hour of superficial conversation'. The following day, they set out on a three-week tour, mostly on foot, across the Scottish Highlands.

By 7 August they had reached the west coast, and Mendelssohn once more braved the ocean, crossing by steamship to the Isle of Mull. That evening, in a letter headed 'On one of the Hebrides', he wrote 'In order to make clear to you the extraordinary effect the Hebrides have had on me, the following occurred to me there'. There follows twenty-one bars of music in short score, with detailed instrumental indications, that resemble closely the opening bars of the *Hebrides* overture in its final form (which was reached, after laborious revisions, some three years later). As in the 'Scottish' Symphony discovery of the previous week, Mendelssohn proves fascinated with the possibility of describing a locale in music, not simply a synaesthetic translation of sight into sound, but a musical mapping out of complex emotional topography. The *Hebrides* overture seems to complete the move – begun in the acutely naturalistic *Calm Sea, Prosperous Voyage*, despite that work's nominal foundations in poetry – from literary to pictorial subject matter, though this, as R. Larry Todd has shown, would be an oversimplification.[6] The roots of the European fascination with these islands were inextricably intertwined with Ossianic poetry, the inauthentic body of ancient Celtic poetry, 'translated' by James Macpherson, which brought with it the tantalising offer of 'an alternative source for the Western classical tradition'. For Robert Schumann, the literary foundations of the *Hebrides* overture were obvious: 'the overtures to *A Midsummer Night's Dream* and *The Hebrides* . . . are to one another as Shakespeare is to Ossian'.

Nonetheless, Mendelssohn's sense of the musical illustration as a natural and worthy counterpart to pictorial illustration had never

9   Engraving of Staffa from Thomas Pennant, *Tour in Scotland and Voyage to the Hebrides*, MDCCLXXII, vol. 2

been more pronounced. In Wales, during a visit of several days at the Coed Du home of mine owner Edward Taylor, Mendelssohn took frequent excursions into the countryside with the three charming daughters of the family – Honora, Susan and Anne. An accomplished artist herself, Anne recalled: 'His way of representing [the hills and the woods] was not with pencil; but in the evening his improvised music would show what he had observed or felt in the past day'. From such musings emerged the 'three Welsh pieces', as Mendelssohn habitually referred to them, ultimately published as op. 16. These vignettes – inspired variously by a rivulet, an arrangement of carnations and roses, and 'little trumpet-like flowers' – he described as 'three of my best piano compositions'.

It may not be a complete coincidence that the only major piece completed by this freshly minted dandy during his months in England was also dedicated to a young woman, long-time Berlin acquaintance Betty Pistor, in whom Mendelssohn seems to have taken some romantic interest (Klingemann and Fanny had actually taken to referring to

Mendelssohn's new E♭-major Quartet, op. 12, as his 'Quartet in B. P.', anticipating the discreet form the dedication on the manuscript finally took). Felix's tendency to link his romantic life with the quartet genre – we recall, too, the 'Ist es wahr?' subject of the A-minor Quartet – was to become a running joke in the family. A few years later, Fanny described the appearance of one of Berlin's young beauties, Rose Behrend, remarking: 'I wish you could have been there for you certainly would have fallen in love and composed some beautiful quartet'. True to form, Mendelssohn produced three quartets in the first sixteen months of his married life, returning to the genre only once more, in an F-minor lament on Fanny's death.

The E♭ Quartet was completed in London on 14 September, four days after his return to the city. As extreme as the A-minor Quartet had been in its dissonance and rhetorical severity, the E♭ Quartet spends much of its time exploring the opposite end of the spectrum. The Allegro of the first movement sets off from an utterance as lyrical as the beautiful opening melody of the A-major String Quintet of two years before, and never strays too far from it. The result is a movement whose lyricism would have seemed daringly pervasive even to Schubert, the first violin spending a large portion of the movement in limpid, conjunct, crotchet melody. Beethoven once more provides the immediate model; the opening gambit of this movement's introduction is rhythmically identical – at least in the first violin – to the opening of Beethoven's 1809 String Quartet in E♭, op. 74, sharing its harmonic thrust as well. The song-like first subject of the Allegro itself is built around a chain of descending parallel tenths that may be related obliquely to the similarly structured first subject of the first movement of Beethoven's recent quartet in the same key, op. 127 (it is to Felix's credit that Pyotr Il'yich Tchaikovsky, probably coincidentally, would begin his 1880 *Serenade for Strings* with a remarkably similar idea).

Though the gestural vocabulary of Beethoven's late quartets informs much of this work almost as strongly as it had the A-minor Quartet, the E♭ Quartet is not as rhetorically sure-footed as its predecessor. The last two movements frequently give themselves over to jagged juxtapositions and sudden changes of direction familiar from late Beethoven, but less frequently with a palpable sense of emotional motivation. Bearing out Abraham's worst fears about his son's interest in the late Viennese master, Mendelssohn rarely feels more mannered than this. Characteristic is the closing minute of the quartet – a close cousin of the closing of the A-minor Quartet – in which the first violin takes off on a brief solo arabesque through which it rediscovers a melody from the development section of the first movement, leading the ensemble then to a reprise of the first subject of the first movement. The whole feels like a calculated effort to revisit the soul-searching events that open the finale of Beethoven's Ninth Symphony, but Mendelssohn imparts little sense of how we arrived here, or why this rediscovery is an important one.

While Mendelssohn had survived the rugged desolation of the Scottish wilds unscathed, London's urban jungle was not so kind. On 17 September, as he reported to his family the following day,

> a stupid little gig crashed into me and robbed me of a pretty piece of skin with the accompanying flesh, black trouser cloth, etc., and Dr Kind has pitilessly condemned me to remain quietly in bed for four to five days. Quietly!

This initial estimate turned out to be extremely optimistic. Mendelssohn remained bedridden for over a month, and was not able to undertake his return trip to Berlin until 29 November, some two months after his projected time of departure. Mendelssohn was well cared for during this time, and received an endless stream of well-wishers, nobility not least among them. When his recovery was almost complete, he removed himself to the Norwood, Surrey, country home of Thomas Attwood, who had been particularly kind to him over these weeks; a couple of months before, in a healthier state, Mendelssohn had accompanied the Taylor girls to a ball at this estate.

No amount of attention from the English could lessen the blow of missing his sister Fanny's wedding, which took place on 3 October in his absence (in the event, she would miss his, too). Nonetheless, there was still his parents' silver wedding anniversary, on 26 December, to look forward to, and Mendelssohn returned to Berlin eager to throw himself into the production of the Singspiel, Heimkehr aus der Fremde ('The Return from Abroad'), he was writing for the occasion. Even with these festivities before him, Mendelssohn lamented his departure from England on 29 November; shortly after landing in Calais, he wrote: 'when its white coast disappeared and the black French coast came into view, I felt as if I had taken leave of a friend'.

★

The silver wedding anniversary came off in a style altogether worthy of Abraham and Lea, and of the gifted circle in which they and their children travelled. Christmas day, the eve of the anniversary, was spent receiving dozens of surprise guests, including extended family and many Berlin friends. The evening's entertainment included a play by Eduard Gans, a poetic recitation by Ludwig Robert, and performances – by the younger generation – of a chorus from Cherubini's Les Deux Journées and of Felix's Kindersymphonie (now lost), composed the previous year. Felix's one-act Heimkehr appeared the following night before a 'private' audience of around 120, following on the heels of a Festspiel – composed in considerable haste – by Fanny.

Despite receiving a number of opera commissions through these years (he had something like a standing offer from Covent Garden in hand as early as June) Heimkehr would be Mendelssohn's last complete vocal work for the stage. Heimkehr doubtless offered the family and their closest circle a form of redress for humiliations of the Camacho fiasco, as if to show – just for the private record – that if he never went on to succeed as an operatic composer, it would not have been for lack of ability. Charming and light-weight, Heimkehr made no pretence to being more than a private occasional piece, though its overture has remained in the repertoire to this day. Karl Klingemann – always the apple of Lea's eye – once more provided the libretto, which concerned the incognito return of a long-lost son, Hermann, in the midst of celebrations commemorating his father's fiftieth year in the mayor's office. A conniving shopkeeper, Kauz, seeks the heart of Hermann's faithful betrothed, Lisbeth, coming to justice only after the son's true identity is revealed; the whole ends in general celebration.

Around this time, the twenty-one-year-old Mendelssohn was offered a position as professor of music at the university. Though flattered, he gave no indications of being tempted. Upon declining the offer, evidence indicates that Mendelssohn recommended Marx, who was offered, and accepted, the position. As Mendelssohn was about to find out, not all quarters were quite so eager to reward his past successes.

In the weeks following his parents' anniversary celebrations, Mendelssohn would complete what he hoped would be another occasional piece, though of a much more ambitious scope, and intended in this case for posterity. The occasion was Berlin's tercentenary celebration of the Augsburg Confession, 25 June 1830. Though this celebration was not formally announced by Friedrich Wilhelm III until 4 April 1830, the important date was obviously well known. Given the success of his Dürer Cantata, of the 'Humboldt' Cantata that soon followed (composed for a convocation of natural scientists under Alexander von Humboldt's supervision), and of the *Passion* revival, Mendelssohn might reasonably have supposed that he would be called on to provide a work for whatever celebration materialised. It is not clear that he ever received such a commission, formally or informally, but the feverish pace at which he worked through the winter towards the completion of his 'Reformation' Symphony strongly suggests that a deadline was in view.

If a commission existed, it fell through; whether Mendelssohn's Jewish ancestry was a factor is a matter of sheer speculation, but the possibility certainly bears raising. The celebration went forward with choral music by Eduard Grell, who had studied under Karl Friedrich Zelter, and two decades later would assume the directorship of the Singakademie.[7] Among the recipients of honorary degrees handed out on this occasion (principal celebrations took place at the university's main lecture hall, with Hegel presiding) was Zelter himself, who claimed to have known nothing about it beforehand. Grell's efforts notwithstanding, the musical motto of the day was, predictably, Ein' feste Burg ist Unser Gott, blasted out by trombones from the city towers around daybreak, then performed, in Latin, by choir and audience at the celebration itself, its opening and closing stanzas bracketing the conferral of honorary degrees. This much, at least, Mendelssohn had gauged accurately; it is around this chorale that his own symphonic finale was organised.

How hard Mendelssohn was hit by this blow – or, indeed, how strong his expectations for a Berlin performance were in the first place – is largely guesswork. Mendelssohn had sufficient faith in the work to take it on the road with him and pursue performances elsewhere. As we shall see, his faith may have been misplaced, and even Mendelssohn's own evident enthusiasm for the piece had waned within a few years. It would not be published in his lifetime.

The symphony begins appealingly enough, with a Palestrina-inspired interlacing of graceful contrapuntal lines, culminating in the 'Dresden Amen' that Wagner would press into service in Parsifal; in the beginning, as in the end, Mendelssohn's models are vocal. But Ludwig Rellstab can perhaps be forgiven for mourning the symphony's pervasive insistence on 'colossal features' at the expense of melody, for the heavy-handed fanfare of a subject that opens the Allegro con fuoco cuts a grim profile indeed beside the introduction. The scherzo that follows is one of Mendelssohn's jolliest symphonic utterances, a foil to the bristly severity of the first movement, with a limpid trio whose tune was discreetly lifted from Ferrando and Guglielmo's second-act duet in Mozart's Così. Similarly operatic is the pathos-laden arioso that opens the ensuing slow movement, though this particular diva might be accused of taking herself, and the depth of her suffering, rather more seriously than anyone else present. The load-bearing movement of the work, from the standpoint of its pro-gramme, is the triumphant finale. Over the closing note of the third movement, a single flute intones the first phrase of Ein' feste Burg (calling to mind the piccolo whose unaccompanied flourish signalled the Prosperous Voyage's first breath of wind). Fragments of the chorale return at various points in the triumphant Allegro maestoso that follows, its first two phrases returning, in a grand *fortissimo tutti*, to wrap up the coda.

Despite its dismal reception during his lifetime, Mendelssohn was justly proud of the work that had ended his five-year hiatus from symphonic composition. Since the composition of his C-minor Symphony, Beethoven had redefined the genre – or set forth a plan for its redefinition – through his 'choral' symphony, in the same key as the 'Reformation'; however appropriate Luther's chorale may have been to the immediate occasion at hand, there seems little question that Mendelssohn's inclusion of the chorale in his 'Reformation' Symphony represented a conscious effort at working out the implications of Beethoven's last word in the genre. This impulse is folded, of course, into Mendelssohn's own fascination with programmatic music, an interest now at its height. Within a few years, this interest in programme music would largely dissolve, along with his eagerness to confront Beethoven's legacy head-on.

Like his departure from London, Mendelssohn's departure from Berlin was delayed, first by his efforts to complete the symphony, finally by a bout with the measles (Rebecka and Paul were also thus afflicted). It was not until 8 May that he and Abraham set off once more, this time heading south. Felix would not enter Berlin's gates again for over two years.

★

Their first stop was in Dessau, Moses' birthplace. Felix spent a few days in town, happy to re-establish ties with Julius Schubring, who had quit Berlin for Dessau only a few weeks before to assume his post as pastor of the Church of St George. While in town, Mendelssohn took part in a small gathering at the home of the organist, Wilhelm Karl Rust, where he played in trios by Beethoven and Haydn, and extemporised on themes from Beethoven's Ninth Symphony.

His next stop-over was in Leipzig. However stung his youthful ego may have been by the 'Reformation' Symphony affair in Berlin, the events of this brief stay put him well on the way to recovery. In the space of a single morning, he managed to sell the A-minor and E♭ Quartets; the first Breitkopf & Härtel snatched up unseen, on the recommendation of Heinrich Marschner (who was himself only familiar with the work from Mendelssohn's keyboard rendition); the E♭ Quartet went to Hofmeister. This prosperous morning was symptomatic of a growing momentum in Mendelssohn's publishing career; publishers would soon be coming to him.

By the end of May, Mendelssohn arrived in Weimar, where several days were spent in the company of Goethe (who, in letters to Zelter, had been anxiously awaiting his arrival since March). The young Mendelssohn could hardly have hoped for a happier or more touching final encounter with the ageing giant, whose benediction was one of the most meaningful events of the composer's life. At the same time, both the music and conversations they exchanged appear to have affirmed and focused Mendelssohn's sense of his own identity against the European cultural landscape.

In the course of several visits, Mendelssohn rehearsed, before this imposing audience of one, a historical survey of music that encapsulated many of the ambitions and convictions that would govern his entire professional career. At Goethe's request, he played representative works spanning the entire history of music as he knew it, in chronological sequence. Mendelssohn's characteristic insistence on including Beethoven, over Goethe's resistance, recapitulated Felix's ongoing struggle with his father's animosity towards the late Viennese master, signifying the depth of Mendelssohn's concern not only with Beethoven's music, but with maintaining the integrity of the musico-historical narrative. An important counterpart to these didactic performances were Goethe's extensive reflections, in their many conversations, on his theatrical experiences, particularly in connection with Schiller. Nowhere would Mendelssohn find a clearer model for his own professional ambitions than in the spirit of 'Weimar Classicism', in Goethe and Schiller's common aim of edification and cultural renewal through self-conscious engagement with the past. At the same time, Mendelssohn's own sense of artistic integrity – an eagerness to downplay concerns of popularity and financial success for which he would soon be defending himself – was doubtless stoked by Goethe's remarks, untinted by remorse, on the amount of his later career that had been spent 'with botany, and meteorology, and other stuff of the same kind, for which no one cared a straw'.

Around the time of Mendelssohn's departure, the old man presented him with a page of the manuscript of *Faustus*, inscribed: 'To my dear young friend F. M. B., mighty, yet delicate master of the piano – a friendly souvenir of happy May days in 1830. J. W. von Goethe'. Mendelssohn would remember him for more than this in the coming days. As he made his way towards Italy, he took up for the first time Goethe's own *Italian Travels*, delighted to observe points of congruence in their experience: 'it is a source of great satisfaction to me to find that he arrived in Rome the very same day that I did . . . indeed, everything that he describes I exactly experience myself, so I am pleased'. Mendelssohn's largest compositional project of the journey was a choral work based on Goethe's text, *Die erste Walpurgisnacht*, about which we shall have more to say later.

Happy days of a more frothy character awaited Mendelssohn in Munich, where nobility and professional musicians alike vied endlessly for his company: 'I played the piano more unremittingly than I ever did in my life before', he wrote to Zelter, 'one soirée succeeding another so closely that I really had not a moment to collect my thoughts'. In the course of early June, he appears to have developed a serious romantic interest in Delphine von Schauroth, a thoughtful, technically stunning pianist four years his junior, for whom he would later produce his G-minor Piano Concerto. So much discussed was this affair that, on Mendelssohn's 1831 return to the city, the King of Bavaria took it upon himself to ask why Mendelssohn resisted formalising the match in marriage. The young composer was as strenuously opposed as his parents to an early marriage, and was in the process of preparing a – most likely inappropriate – rebuke to the king when the conversation abruptly moved on to other subjects. Felix's own romantic life would do the same before too long.

After frustrations in Salzburg – Mendelssohn there encountered an aristocratic relative, but did not figure out who she was until several miles too late – he continued on to Vienna. Rarely had he spoken so pointedly of the decline of German music as in his letters from this city. Despite the popularity of Beethoven's 'Battle Symphony', and other occasional music written for the Congress of Vienna, the bourgeoisie who formed the core of the concert- and opera-going public had tended to look on Beethoven, in Sigrid Wiesmann's words, 'as something of a monument admired preferably from afar'.[8] Since the explosive arrival of *Tancredi* and *L'italiana in Algeri* in 1813, Rossini fever had established for Italian opera a pre-eminence which would continue for decades, while regular orchestral concerts were slower to materialise here than in London or Paris. In 1836, Frances Trollope – one of her generation's most popular authors of travel literature – reported bleakly: 'Handel, Mozart, Haydn, and the like are banished from "ears polite", while Strauss and Lanner rule the hour'. Mendelssohn similarly discerned in the Viennese musical public a frivolity, and in the musicians themselves a listlessness, altogether unworthy of the mighty legacy of Viennese Classicism. In a letter to Rebecka, complaints about having no one to flirt with lapse seamlessly into a playful, but obviously heartfelt, tirade:

> I certainly can't flirt with Hauser; he is much too grumpy . . . Simon Sechter is no young lady, either, but an old counterpointist . . . There isn't much more to Thalberg than a pretty hooked nose and stupendous fingers; Merk smokes a cigar while performing a gloomy Adagio and certainly doesn't let it go out. Czerny is like a tradesman on his day off, and says he is composing a lot now, for it brings in more than giving lessons . . . Beethoven is no longer here, nor Mozart or Haydn either, and when Stadler shows me the piano on which Haydn composed the *Seasons*, it doesn't help me much either – in short, I'm not pleased with the world.

From Vienna, Mendelssohn struck out for Pressburg, where he witnessed the magnificent spectacle surrounding the coronation of

Ferdinand V, King of Hungary. After a brief return to Vienna, he turned south once more.

★

Though his arrival in Italy did not come as the 'sudden explosion, violent and startling' he had imagined it would be, Mendelssohn's first communication from Venice, of 10 October, sets the happy tone that would define the months ahead: 'That [probably referring to the city named in his heading] is Italy. And what I have thought of, since I have been able to think, as life's greatest joy, that has begun now, I am basking in it.'

In his *History of the Popes* – which contains strong overtones of the travelogue – Berlin historian Leopold von Ranke suggested that Italy's greatest attraction for the northerner might well be that it was 'adorned with matchless works of art'. Mendelssohn proved the model German tourist in this respect; apart from the glorious weather (Venice offered a very different autumnal visage than Berlin) the most overwhelming aspect of the city was its supply of Titians: 'today I have seen the finest pictures in the world', his first letter proudly proclaimed. Detailed, often insightful, accounts of his encounters with visual art make up a substantial fraction of his Italian letters.

Two weeks later, as he journeyed southward, Mendelssohn found himself immersed in Italy's second great attraction: its scenic splendour. 'The fair land of Italy' commenced, he reported, about an hour outside of Florence, a moment his first letter from that city paints in fine brushstrokes:

> there are villas on every height, and decorated old walls, with sloping terraces of roses and aloes, flowers and grapes and olive leaves, the sharp points of cypresses, and the flat tops of pines, all sharply defined against the sky; then handsome square faces, busy life on the roads on every side, and at a distance in the valley, the blue city.

By the beginning of November, the first leg of his journey ended with his arrival in Rome. Here he would spend his first winter away from home.

Mendelssohn found himself welcomed at once into the city's most elite circles, spending the next six months in the company of figures like papal choir director Giuseppe Baini, Prussian ambassador Baron von Bunsen, music collector Fortunato Santini, and a close-knit circle of German artists that included Eduard Bendemann and Wilhelm Schadow. In June, he struck up an especially warm friendship with Horace Vernet, the director of the French Academy, who was so moved by Mendelssohn's improvisations on themes from *Don Giovanni* (which 'caused him a degree of delight far beyond what I ever knew my music to produce in any one') that he demanded, on the spot, to be allowed to paint Mendelssohn's portrait. Despite exchanges of this kind, and a friendship with Schadow that would grow extremely close in the years ahead, Mendelssohn never established, in Rome, a close circle of companions comparable to his English friends – 'I feel much the want of a *friend* here, to whom I could freely unbosom myself' – and he soon resigned himself, contentedly enough, to an existence in which nature and art were his closest companions.

The impoverishment of Rome's musical life became clear at once: 'The orchestras are beneath contempt . . . The papal singers even are becoming old; they are almost all unmusical, and do not execute even the most established pieces properly.' Even opera had fallen into serious decline, the best singers having quit the city long since for the infinitely more lucrative markets of Paris and London. The musical offerings this winter were put in an especially depressed state by the death of Pope Pius VIII a few weeks after Mendelssohn's arrival. The musical high point of Mendelssohn's stay (rather, his return after an excursion southward) was the papal choir's music during Holy Week, critically surveyed in a brilliant, lengthy letter to Zelter; even here, though, 'the negligence and bad habits of the whole previous year have their revenge, consequently the most fearful dissonance sometimes occurs'. Mendelssohn was much in demand at private gatherings, and offered 'a small Fantasie' at one of the modest Philharmonic concerts around the new year, to tumultuous applause. But he soon abandoned hope of a major concert appearance.

Among Mendelssohn's closest musical associates during this stay was Hector Berlioz, who had won the coveted *Prix de Rome* (not on his first attempt) with his cantata, *La mort de Sardanapale*. Though Berlioz much admired Mendelssohn as a pianist, a composer and a person, the feeling was hardly mutual; Mendelssohn found Berlioz's music self-indulgent and inept, once writing of the *Francs Juges* overture, 'his orchestration is such a frightful muddle, such an incongruous mess, that one ought to wash one's hands after handling one of his scores'.[9] Though Mendelssohn made no secret to Berlioz of their artistic incompatibility, as he saw it, he never made these feelings public, and would have occasion in later years to perform more than one professional good deed on Berlioz's behalf, as we shall see. Though the two spent a good deal of time through these months in rambling, broad-ranging conversation, Mendelssohn was repelled by Berlioz's eagerness to play the irreverent genius, and resented his casual denigration of Mozart and Haydn. In his *Mémoires*, Berlioz would look back fondly on these days, but the relationship never became close.

The lack of good performed music in Rome did not keep Mendelssohn from joyfully revelling in musical offerings of a different kind. Since his London sojourn, he had made a habit of hunting down the most significant manuscript repositories at each major destination – those of the British Museum in London, for instance, and of Breitkopf & Härtel in Leipzig. He found in Santini's and Baini's collections a treasure-trove of sixteenth- and seventeenth-century polyphony, in which he happily lost himself for hours on end.

His pleasure in work of this kind is only one symptom of a historical sensibility that was becoming increasingly refined through these years, an impulse that finds important expression in his meditations on visual art. Unlike music, which lived or died (as he knew well) according to the vicissitudes of fashion and performance practice, visual art remained – in the absence of damage or the grossest neglect – more or less permanently in the state of its initial creation. Mendelssohn's fascination with the sense of authorial immediacy borders, at times, on mysticism. In gazing at a pair of Venuses in the Tribune, he remarked, 'their loveliness inspires a feeling of piety; it is as if the two spirits who could produce such creations were flying through the hall and grasping at you as they passed'. In response to another painting: 'We feel as if the painter belonged to it, and still ought to be sitting before his work, or had only this moment left it'. Just as informative is the profundity of his frustration with living artists who refuse to adopt the same pious stance; outbursts on the subject form some of his most forceful articulations yet of the attitude towards the past – with overtones of authorial self-abnegation that we have witnessed in several other guises – that seems to lie close to the heart of his own craft. About Munich's artists, he wrote to Devrient:

> They are wanting in the first quality that I think an artist ought to have, and that is reverence. They speak about Peter Paul Rubens as if he was one of them, or indeed scarcely so high; and think they glorify Cornelius when they arrogantly disparage another great artist, whose worst picture they will never understand. I wish the devil would take this odious vanity that is the order of the day now! By heaven! These people do not know anything beyond their tiresome 'I'...[10]

During his winter in Rome, Mendelssohn was facing his own set of delicate compositional negotiations with the past, centred on the continuing question of what implications J. S. Bach's recrudescence might hold for modern composition.[11] Shortly before Mendelssohn's departure from Vienna, Franz Hauser – an opera singer who had met Mendelssohn through Schelble five years earlier – had given him a volume of Lutheran hymns. The gift turned out to be a more significant creative catalyst than Hauser could possibly have imagined. From Venice, two months later, Mendelssohn wrote to Zelter: 'on reading them [Luther's hymns] over I was again much struck by their power, and I intend to set several of them this winter'. The letter sets forth an ambitious compositional programme including a half-dozen sacred works, pieces which turned out to comprise a substantial fraction of Mendelssohn's compositional activity in Rome (which also encompassed a completed draft of the *Hebrides* overture and early work on the secular cantata, *Die erste Walpurgisnacht*). This 'Lutheran project' included four multi-movement chorale cantatas – the last, *Ach Gott vom Himmel sieh' darein*, not finished until 1832 – which continued the series initiated with *Christe, du Lamm Gottes* in 1827. Also included were two smaller works, *Aus tiefer Noth* and *Mitten wir im Leben sind*, published (along with a slightly earlier *Ave Maria*) as op. 23.

The following summer, Devrient objected that Mendelssohn's choral music was beginning to bear the imprint of Bach perhaps too strongly. Mendelssohn's startling – if seemingly matter-of-fact – response affords a keen insight into his distinctive conception of the past and its musical legacy, which we have glimpsed already in the *Sieben Characterstücke*. Mendelssohn suggests that older musical styles are not confined to their historical point of origin, but enjoy a kind of permanence; Bach's language, it seems, is no less available to Mendelssohn than it was to Bach himself:

> If it bears similarities to Sebastian Bach, I can do nothing about it, for I wrote it according to my mood, and if the words inspired in me the same mood they inspired in old Bach, I shall love it all the more. For I am sure you do not think that I would merely copy his forms, without the substance [Inhalt].

Though Mendelssohn would not, in fact, publish his most frankly Bachian works (the chorale cantatas), claims like this one afford key insights into the conceptual origins of the conservative – at times retrogressive – tendency in much of his published output that has been a major sticking point for critics from the start.

The 'Lutheran project' has a broader significance of another kind, as well. In works of this type, Mendelssohn seems to situate himself self-consciously, almost polemically, as a religious, artistic and linguistic Other in his Italian cultural landscape (in a similar sense, though the German 'Nazarene' painters who had set up shop in Rome two decades earlier were more unreflectively invested in Italy's indigenous Catholic art, their 1819 exposition had the important distinction of being, as Elizabeth Holt observed, 'the first exhibition of the work of German-speaking artists grouped on a "national" basis any-where'[12]). Indeed, the spirit of proud resistance discernible in this outpouring of Lutheran choral music characterised Mendelssohn's whole sense of identity in the course of these years of travel, years through which his self-identification as a German was not compromised, but brought into focus. 'The French say I am *cosmopolite*', he would write from Paris towards the end of his journey; 'Heaven defend me from being anything of the kind!' He would proclaim in a letter to Devrient, penned in the summer of 1831, around the conclusion of his Italian sojourn: 'The land of artists is, once and for all, Germany. Long may it live!' From Paris, he related to Zelter the experience of passing through Germany again after the Italian expedition, 'I noticed that I was a German and wanted to live in Germany, as long as I could do so'.

*

On 10 April, Mendelssohn left Rome for a stay of almost two months in and around Naples, much of it spent in the company of painters Eduard Bendemann and Wilhelm von Schadow. Julius Benedict, the former pupil of Weber who – along with his teacher – had first met Mendelssohn in Berlin around the time of the *Freischütz* première, was vacationing there, too, for the first days of Mendelssohn's stay. Though Mendelssohn dutifully acquainted himself with the most important figures in the local music scene, not even their leader, Donizetti, escaped his scorn; the condition of opera, Mendelssohn soon announced, was worse than in Rome.

Despite the bountiful distractions of nature and the teeming life of the city – 'I have not yet been able to compass one serious quiet reflection, there is everywhere such jovial life here, inviting you to do nothing' – the stay witnessed further progress on *Die erste Walpurgisnacht* and the A-major Symphony (though two more years would pass before the first draft of the latter was completed). Anxious about his son's safety amid the general environment of political unrest, Abraham forbade Felix an excursion to Sicily, which the youngster grudgingly crossed off his itinerary. In early June Mendelssohn returned to Rome for a couple of weeks, just long enough to tie up his affairs there, pay farewell visits to his acquaintances, and take in the lavish music of Holy Week.

By early July he had made his way, via Florence and Genoa, to Milan. Though he had placed little emphasis on making new acquaintances in the course of these peripatetic weeks, Milan offered him one of the happiest personal encounters of the trip. In an act of remarkable bravado (a keen illustration of just how much a man-of-the-world Mendelssohn had become) he decided to pay a visit – notwithstanding his lack of a letter of introduction – to Baroness Dorothea von Ertmann. An accomplished pianist, the Baroness had known Beethoven well; some have even suggested that she may have been Beethoven's 'Immortal Beloved', though Maynard Solomon's biography of the composer put this possibility soundly to rest. Mendelssohn knew Ertmann only as the dedicatee of Beethoven's op. 101. Upon entering the home, Baron Ertmann himself happened to be the first person Mendelssohn encountered ('This', Felix reported coolly, 'was unpleasant'). To the great relief of the flustered youth, the retired General recognised his name, and he soon found himself warmly welcomed into their home. Mendelssohn and Madame Ertmann spent hours playing to one another, bonding at once through their mutual admiration for Beethoven, whose works 'there was not a person in Milan who cared to hear'. Her memories of the late master – including the heart-breaking story of the hour-long improvisation through which he had consoled her after the death of her last child – left Mendelssohn with as strong a sense of personal connection to the late master as he had ever felt.

At the end of July, Mendelssohn passed out of Italy into Switzerland, where he spent the better part of a month wandering through the mountains on foot. Days of torrential rain, with the devastating floods that attended it, only added to the sense of high adventure. The staggering beauty of the letters from this period afford a worthy counterpart to the music nature had inspired; his first communication from Switzerland, from a valley he and his family had visited before, sets the tone:

The snow through the blue, dark air so pure, and sharp, and near; the glaciers thundering unremittingly, as the ice is melting: when clouds gather, they lie lightly on the base of the mountains, the summits of which stand forth clear above . . . I wished to sketch the outlines of the mountains, so I went out and found an admirable point of view, but when I opened my book, the paper seemed so very small that I hesitated about attempting it. I have indeed succeeded in giving the outlines what is called correctly, – but every stroke looks so formal when compared with the grace and freedom which everywhere here pervade nature. And then the splendour of the colour! In short, this is the most brilliant point of my travels; and the whole of my excursion on foot, so solitary, independent and enjoyable, is something new to me, and a hitherto unknown pleasure.

★

Around noon on 5 September, Mendelssohn crossed 'the wild grey Rhine' by ferry, and set foot once more on German soil. By the 1st of October, he found himself again in Munich, where he threw himself almost at once into preparations for a concert that took place on the 17th. The evening – 'much more brilliant and successful than I expected' – included Mendelssohn's C-minor Symphony, the *Midsummer Night's Dream* overture, and his just-completed G-minor Piano Concerto, op. 25. This last piece, which he had been kicking around in his head for almost a year before, was dedicated to Delphine von Schaurath, whose *grande affaire* with the composer was then at its height, though nearly at its end.

After the impressive handful of concertos composed between 1822 and 1824, Mendelssohn had not touched the genre for seven years. The G-minor Concerto speaks from a different world than the earlier works, Mendelssohn's rethinking of the genre evidently taking Weber's *Konzertstück* as its starting point. The magisterial breadth of his early concertos gives way here to a breathless economy; the whole piece could be performed comfortably in the time it takes to perform the first movement of the A♭ Double Piano Concerto. The three terse movements of the G-minor Concerto, like the four of the *Konzertstück*, are connected with transitions.

Weber had dispensed with the double-exposition structure of the traditional concerto – with main material played first by the orchestra, then by the soloist – by allowing piano and orchestra to join in a single exposition. Mendelssohn's first movement offers an even more radical, more propulsive conception. After an ear-catching opening crescendo from the orchestra, the piano abruptly enters, but not with anything that could properly be called a subject. For twelve dazzling bars, flashes of virtuosity fly out in fits and starts; though the piano makes its way through an array of harmonic regions, these do not include a firm sounding of the G-minor tonic. After a gentle prod from the orchestra, the piano produces the beginnings of a theme, but soon loses itself once more in virtuoso amblings. Only in the hands of the orchestra, on its tutti return, does the subject coalesce. The piano displays even less interest in the subject on recapitulation; after its brief reintroduction by the orchestra, the piano intrudes with lyrical musings that move almost immediately into the song-like second subject.

The behaviour of Mendelssohn's soloist here must be situated within a general tendency in the concertos of Hummel, Field, Weber, and others 'to define a personality . . . in the solo part', as Steven Lindeman puts it, 'that resisted, through either virtuoso defiance or lyric escape, the world proposed by the orchestra'.[13] But Mendelssohn brought to the Concerto his own quite personal psychological baggage, which may account for the extremity of his vision. Since his first visit to Paris, Mendelssohn had been lamenting the vacuity of much contemporary virtuoso music; a letter to Moscheles from the following summer offers a typical tirade:

> But why should I hear those Variations by Herz for the thirtieth time? They give me as little pleasure as rope-dancers or acrobats: for with them at least there is the barbarous attraction that one is in constant dread of seeing them break their necks . . . I only wish it were not my lot to be constantly told that the public demand that kind of thing. I, too, am one of the public, and demand the very reverse.[14]

It is tempting to perceive in the opening of the G-minor Concerto a light-hearted reflection of Mendelssohn's very serious anxieties concerning the insidious (as he saw it) impact of empty virtuosity on contemporary concert life, indeed, of his ambivalence towards his own status as a world-class virtuoso. '[W]henever I get to a piano here', he had written to his father during his first London visit, 'I slip into incessant practising of virtuoso passages and similar stuff, and come away without profit or new ideas'. Ideas are precisely what the pianistic virtuosity of this first movement forestalls. Its soloist refuses to be bothered by any sense of responsibility to the principal theme around which the whole musical structure was to be organised.

In the course of this Munich visit, Mendelssohn completed a preliminary draft for another work, the single-movement *Capriccio brillant*, which seems to address precisely these issues in an even more thoroughgoing way. The orchestration of the work was completed the following May, just in time for its London première. Here the crux of the musical argument lies in the peculiar character of the 'second subject', the melody that articulates the arrival of a new, contrasting key area. The boisterous march for the orchestra bears a striking similarity to the *tempo di marcia* third movement of Weber's *Konzertstück*, a connection that many members of Mendelssohn's London audience might well have made at once. But as a second subject, this march makes no sense whatever, its *fortissimo* bravado cutting quite a different profile from Mendelssohn's customary second-subject lyricism (Philip Radcliffe, in his biography of Mendelssohn, remarked that the *Capriccio brillant* 'is spoilt by a second subject of startling banality'[15]). On the return of this material in the recapitulation, however, the piano takes the march instead of the orchestra, recasting it in an altogether more formally suitable guise; in the piano's hands, it appears at a gentle *pianissimo – leggiero*, no less. We may discern here an act of musical self-mythologising. Mendelssohn seems to make reference to the furthest extreme of virtuoso piano music with which he had associated himself – the *Konzertstück* – only in order to cast its jolliest moment in the form of a musical problem. He, in the persona of the pianist, swaggers in at the eleventh hour to regularise this wayward impulse, to bring it into the fold of classical normalcy; in this reading, the piece emerges as little short of an aesthetic manifesto. (As if to affirm the association with Weber, Mendelssohn's soloist offers, in the coda of the *Capriccio brillant*, a direct quotation of the opening bars of the *Konzertstück* march.)

But the *Capriccio brillant* takes us ahead of our story.

★

By the time Mendelssohn left Munich, he had contracted with the theatre directory to compose an opera. On his way through Düsseldorf, he approached Karl Immermann with the idea of an opera based on *The Tempest*, and Immermann consented to undertake the project. Though this enterprise met the same abortive end as dozens of other operatic projects in the coming years, Mendelssohn did make other important contacts in Düsseldorf, the results of which will concern us in our next chapter. By the middle of December, in any event, Mendelssohn had arrived in Paris, where he spent the second winter of his journey.

Mendelssohn was baffled by the heated political discourse that had, since the July Revolution, been the order of the day, politics being 'a subject that I wish to avoid for at least a hundred and twenty reasons; and chiefly because I don't in the least understand it'. Though a dedicated liberal – he preferred the term 'radical' – Mendelssohn kept his distance from the whirl of revolutionary fervour that was casting forth, at just this time, the most politically charged work of Hugo, Stendhal, Balzac, Delacroix and Delaroche.

With his own reputation on the ascent, Mendelssohn quickly made, or re-established, contact with a dazzling array of musicians in the city: the violinist Baillot, 'the grumbling Cherubini', Herz, Habeneck (the director of the *Société des Concerts*) and Meyerbeer, whose *Robert le Diable* was the toast of the town. Mendelssohn, for his part, found *Robert* 'thoroughly frigid and heartless', and did not warm to its composer; to suggestions that he and Meyerbeer resembled one another in appearance, Mendelssohn responded by having his hair cropped. These were heady days, and at first happy ones. In his *Recollections*, Hiller tosses off lightly anecdotes that would have seemed epoch-making in any other city. One memorable episode finds Mendelssohn, Chopin, Liszt and Hiller gathered before a café on the Boulevard des Italiens. In a scene worthy of a Beatles film, this foursome descend on Kalkbrenner, who had the misfortune of passing by on the sidewalk, to torment him with their lightning repartee. 'Youth', Hiller tells us, 'has no mercy'.[16]

Mendelssohn found himself more impressed than ever with the state of orchestral music in the city, not least in the polished Beethoven performances for which the Société des Concerts had become famous. Beethoven's popularity among the Parisians was a recent, and rather sudden, development. At the Paris première of his First Symphony in 1807, the *Tablettes de polymnie* set the tone for two decades of Beethoven reception in Paris, finding the work 'a dangerous example for musical art . . . multiplying the most barbarous dissonances and making the greatest noise with all the instruments of the orchestra. . . Alas! this only grates on the ear without speaking to the heart'.[17] What little following Beethoven amassed through the 'teens and early 'twenties was largely due to the efforts of Baillot, who ardently championed the early quartets. An electrifying performance of the *Eroica* Symphony at the recently established Société des Concerts on 9 March 1828 was greeted as a revelation; the *Journal des Débats* proclaimed, 'a revolution has just occurred in the musical world'. By the time of Mendelssohn's arrival in the city in 1831, Beethoven's symphonies were firmly ensconced at the centre of the city's concert life.

Mendelssohn's music, too, was making significant headway. During his visit, Baillot and his quartet offered superb performances of the A-minor and E♭-major Quartets; the Octet, too, was much played and admired. Habeneck took a keen interest in promoting Mendelssohn at the Conservatoire concerts, and conducted the polished French première of the overture to *A Midsummer Night's Dream*.

Though Mendelssohn was offered the chance to perform a Beethoven sonata himself, he successfully negotiated for Beethoven's G-major Concerto, still little known in Paris, which came off famously.

A planned performance of the 'Reformation' Symphony met a less happy fate. In a letter of 13 February 1832, Mendelssohn found his excitement at the prospect difficult to contain: 'I look forward with the utmost delight to the Symphony in D minor, which is to be rehearsed next week; I certainly never dreamt that I should hear it in Paris for the first time'. In the event, he never heard it in Paris. Though his own letters make almost no reference to the event, the symphony was quietly shelved after a single rehearsal. The musicians – Hiller tells us from a second-hand report – pronounced it 'much too learned, too much *fugato*, too little melody'.

Nor was this the hardest blow he received in Paris. On 3 February, his twenty-third birthday, he received news that his childhood friend Eduard Rietz, the violinist to whom the Octet was dedicated, had died. Mendelssohn was overwhelmed at the loss: 'A new chapter in my life has begun', he wrote the next day, 'but as yet it has no title'. A few weeks later he received word that a new chapter had begun for Germany's cultural life, as well; Goethe had died on 22 March. 'It is another of those mournful events connected with my stay here', he wrote home of Goethe's death, 'which will always recur to my mind at the very name of Paris'. By this point, cholera – 'the spectre' as it was known – had swept the city. Mendelssohn himself would survive a mild case before quitting Paris, with relief, in mid-April.

The last weeks of Mendelssohn's Grand Tour were spent in London, reliving the glories of his earlier stay. By late June, he had taken part in five concerts, which included performances of the *Hebrides* overture, the new *Capriccio brillant*, the overture to *A Midsummer Night's Dream*, and – in his most splendid success of the season – the G-minor Piano Concerto. 'When the man played his Munich concerto at the Philharmonic', Klingemann wrote to Berlin, 'the triumph was ridiculous'.

News of Zelter's death on 15 May did not come as a surprise to

Mendelssohn; he had predicted that his teacher would not long outlive Goethe. But the event did leave a conspicuous void at the head of the Singakademie, and the question had already arisen whether Mendelssohn might be the one to fill it. As he headed back towards Berlin in the last week of June, it was with a blend of hope and anxiety that he had articulated in one of his last communications with Zelter:

> I hope that in Berlin I shall be able to find my own livelihood and that which is necessary to it, and that I shall not feel less at home there, where I have you and my parents and siblings and friends, than in all of the rest of the other German locales.

Berlin would disappoint him.

5 Frustrations in Berlin and Düsseldorf

[A] large public deserves to be respected, and not treated like children from whom you take money. If, by showing them what is good, we develop in them a feeling or taste for what is good, they will be all the more willing to pay their money because they will have nothing to reproach themselves for. They can be flattered like a child you wish to improve and help towards greater intelligence, not like a rich grandee to perpetuate his failings from which one profits.

Johann Wolfgang von Goethe, *Wilhelm Meister*[1]

It was doubtless with a heady, bewildering mixture of feelings that the fifty-four-year-old Carl Friedrich Rungenhagen awoke and prepared for the events of 18 May 1832. Karl Friedrich Zelter, the teacher and friend whose confidence in him had brought Rungenhagen the happiest days of his life, had died three days earlier. Rungenhagen had been a member of Berlin's Singakademie for almost as long as Zelter had been its director – over thirty years. In 1814, Zelter had made him deputy director. Though Rungenhagen never fancied himself as another Handel, he was a competent composer and conductor whose affability, industriousness and reliability served him well under Zelter's guiding hand. Putting to rest his father's deep-seated misgivings about the value of a career in music (he had only turned in this direction after his father's death), Rungenhagen's modest gifts and abundant enthusiasm had brought him respect and a limited sort of fame. At last, in the midst of the cold spring of 1832, it fell to Rungenhagen to conduct the Singakademie at the funeral of its beloved director, a major civic event at which Friedrich Schleiermacher himself was delivering the oration. He had conducted before this public countless times before, but on this occasion, the eyes of the city would fall upon him with a new intensity, seeking, as one, the answer to a single question: how worthily would Zelter's right-hand man, and obvious successor, fill the void whose enormity they had all gathered to acknowledge? Rungenhagen himself felt this void as painfully as anyone, but recognised, too, that this day signalled a major point of arrival in his musical career.

Acquitting himself more than adequately at the funeral, Rungenhagen turned to preparations for an even more important event, the Singakademie's own memorial service for its fallen leader. On 7 June, he directed them in a moving performance of Mozart's *Requiem* and a selection of Zelter's own motets. Though it would be another seven months before the Singakademie would formally elect a new director, Rungenhagen had already shown that their collective artistic life could indeed continue without Zelter. The torch had already been passed to him in spirit; the Singakademie had only to determine whether there was any serious reason to contemplate handing it to another the following January.

The only serious contender for the position had not been heard from for over two years; scattered, irregular reports suggested that he had spent this time of general mourning frolicking through his second glamorous concert season in London. It was true that the dashing, handsome Felix Mendelssohn had brought the Singakademie their finest hour; the *St Matthew Passion* revival three years earlier had brought the organisation a flattering splash of international attention, spurring a revival of interest in Bach's choral music that seemed to vindicate the vigilant attention Zelter had paid to the old master for decades. And however one might grouse in private about the insular hyper-intensity of the education his somewhat aloof parents had provided him, Mendelssohn's musical memory, his skills at the keyboard, and the sheer clarity of musical thought behind his conducting were nothing short of a phenomenon. At the same time, not only Felix and his sister, Fanny, but over a dozen other members of their extended family had been members of the Singakademie; the core holdings of the organisation's library were gifts from Felix's father, and from his mother's aunt, Sara Levy. But Felix had been gone for most of Zelter's last three years. His family had never participated fully in Berlin's civic life – not even as fully as their conversion to Christianity might have enabled them to – and Felix's own long absence could hardly be taken as a sign of devotion to his hometown.

Events behind the scenes at the Mendelssohn house would hardly have put these reservations to rest. Despite prodding from Fanny and Abraham, Felix refused to hasten his trip home to increase his chances of being appointed as Zelter's successor; he arrived in Berlin at the end of June. In the feverish wake of the St *Matthew Passion* performance, Felix had been highly receptive to overtures from one of the Singakademie's directors, Professor Lichtenstein, who seems to have suggested privately that Felix would make a good successor to Zelter. Indeed, Felix seemed convinced, in 1832, that he had actually been offered the post at this earlier time, and grudgingly told his father that he would honour this agreement if the Singakademie pressed the matter. But by the time of his return from abroad, Mendelssohn had come to think the Singakademie directorship a modest reward indeed for his new-found European celebrity. He wrote to his father from London on 18 May:

> Considering the peculiar position of the Academy, the small salary they give, and the great influence they might exercise, the place of Director seems to me only an honourable post, which I have no desire to sue for. If they were to offer it to me, I would accept it, because I promised formerly to do so, but only for a settled time and on certain conditions.[2]

It was only with the most urgent prodding from his family, and from Eduard Devrient, that Felix was moved to formalise his candidacy at all. In a 4 August letter to Klingemann, Felix – certain that

Rungenhagen 'will receive, or rather retain' the position – reveals that he would not even consider it 'without stunning conditions: a fine salary, complete authority and leave to travel'.[3] After a general meeting in October, Felix was more convinced than ever that Rungenhagen's election was both certain and fully appropriate. Rungenhagen seems to have agreed: when a subcommittee comprised of Devrient, Schleiermacher and G. H. Köhler concocted a plan for Mendelssohn and Rungenhagen to split the job, granting Mendelssohn chief authority in musical matters, Rungenhagen himself rejected the idea over Mendelssohn's own tentative acceptance.

On 22 January 1833, the matter at last came to a vote, which proved decisive. 148 votes were cast for Rungenhagen, eighty-eight for Felix, four for Eduard Grell. In Eric Werner's estimation, this blow constituted 'the severest trauma of his life. The wound in Felix's soul never healed fully.'[4] William A. Little suggests, in more restrained tones, that 'the business with the Singakademie seldom seemed to amount to anything more than a persistent nuisance'.[5] Felix understood as well as anyone Rungenhagen's worthiness of the post, and does not, in his known correspondence, make recourse to murmurs of anti-Semitism that some of those around him did (probably with some justification). Though a sense of humiliation was inevitable, Felix had not wanted the job, and his prospects elsewhere were improving all the time.

His family, however, took the decision as an unforgivable insult, and felt honour-bound to withdraw from all involvement in the Singakademie, effectively estranging themselves from a large segment of Berlin's musical public. Obviously the individual who actually had the most to lose in all of this was not Felix himself – for whom the possibility of mobility was a foregone conclusion – but Fanny, whose musical horizons had already been limited enough. Indeed, her later remarks on the Singakademie suggest a bitterness much more profound than Felix's own. In February 1834, she reported to Felix: 'On Thursday the Academy will perform the b-minor Mass, which will probably be dreadful'. A year later, she laments that Felix was not there to conduct a recent Bach performance, remarking 'what the fools themselves have attempted has once again sunk without a trace'. Not even more objective commentators have attempted to mask the fact that the Singakademie decidedly failed, under Rungenhagen's direction, to live up to the potential significance it had shown in the last years of Zelter's direction, and was soon outpaced by similar organisations elsewhere.

Though his failure to obtain the Singakademie directorship may not have come as a crippling blow to Felix's professional aspirations, it was the most palpable manifestation of a sad fact which Felix had discovered at once on his return home: he was extremely unhappy in Berlin. The summer after his return had been a cold and wet one, much of which Fanny, Abraham and Felix himself spent battling off illness. The musical contours of his personal life had changed a good deal since his teenage years: two of his closest friends – Zelter and Eduard Rietz – were dead, his relationship with A. B. Marx was beginning to cool, and Fanny was married and caring for a young child. The whole tenor of the city's public life, inasmuch as he had ever been a part of it, had grown more and more conservative, dampened by an environment of increasing governmental regulation under the ageing Friedrich Wilhelm III. Felix found himself 'more uneasy and restless than I have ever been'. '[T]he most bitter moments I ever endured, or ever could have imagined', he wrote the following April, 'were during last autumn'.

Not all had gone badly for him. In November 1832 he received a commission from the Philharmonic Society for 'a symphony, an overture and a vocal composition'; the following months witnessed the completion of the 'Italian' Symphony, begun two years earlier, which would form the first instalment in this series. Mendelssohn also gave a series of concerts (on 15 November, 1 December and 20 January) through which the Berlin public had – and seized upon – the opportunity to applaud his most accomplished works: *Die erste Walpurgisnacht*, the *Midsummer Night's Dream* overture, the *Meeresstille und glückliche Fahrt* overture, the *Hebrides* overture, the 'Reformation' Symphony, the G-minor Concerto, and the *Capriccio brillant*. The city's most influential critic, Ludwig Rellstab, abandoned his usual reserve for the occasion: 'These three musical evenings were more meaningful for the art than a whole year of the usual concerts'.[6] Even so, the whole tenor of civic life in Berlin had taken a turn for the conservative, and it was more clear than ever that the musical institutions of the city – which was still struggling to get an orchestral establishment off the ground – formed a poor canvas for Mendelssohn's artistic life's work. The day after Christmas – the third anniversary of the première of his *Heimkehr aus der Fremde* – he wrote to his librettist, Klingemann, comparing 1832 to 1829:

> Things are no longer what they were at the time of the 'Liederspiel', and although I really have completely overcome all feelings of depression at the change, it was no easy task and I still have a very strange sensation when I compare conditions. Only my parents are completely unchanged, or rather, even kinder and less reserved; when I am with them, I miss nothing, and the same thing with my sisters. But outside of our home every step reminds me how the city has stopped dead, and therefore gone backward. Music suffers, people have grown more narrow-minded than ever, the best of them have passed away, others who once nursed fine plans are now happy philistines and sometimes remember the days of their youth . . .[7]

As encouraging as the commission from the Philharmonic Society had been, an invitation of even more far-reaching significance had arrived by the end of February, when Mendelssohn was asked to come to Düsseldorf to conduct the Lower Rhein Music Festival. Though he had already arranged to be in London in early May for the première of the 'Italian' Symphony, and the festival was slated to begin on the 26th of that month, he eagerly returned his assent. Thus, in mid-April he left his hometown once more, with prestigious engagements before him and a strong desire for an opportunity that might take him out of Berlin for the long term. For this he did not have to wait long.

★

10   First page of the manuscript of Mendelssohn's 'Italian' Symphony

Mendelssohn's joy at being out of Berlin was amplified by the triumphant reception of his 'Italian' Symphony in London, where he arrived in late April after a brief stop-over in Düsseldorf. As we have seen, the rejection of the 'Reformation' Symphony – his first fully mature work in the genre – by the Conservatoire Orchestra was one of the greatest humiliations of his career to date. The *Harmonicon* at once hailed the

'Italian', after its 13 May première, as 'a composition that will endure for ages, if we may presume to judge such a work on a single performance'.[8]

Even so, Mendelssohn had serious misgivings about the work; its genesis had been protracted, and it would undergo another overhaul in the months ahead (though his final version of the work was not the version published after his death, and universally familiar today). Mendelssohn had, by this point, fallen into a habit of almost compulsive revision, from which hardly any mature work was exempt. The Octet, the String Quintet that had followed, the *Meeresstille, glückliche Fahrt* overture, the *Hebrides* overture, and *Die erste Walpurgisnacht* were all withheld for years from publication, finally released only in forms substantially different from their initial ones. In the case of the 'Italian' Symphony, Mendelssohn would never feel sufficient confidence in the work to publish it. Fanny had complained about his proposed revisions to the work, 'I feel you are only too ready to change a successful piece later on merely because one thing or another pleases you more then'.

Where the 'Reformation' Symphony represented one extreme in Mendelssohn's programmatic imagination – suggesting the clearest narrative progression of any of his programmatic works – the 'Italian' Symphony is firmly rooted in the more pictorial language of the *Meeresstille* and *Hebrides* overtures. Indeed, the sunburst of winds with which the piece begins is lifted more or less directly from a colouristic wash early in the 'Prosperous Voyage'. The happy opening subject, after being silenced in the middle of the movement in a sobering encounter with a new minor-mode fugue subject, comes into its own at last in the coda, where it is rendered as a triumphant fanfare for every brass instrument in the house. Those with any taste at all for anthropomorphic readings might well discern here a struggle – autobiographical, perhaps – between the bright-lit musical landscape of the south and the strict, arch-German fugal processes that had been a central component of Mendelssohn's symphonic style for a decade.

By the time of the symphony's première, Mendelssohn had already appeared at the keyboard in Moscheles' 1 May concert, where they premièred their jointly composed variations on the gypsy march from Weber's *Preciosa*. Moscheles had visited Berlin the previous October, and the two were closer than ever (if Mendelssohn had not, in the eyes of some, proven sufficiently Christian to serve as the Singakademie director, he had received a more welcome honour in being made godfather and namesake to Ignaz and Charlotte's first son, born in February). Though Paganini – whom Mendelssohn profoundly admired – had approached him, too, with the idea of playing Beethoven sonatas together, the violinist required a painful jaw surgery that made this impossible.

The day after the A-major Symphony's première, Mendelssohn set off once more for Düsseldorf to undertake preparations for the Lower Rhein Music Festival. The first day of the festival was to feature Handel's *Israel in Egypt*, the first of a series of oratorio performances through which Mendelssohn, over the coming years, would emerge as one of Handel's most important advocates in Germany. Mendelssohn had planned on relying on the Berlin Singakademie's score and orchestral parts for the occasion, an arrangement in which Mendelssohn doubtless took a good deal of private pleasure. In the event, he was able to do the Singakademie one better. In the course of his London visit, Mendelssohn managed to unearth Handel's original score for the work, which included many numbers not in the Berlin copy. The 26 May opening of the festival thus became a revival vaguely comparable to the *St Matthew Passion*, one of the first major public rewards of Mendelssohn's tireless archival work. 'My dear Felix', Fanny wrote of the find, 'you possess great powers of judgement but good luck in no less measure: another stroke of fortune'.

We are able to glimpse the events of the festival itself through the eyes of Abraham, whom Mendelssohn invited down for the event. The two would spend much of the next four months together, with Felix making his first decisive steps into a life outside of his parents' home, and Abraham making what seem decisive physical and psychological steps towards old age. The gentle – though not always subtle – shifts of power in the relationship over these months left them as close as ever, and were critical in preparing them both for the new era that lay before them.

Not for the last time, Abraham's very domestic circumstances served as an expression of his son's fame: he found himself lodged in the house of Regierungspräsident von Woringen himself. 'I have never seen . . . anybody so petted and courted as he is here', Abraham wrote to Lea of their eldest son; 'he himself cannot enough praise the zeal of all the performers, and their perfect confidence in him; and as it always has been, his playing and his memory astound everybody'. In watching Felix rehearse the amassed chorus, Abraham joyfully recognised in his son a happy fulfilment of the bourgeois fantasy of power, respect and influence won through industry and charisma:

> To me at least it does appear like a miracle that four hundred persons of all sexes, classes and ages, blown together like snow before the wind, should let themselves be conducted and governed like children by one of the youngest of them all, too young almost to be a friend for any of them, and with no title or dignity whatever.

With this chorus, an orchestra of around a hundred, and over 1,000 spectators, the festival's first day set off with Mendelssohn's 'Trumpet' overture (a non-programmatic work composed some seven years earlier, but revised over the previous months) and *Israel in Egypt*. After a festive evening of toasts and general levity, the same forces arose the following day for Beethoven's Pastoral Symphony, his *Leonore* overture No. 3, an Easter Cantata by Weimar Kapellmeister Ernst Wilhelm Wolff, and a cantata *Die Macht der Töne* ('The Power of Music') by Peter von Winter. Spirits were running sufficiently high that, for the first time in the fifteen-year history of the festival, a third concert was announced for the 28th. This included, among other things, a reprise of Felix's overture, a scene from Weber's *Freischütz*, Weber's *Konzertstück* (with Mendelssohn at the keyboard), an aria from Mozart's *Figaro*, and the second part of Handel's *Israel*.

The summary of these events in the *Düsseldorf Zeitung* – penned by

Beethoven's much-maligned confidant, Anton Schindler – captures fully the feverish enthusiasm of Mendelssohn's reception:

> I have words only of deep admiration for everything which the artists have accomplished with this music festival. The goodwill and dedication to the noble art of music expressed themselves in the tenacity with which the many strenuous rehearsals were undertaken with a zeal such as I have never before witnessed. The exactness and indefatigable industry of the General Director, the excellent Felix Mendelssohn-Bartholdy, are responsible for the quality of the performance. It is due to him alone that the fifteenth Lower Rhein Festival was incomparably superior to all preceding ones.

It was largely due to Mendelssohn's impact that an invitation to conduct the Lower Rhein Music Festival became one of the highest honours a composer could enjoy; Mendelssohn himself would direct six more, and its future conductors included Liszt, Brahms, Richard Strauss, Ferdinand Hiller and Niels Gade.

The successes of these three days brought a more immediate benefit for the young conductor, as well. He received, and accepted, a commission to become Düsseldorf's music director. The salary was set at 600 Thaler, and he was permitted three months' vacation each year. Felix described his duties, and his private motivations, to Schubring in September:

> I've decided on taking up my abode there for two or three years, nominally in order to direct the church music, and the Vocal Association, and probably also a new theatre which is now being built there, but in reality for the purpose of securing quiet and leisure for composition. The country and the people suit me admirably.

Though the town seemed happily infused with a genuine love for, and devotion to, its music – the president and his daughters themselves sang in the chorus, as did many among the famous school of painters lodged there around Mendelssohn's friend, Wilhelm von Schadow – there was some uncertainty here. The orchestra was fourth-rate, and it was not clear if the fault lay in disorganisation or in an actual dearth of skill; the particular nature of Felix's obligation to the theatre had not been defined, either; Mendelssohn would have to make his peace, too, with being director of sacred music in a Catholic city, raised though he was by a mother who was prone to vehement expressions of the anti-Catholic sentiment that characterised much of German Protestantism. Whatever Woringen and the other Düsseldorfers might have imagined, there was little sense, on Mendelssohn's part, that this position was likely to prove more than a short-term arrangement – Abraham referred to 'the useful and important school it will be for him'. But the Düsseldorf commission was a strong vote of confidence, and afforded a first opportunity at what Mendelssohn, the emerging professional, most ardently sought: a firm institutional framework within which to express the artistic ideals and ambitions that had thus far been expressed in the more personal forms of letters and compositions, only intermittently through performance.

★

As his Düsseldorf duties did not begin until 1 October, Felix and Abraham decided to enjoy the emotional afterglow of the youth's recent successes in London. They left on 3 June. Though overwhelmed by the size and density of the city, Abraham was appalled by the face of its poor, and by an air pollution whose like he had never seen. Even the obvious prosperity of many quarters were no match, as Abraham reported to Lea, for 'the grand aspect of the Tuileries, the Place Louis XV, the Champs Elysées, the Boulevards and Quais which encircle it all'. Abraham spoke hardly any English, and found himself more dependent than ever on his son, whose friends lavished every kindness on the pair. His letters offer us glimpses at a new spirit of humility, and a new confidence on Felix's part. One emblematic episode was a visit to an art exhibition in June, the whole of which Abraham pronounced 'a heap of rubbish'. 'Felix does not quite agree with me', he continues: 'he thinks a painting by Wilkie . . . interesting and good, and for the sake of peace I give in and acknowledge one half of his praise'. Five years before, such an outcome would have been unthinkable.

In late July, Abraham found himself in a position a good deal more humble than he had planned. Just as Felix had on his own first visit to the city, Abraham sustained a leg injury which – probably through infection – became serious enough to keep him immobile for several weeks. If his whole visit to England had smacked of a vaguely infantil-ising journey into a world in which his entire existence, and most of his contacts with the outside world, were mediated by his son, his weeks of recovery strongly enhanced this dynamic. Abraham's reflec-tions on Felix's attentive care through this period lapse into language that might well describe the debt of a child to a parent:

> I owe my recovery to one whom, away from you, I like best being indebted to, and that is Felix. I can never tell you what he has done for me, what treasures of love, patience, perseverance, grave kindness and tenderest care he has lavished on me; and much as I am obliged to him for the thousand marks of kindness and attention I received at other hands for his sake, the best ever came from himself, and my best thanks are to him.

Despite the injury, this summer was as full of joy as the last had been of despair. In addition to the pleasures of his father's company, Felix watched closely the course of debates in the House of Commons on a measure that would remove the few remaining legal restrictions on British Jews. Felix's report on the measure's ultimate success was jubilant. Events back in Berlin gave cause for celebration as well. Felix's younger sister, Rebecka and her husband, mathematician Peter Lejeune Dirichlet, celebrated the birth of their first child, Walter, on 2 July.

It was, finally, in the spirit of uncharacteristic youthful levity that Abraham wrote home of his imminent departure from England, announcing that he would soon be arriving in Berlin with a comely young French painter, Alphonse Lovie. On their 13 September arrival, 'Alphonse' turned out to be none other than Felix himself, concerned enough about his father's health to insist on returning with him. Felix's stay was brief, and spent almost entirely with family. He was there not as a citizen, but as a guest in his parents' house. When, on 25

September, he ventured forth once more, it was in the full knowledge that he might never return there as anything more than a guest.

★

A few weeks before Zelter's death, Mendelssohn had written him a long, heartfelt letter revealing that his years abroad have left him more convinced than ever that he wanted to settle in Germany. Much of the letter is spent singing the praises of his friend, Johann Nepomuk Schelble, the founder and director of the Frankfurt Caecilienverein. In his moving account of Schelble's impact on Frankfurt's musical life we can discern a map of Mendelssohn's own professional agenda:

> the Caecilienverein is there, which alone is enough to make one glad to be in Frankfurt; these people sing with so much fire and are so in unison that it is a joy to behold . . . One can scarcely believe what an effect a single person who wants to accomplish something can have on all the others; Schelble is not alone in this, of course, and a taste for serious music is not primarily restricted to Frankfurt, and yet it is remarkable with what joy and how well the amateurs there play the *Well-Tempered Clavier*, the *Inventions*, and all of Beethoven, how they know everything by heart, fix every wrong note, how really musically trained they are. He has built up a very important circle of influence and brought people further along in the truest sense.

Even as Mendelssohn grew increasingly frustrated with the incompetence of the amateur orchestra ('they are too inept, and good intentions alone are not enough') and with his irksome duties in the rarefied, highly professionalised atmosphere of the theatre, his two-year stay in Düsseldorf brought into sharp focus Mendelssohn's vision of the popular choral ensemble as the foundation of widespread reform in musical taste.

The first reform he sought to undertake was in the realm of church music. Lutheran though he was, Mendelssohn's encounters with Thibaut, and with the rich archival holdings of Rome, had left him with no shortage of opinions on the subject of Catholic liturgical music. Nowhere in Düsseldorf, he reported to Rebecka, could there be found 'even one tolerable solemn mass, and not a single one of the old Italian masters; nothing but modern showiness [*Spektakel*]'. Even before settling into his rooms in Wilhelm von Schadow's house, he set off by carriage to cull the region: Elberfeld yielded scores of Palestrina, Allegri and Bai; he found Lotti, Pergolesi, Leo and more Palestrina (six masses) in Bonn; Cologne offered 'the best old Italian pieces which I as yet know, particularly two motets of Orlando Lasso'.

Mendelssohn returned from this journey to discover the town in the throes of preparation for the visit of the Crown Prince of Prussia. This visit was celebrated with a collaborative undertaking that formed, for Mendelssohn, a happy welcome into the artistic circle with whom he would spend most of his time in the coming years: *Israel in Egypt* was reprised, with Mendelssohn at the piano, accompanied by *tableaux vivants* designed by Wilhelm von Schadow and his students Eduard Bendemann and Julius Hübner. The Crown Prince already sensed keenly what the Prussian capital stood to lose in cutting ties with a musician of Mendelssohn's stature and promise, telling his 'dear Mendelssohn' that he 'was really quite angry at my forsaking both him and Berlin for so long a time'. Mendelssohn was soon made aware just how earnest these sentiments were: by the end of the year, he had been named a member of the Academy of Art in Berlin. When the Crown Prince took the throne, as Friedrich Wilhelm IV, seven years later, he at once set about crafting an offer Mendelssohn could not refuse (though he should have).

Israel was only the first of a handful of Handel oratorios that would form a cornerstone of the town's musical life under Mendelssohn's guidance. His first concert, of 22 November, included *Alexander's Feast* – whose score and parts he had discovered in Elberfeld – as well as Beethoven's C-minor Piano Concerto and *Egmont* overture. Over the next two years would follow performances, in part or in whole, of four more Handel works: the *Dettinger Te Deum* on 17 August 1834, the first part of *Samson* on 23 October 1834, the first part of *Judas Maccabaeus* on 18 December 1834, and *Messiah* on 12 March 1835 (he had directed it in Elberfeld a year earlier). Handel's *Solomon*, in a translation by Karl

Klingemann, was the centrepiece of the 1835 Lower Rhein Music Festival in Cologne, once more placed under Mendelssohn's direction (the 1834 festival had been conducted by Beethoven's pupil, Ferdinand Ries). Under Mendelssohn's guidance, the Düsseldorf Musikverein also braved Haydn's *The Seasons* and parts of *The Creation*, Beethoven's C-minor Mass, Mozart's *Requiem*, Cherubini's C-minor Mass, cantatas of J. S. Bach (Simrock had begun publishing A. B. Marx's editions in 1830), and Mendelssohn's own *Verleih' uns Frieden*. Instrumental offerings reflected no less strongly Mendelssohn's investment in Germany's emerging canon, including overtures of Gluck, Mozart, Cherubini and Weber, and a number of Beethoven's symphonies. Mendelssohn's early contentment with the state of things in Düsseldorf is captured, in his own English, in a letter of 3 April 1834 to his English friend, William Horsley:

> My occupations here are all most all pleasant and interesting; the 'Musikverein' or 'vocal Society' is as noumerous as it possibly can be in such a small place as this is; there are 113 members, merely amateurs, who meet every Tuesday, and spend the evening with singing Choruses at the Piano, there are some excellent voices amongst them and even the Choruses go sometimes so well, that it is quite astonishing to me. I wish you could hear some of Handels oratorios, particularly *Israel*, *Maccabaeus* and *Samson*, which they sing with a true enthusiasm. Besides there is an 'instrumental Society' (less noumerous between twenty-and thirty) and then the military bands of three regiments, and the orchestra of the theatre, although all the three contains a great many sholking fiddlers. I hope I shall be able to form a pretty good orchestra in selecting the good performers and leaving the bad ones behind.

The inadequacy of local instrumentalists – a frustration which would only worsen in the course of 1834 – was only one of the difficulties Mendelssohn encountered in his efforts to reform the theatrical life of the town. Though prospects seemed promising enough at the outset, the irritations of his operatic dealings became a burden that more than balanced out the joys of his choral activities.

With the model of Goethe's turn-of-the-century reforms in Weimar's ducal theatre before them, Mendelssohn and dramatist Karl Immermann sought to establish a theatre in Düsseldorf whose scope would include both opera and spoken drama. In Immermann, Mendelssohn found a collaborator whose frustrations with the decrepitude of much of Germany's contemporary cultural life closely matched his own. Through the period of their partnership, Immermann was beginning work on a novel, The Epigones (published in 1836), which articulated anxieties and desires closely akin to those at the heart of Mendelssohn's own artistic world-view, seeking to navigate a difficult course between the cherished artefacts of the late eighteenth century and the spiritual and aesthetic impoverishment of the present:

> To express the whole misery in one word, we are epigones and bear the burden with which each successor and later generation is usually stuck. The great endeavour in the realm of the spirit undertaken by our fathers from their huts and cottages supplied us with numerous treasures that are now spread out on all market tables . . . But with borrowed ideas it is as with borrowed grain: anyone who traffics foolishly with foreign goods always becomes poorer.[9]

Even before the establishment of the new Theatre Association on 10 March 1834, Mendelssohn and Immermann embarked on a series of 'classical performances' which they hoped would set a new standard of theatrical excellence. It was not at all clear, from the first performance, that the Düsseldorf public was ready for such a revolution, or at least for the cost it entailed. In December 1833, after some twenty rehearsals, Don Giovanni hit the stage under Mendelssohn's direction; it was the first opera he had conducted in public. Disgruntled by the increased price of tickets necessitated by production costs, the audience's vocal protests became vehement enough that the curtain had to be raised and lowered three times before the second act could get underway. Though the crowd at last fell into silence, and applauded heartily at the close, Mendelssohn took the occasion to grandstand in the name of the dignity of the enterprise: 'I declared that until the company and I had received some apology I would not again conduct the opera'. The apology came (in the form of a manifesto from the Association for the Promotion of Music), and performances resumed, if a few days behind schedule.

The public was persuaded that Mendelssohn had, in this case, acted justifiably in defence of his art; he was greeted with a three-fold flourish of trumpets at the next performance, and the operas that followed were generally acclaimed. But the incident offered a glimpse of a personality whose insistence on perfection, and on maintaining absolute authority, could border on petulance. At a particularly frustrating rehearsal of Beethoven's incidental music for *Egmont*, Mendelssohn proudly reported tearing the score in half in his rage at 'the stupid musicians'. Though the production of Cherubini's *Wasserträger* later in the winter of 1833 was a dazzling success, Mendelssohn lamented that he 'was obliged to undertake the regulation of everything – the acting, the scenery and the dialogue, – or it would all have gone wrong'. In a brief letter of the following October, he summarily (and briefly, as it turned out) resigned his post as director of church music 'until circumstances allow for the appointment of a different organist to the one who rendered his services for today's Mass . . . His incompetence makes impossible any successful performance.'

Mendelssohn took genuine pride in his operatic successes – productions included Marschner's *Hans Heiling*, Weber's *Freischütz* and *Oberon*, Auber's *Fra Diavolo*, and Mozart's *Entführung* and *Zauberflöte*. But his functions as 'intendant' of the new theatre soon became oppressive. In spite of repeated efforts to distance himself from the daily drudgery and irritations of theatrical life (he promptly deputised Julius Rietz, younger brother of his late friend Eduard, as the theatre's musical director), Mendelssohn found himself responsible for assembling an orchestra and a roster of singers in the autumn of 1834. His life as a composer was suffering profoundly:

11 Pencil drawing of the composer at age twenty-five by his friend and landlord,
    Wilhelm Schadow

When I sat down to my work in the morning, at every bar there was a ringing at the bell; then came grumbling choristers to be snubbed, stupid singers to be taught, seedy musicians to be engaged; and when this had gone on the whole day, and I felt that all these things were for the sole benefit and advantage of the Düsseldorf theatre, I was provoked.

Mendelssohn's initial amicability with Immermann had cooled considerably in the course of 1834; by the end of the year, the two were hardly on speaking terms. The seeds for this falling out had been sown much earlier, despite Mendelssohn's genuine respect for Immermann's work in Düsseldorf. Mendelssohn had rejected Immermann's libretto for The Tempest, backing out of a projected collaboration they planned in the autumn of 1831. Immermann had also had a heated altercation with Wilhelm von Schadow – Mendelssohn's landlord and close friend – just before Mendelssohn's arrival in Düsseldorf, leaving the composer in a delicate position from the start. If Mendelssohn could be uncompromising and, at times, abrupt, Immermann's, too, was a difficult personality. His guarded, often defensive manner was exacerbated by the struggles of maintaining a private life centred on a decade-long affair, by which many in Düsseldorf were scandalised, with Elisa von Lutzow. Elisa had divorced her husband (a Prussian general) in 1825, but refused to marry again. Fanny Mendelssohn, who met Immermann in Berlin in the autumn of 1833, found him 'much friendlier than his reputation in that regard', though still 'very tight-lipped and far too reflective'. A year later, her brother would be much less charitable in his characterisations of the author.

On 2 November 1834 – thirteen months after arriving in Düsseldorf – Mendelssohn abruptly resigned his post at the theatre, agreeing to be involved only as a conductor. This decision set in motion a process of withdrawal from his Düsseldorf commitments that was completed the following summer. His last concert in the town took place on 2 July 1835.

★

Mendelssohn's frustration becomes understandable in light of the rather meagre output of these years. By the time of his departure from Düsseldorf, it had been over five years since the completion of the E♭ String Quartet, his last major chamber work. He had not returned to the A-minor Symphony, begun in Scotland, that he had spent much of his Italian tour contemplating. The *Rondo brillant* for piano and orchestra he did complete – dedicated to Moscheles and performed by him to general acclaim – made no claim to particular significance. Mendelssohn's own fondness for the overture to *Die schöne Melusine*, premièred in London under Moscheles' direction, on 7 April 1834, was not much consolation for its cool initial reception (to Felix's great irritation, Fanny herself seemed somewhat bewildered by the piece, and echoed George Smart's suggestion that a fuller programme would be of use in making sense of the work). Most frustrating for Felix was the painfully slow progress of the work he probably considered his most significant undertaking to date, the oratorio, St Paul, that had been commissioned by Schelble's Caecilienverein early in 1832 (again, Catholic surroundings brought out one of his most decidedly Protestant projects).

During Mendelssohn's time in Düsseldorf, the role of composition in his professional life changed fundamentally, as he knew it would. Superb conductor and pianist that he was, he had formerly been a composer first and foremost, who performed as suitable occasions arose. With the move to Düsseldorf, his obligations as conductor and administrator took priority, composition thriving or suffering according to how much time other duties permitted. Though his frustrations with his manifold duties prompted him to insist on twice as much annual leave in his next post (the three months' vacation in Düsseldorf became six in Leipzig), his very frustrations with the incompetence of the Düsseldorf instrumentalists underline the personal investment he had in his work outside of composition. The concerts he organised – particularly in their promotion of older music – were just as legitimate an artistic outlet as composition itself.

Mendelssohn's daily immersion in the business of music-making had implications not only for the amount of composing he did, but for its nature. If we take the late twentieth-century concert hall as our judge, one significant result of Mendelssohn's increasing attention to non-compositional matters was a precipitous decline in the sheer calibre of his work. After the assumption of his position in Düsseldorf, it would be nine years before he would complete a work (the 'Scottish' Symphony) whose later reception would rival that of his most popular earlier works: the three title-bearing overtures, the 'Italian' Symphony, the Octet, or the *Rondo capriccioso* for piano. The recent explosion of interest – on the part of scholars and performers alike – in formerly obscure pockets of his output has generally exacerbated the tendency to locate the load-bearing compositions of his career in its early years, with new attention to the string *sinfonie*, the early dramatic works, and the chorale cantatas. Greg Vitercik, in kicking off his insightful analysis of a handful of early works, points to the shadow Mendelssohn's later career has even tended to cast over his whole critical reception: 'if the composer's "mature" works are so distressingly weak, what could anyone expect to find in his youthful creations?'[10]

Though neither Mendelssohn himself nor the bulk of his contemporary critics observed this decline in quality, he does indeed seem to have been in the process, in the early thirties, of reconfiguring his creative sensibilities to reflect more fully the circumstances in which he composed. To employ the blunt, awkwardly over-sized nomenclatural tools of music historiography, this might be described as a move towards the 'Biedermeier', away from the more robustly Romantic instincts of his youth. The mid-nineteenth-century poet, Gottlieb Biedermeier, from whom this sensibility takes its name, never existed, but was invented by medical student Adolf Kussmaul and his friend, Ludwig Eichrodt. The parodistically vapid, four-square verse they published under this name – the first series appeared in 1855 in Munich's *Fliegende Blätter* – was embraced as the embodiment of all that was insufferably decorous, comfortable, complacent and respectable in the conservative German culture of the decades following the

Napoleonic Wars. 'Biedermeier' music, as the term came to be used, was conservative in outlook, emotionally restrained, and firmly rooted in the musical practices of the society for which it was created: '"Biedermeier"', Carl Dahlhaus observed, 'can be seen as the very quintessence of a successful mediation . . . between the history of composition and the history of institutions'.

Mendelssohn would very likely have gratefully accepted such a description as a compliment. Indeed, this is precisely the impulse at work in his account of the compositional motivations behind the four-part songs for mixed voices to which he had lately turned his attention. Looking over Mendelssohn's settings of Heine's *Volkslieder* – which would appear among his first published collection of songs for this ensemble in 1838 – Fanny was at a loss as to why he had departed from a standard piano/voice arrangement: 'I don't think the text warrants such a texture nor is it suited to your conception'. Felix replied:

> I think this is the only way that one can write *Volkslieder*, because any piano accompaniment smacks immediately of the chamber or the music chest, and because four voices without an instrument can therefore most easily carry such a Lied. And if the reason is too aesthetic, then accept the reason that I really wanted to write something of the sort for the Woringens, who sing such things in a charming manner.

These Lieder, like much that Mendelssohn would create from this point onwards, embody the ideal underlying Paul Hindemith's notion of *Gebrauchsmusik*, compositions in which abstract artistic considerations are balanced against, and qualified by, consideration of the people and the institutions for whose use they are intended.

If the 'Biedermeier', as a critical angle of attack, is most useful in explaining the largely forgotten choral works of Mendelssohn's later years, it is just as important in assessing the most novel new form in which Mendelssohn had begun working, the *Songs Without Words*. The first set of these lyrical piano miniatures – which he had evidently been composing under this title since the late twenties – was published in London, Bonn and Paris in July 1832, just after his return from abroad. Another followed in 1835; three more sets would follow before his death. All were dedicated to women (including one set to each of the Woringen daughters, Rosa and Elise). Though the *Songs Without Words* include some pieces of considerable technical challenge, and they were certainly performed in concerts, these works were geared towards private use by the cultivated amateur, an audience which had at its demographic centre the young, single woman.

The enthusiasm Mendelssohn habitually kindled among this cohort was legendary (his mother was only the first to suggest that the outcome of the Singakademie's decision might have been different had under-aged women not been denied a vote in the election of the new director). Whatever their musical worth, the *Songs Without Words* offered to the 'secretly enchanted'[11] female fan musical works around which to spin fantasies of quiet domestic union with their handsome author. Robert Schumann's characteristically impressionistic musings on these works situate them tellingly in just such intimate surroundings: 'Who of us in the twilight hour has not sat at his upright piano . . . and in the midst of improvising has not unconsciously begun to sing a quiet melody?' Fanny's report on the Berlin reception of the *Songs Without Words* suggests that the works had struck home: 'I play them everywhere, and a pair of ladies regularly fall into a dead faint nearby'. Particularly telling is an episode in the novelistic tribute to Mendelssohn, *Charles Auchester*, authored soon after his death by a teen-aged English fan, Elizabeth Sheppard. When Mendelssohn's character, 'Seraphael', arrives on the campus of a fictionalised Leipzig Conservatory for the first time, he sneaks into the back of the auditorium unnoticed while a performance is in progress. He is spotted in the midst of a virtuosic sonata by a local pedant and resoundingly charged to take the stage himself. After some coaxing, he steps up to the piano, speaks not a word, and plays (perhaps improvises) a song without words. The crowd, needless to say, is spellbound.

Another fundamental shift in the direction of Mendelssohn's composition concerned his abandonment of the programmatic bent that had informed so much of his output to this point. *Die schöne Melusine*, premièred in London on 7 April 1834, marked his last such work. He contemplated further works in this vein; a few months after this première, he and Fanny discussed seriously his desire to write another overture on Shakespeare (she pushed for *Macbeth*), and he contemplated a companion piece to a three-volume collection of engravings, *Views of Granada*, she had sent him early in 1835. But apart from the 1842 completion of the 'Scottish' Symphony (which was published without this title), descriptive music appears to have lost its appeal.

The immediate inspiration for *Die schöne Melusine* was Conradin Kreutzer's operatic setting of the fairy tale, which Mendelssohn saw – and despised – in Berlin in the spring of 1833. The subject afforded him the opportunity to take up once more the aquatic orientation of the *Hebrides* and the *Calm Sea, Prosperous Voyage* overtures, this time in a babbling subject for the clarinet that frames the whole (and from which Wagner's *Rheingold* motif took its cue). After their visit to the art exhibit in London in the summer of 1833, Abraham had written: 'I still do not understand why [the English] should not have, nor ever have had, a marine painter'. Whether Mendelssohn was self-consciously seeking to redress this lacuna in his own chosen medium we can only conjecture.

★

Though Mendelssohn's frustrations in Düsseldorf were real and pressing, it seems unlikely that he would have been quite so quick to abandon his post had he not already received much more alluring offers. By October 1834, it had been made clear to him that certain powerful figures in Leipzig's musical scene might be interested in his services. On 2 January he received an offer of a professorship at the university there, which he turned down ('I am in no way in a position to speak on music properly for even a half hour, let alone throughout an entire colloquium'). What crystallised soon thereafter was one of the most attractive offers any German musician could hope for: the directorship of the Leipzig Gewandhaus Orchestra and the Singakademie, with six months of vacation. With his salary finally fixed at 600 Thaler (half again what was initially offered), and the assurance that no other musician would be forced out through his acceptance, Mendelssohn took the job. On 26 January he wrote to Conrad Schleinitz (president of the Gewandhaus board of directors with whom he had been in negotiations): 'it is my only desire to further the cause of music down the path which seems right to me, and . . . gladly accept a calling which would place the means of doing so within my reach'.

6 Scaling the heights in Leipzig

Thank God! At last the morning light
Bursts through my windows: French and bright.
My wife is coming – fair as day –
And smiles my German cares away.
Heinrich Heine, 'Night Thoughts'[1]

Mendelssohn arrived in Leipzig at the end of August 1835. After the stultifying philistinism of Berlin and the provinciality of the Düsseldorfers, however well-intentioned, his new home cut an attractive profile indeed. By early October, he was able to write home: 'I cannot tell you how much I am satisfied with this beginning, and with the whole aspect of my position here'.[2] Eight months later, the young composer – recently named an Honorary Doctor of Philosophy and Master of Fine Arts of Leipzig University – proclaimed the arrangement permanent:

> I am now fairly established in Germany, and shall not need to make a pilgrimage into foreign countries to secure my existence. This, indeed, has only been evident . . . since my being placed at Leipzig.

The first decades of the nineteenth century had not been kind to the Kingdom of Saxony. King Friedrich Augustus I had supported Napoleon during the wars, and was rewarded, at the Congress of Vienna, with the loss of over half of his territories to Prussia. Despite the relative economic hardship of these years, Saxony's second city, Leipzig (Dresden was the capital), continued to enjoy a central position in the German commercial and intellectual landscape. With a population still well under 50,000, Leipzig's cultural influence outpaced its size. Its trade fairs had, in the eighteenth century, earned it the name 'little Paris'; the university stood at the centre of a teeming intellectual environment that supported well over a hundred bookshops and dozens of publishing houses.

Though Mendelssohn was vehemently uninterested in music criticism, the proliferation of music-related periodicals was a powerful indicator of the city's lively intellectual engagement with its own robust musical affairs. Leipzig's *Allgemeine musikalische Zeitung* had been one of Europe's leading music periodicals since its founding in 1798, indeed, the first German music periodical to remain in print for any length of time. The year before Mendelssohn's arrival in the city, Robert Schumann – a struggling, obscure composer of twenty-four years, still trying to figure out what to do when he grew up – had founded the more progressive *Neue Zeitschrift für Musik*, in which reviews of several of Mendelssohn's early works for piano had already appeared. The *Zeitung für die elegante Welt* also housed a steady stream of non-technical music reviews.

Leipzig was a centre of music publishing, as well. Mendelssohn had a close ongoing relationship with the city's leading music publisher, Breitkopf & Härtel (the publisher of the *Allgemeine musikalische Zeitung*), which he had long considered one of Germany's leading lights in the business. Shortly after Gottfried Christoph Härtel's 1795 purchase of the firm from the grandson of its founder, he had begun issuing complete editions of Mozart and Haydn. In the early years of the nineteenth century the firm issued landmark editions of J. S. Bach's motets and chorale preludes, with the *Well-Tempered Clavier* following in 1819. Härtel had published, among other things, the three concert overtures on which Mendelssohn's considerable popularity in Leipzig was founded, and had already begun making noises about a complete edition of Mendelssohn's work.

12 Interior of the Gewandhaus: watercolour by Gottlob Theuerkauf

Where Düsseldorf had offered Mendelssohn a musical environment richer in potential than achievement – and not, as it turned out, sufficiently rich even in the former – Leipzig boasted a handful of well-established musical institutions: the choir of the Thomaskirche, the Singakademie, the opera, the 'Euterpe' (a thriving amateur vocal and orchestral organisation), and, at their head, the Gewandhaus Orchestra. The young conductor wasted no time in proving that the Leipzigers' confidence in him was well-placed. His first concert, on 4 October, included his own *Calm Sea, Prosperous Voyage* overture (already a popular work in the city), a scene and aria from *Der Freischütz*, Louis Spohr's Violin Concerto no. 8, the overture and Introduction to Cherubini's *Ali Baba* (with Singakademie and Thomaskirche choir), and, in the second part, Beethoven's Fourth Symphony. 'F. Meritis stepped forth and a hundred eyes flew to him in the first moment', Schumann reported. Quick to clear up whatever confusion might surround his new appellation for the conductor – whom he deeply admired – he continues: 'Meritis conducted as if he had composed the overture himself, and the orchestra played accordingly'.[3]

The orchestra – some twenty-six strings, eight woodwinds, four brass and two percussionists at the time of Mendelssohn's arrival – was still performing in the old Gewandhaus, accommodations that were, as Chorley observed, 'infinitely too small for the audience who crowded it'.[4] The women sat in two sections facing one another, at right angles to the stage. The men stood in an unruly mob behind them on either side.

Humble as these surroundings were, it was here that the Gewandhaus Orchestra and its energetic, beloved director spent the next six years laying – or at least consolidating – the foundations of the modern professional symphony orchestra, an achievement whose historical impact must be considered far greater than the aggregate impact of Mendelssohn's compositions. Where the Gewandhaus Orchestra had formerly been led by the concertmaster, Mendelssohn now directed with the baton, adumbrating through the sheer clarity of his musical vision the *auteur* status of the modern conductor. Where the ensemble had formerly been appallingly recompensed for their labours, Mendelssohn struggled successfully to increase their salaries, and personally undertook the establishment of a pension fund. And while he vigorously sought out and programmed worthy new creations, the Gewandhaus concerts of these years consolidated a repertory – the concept of which we take fully for granted today – centred around a fixed, stable canon of German masterworks. We must, of course, guard against mapping Romantic narratives concerning the originality of genius on to Mendelssohn's role in this last process; he no more invented the canon than Haydn invented the symphony (nor was he, for that matter, the first to use a baton; Louis Spohr and Peter Joseph Lindpaintner were conspicuous predecessors). But never had a musician so singularly dedicated to the consolidation of a canon of German masterworks – and so distinctly equipped with training, personal charisma and innate musicianship to bring to the peak of their capabilities whatever ensemble was placed before him – been placed in charge of a cluster of ensembles so capable of realising his vision.

At the heart of the canon *chez* Mendelssohn were the overtures, symphonies and concertos of Beethoven and Mozart, with Haydn, Gluck and Weber not far behind. Hiller, who knew well the legendary Beethoven performances of the Conservatoire orchestra in Paris, found even stronger praise for Mendelssohn's achievement: 'no one had ever imagined so deep a conception, or such artistic finish in the performances of the great symphonies'. Handel, too, remained central to Mendelssohn's project. Spurred on by his new thirty-two-volume edition of Handel's complete works – an expression of thanks from the committee of the 1835 Lower Rhein Music Festival – Mendelssohn became fascinated with the possibility not only of promoting Handel in Germany, but of reviving these works in their original form, without the added brass parts that had become customary by the early nineteenth century. November 1836 saw two massive Leipzig performances – with some three hundred singers before an audience of 2,000 – of *Israel in Egypt* in this form. One among the audience,

William Sterndale Bennett, found the Leipzig product no match for the polished Handel performances in England: 'The singers for the soli parts were anything but good, the orchestra wanted point, and the organist was continually lugging'.[5] But the Leipzig press, like the conductor, were euphoric. *Messiah* followed on 16 November the following year, to similar acclaim.

Mendelssohn's advocacy of older music came into particular focus in a series of four 'Historical Concerts' offered early in 1838. Following the model of the historical survey he had performed at the keyboard for Goethe, these concerts were laid out chronologically. The first, of 15 February, included Bach's D-major Orchestral Suite (his concerto for three keyboards had already become a staple of the Leipzig repertoire), together with works of Gluck, Handel and Viotti. The second concert, on 22 February, moved on to Righini, Cimarosa and Naumann, closing with Haydn's 'Farewell' Symphony. To the great delight of the packed house, the musicians actually blew out their candles and left the stage one by one, as they had in Haydn's day, in the closing pages of the final work. On 1 March came Mozart, Salieri, Romberg and Méhul; a week later, Vogler, Weber and Beethoven. This extremely popular series was followed by a second in 1841, this time with the first concert dedicated exclusively to Bach and Handel, the second to Haydn, the third to Mozart, the fourth to Beethoven. The massive final concert of this series included *Leonore* overture no. 3 (the orchestra had performed all four *Leonore* overtures at a single concert a year earlier), the Kyrie and Gloria from the C-major Mass, the Violin Concerto, and the Ninth Symphony, which Mendelssohn had conducted at the 1836 Lower Rhein Music Festival in Düsseldorf. A third series of historical concerts followed, partly under the direction of concertmaster Ferdinand David, in 1847.

A musical landmark of a much more personal nature came with Mendelssohn's organ concert in the Thomaskirche in August 1840 for the erection of a Bach monument. (The monument was erected three years later, on Bach's birthday, under the windows of his old rooms in the Thomasschüle.) The concert – an all-Bach affair apart from a brilliant closing improvisation on *O Haupt voll Blut und Wunden* – was a revelation to the Leipzigers; an enraptured Schumann wrote, 'there is nothing greater in music than the enjoyment of the twofold mastery displayed when one master gives expression to another. Fame and honour to young and old alike'.[6] Elise Polko recalls Johann Friedrich Rochlitz (the ageing critic who had edited the *Allgemeine musikalische Zeitung* for the first twenty years of its existence) embracing Mendelssohn after the performance with the words: 'I can now depart in peace, for never shall I hear anything finer or more sublime'. Rochlitz would live, however, to see Mendelssohn's next great musical offering to his predecessor, the triumphant performance of the *St Matthew Passion* on Palm Sunday 1841.

As joyfully as he undertook the task of promoting the music of the dead, Mendelssohn proved no less energetic in his pursuit of worthy new works. His position as north Germany's leading arbiter of musical taste – Schumann described him as his own 'highest, final reference' – was not always an easy one: 'Six new symphonies are lying before me', Mendelssohn lamented in a 10 January 1837 letter to Hiller; 'not one of them pleases me'. Hiller himself pleased Mendelssohn immoderately; he received this letter in the midst of a season that featured two of his overtures, and Mendelssohn would direct the 1840 première of his oratorio, *Destruction of Jerusalem*. The work of Julius Rietz appeared, as well, and William Sterndale Bennett, along with many whose names history has barely seen fit to record: Reissiger, Lechner, Vogler, Täglichsbeck, Bergmüller. Though Mendelssohn refused, in a series of now-famous letters, to encourage Fanny to publish, he eagerly programmed a song of hers that had been put out by Schlesinger in 1837. There was, the proud brother reported, 'much applause when it was over'.

Mendelssohn's relationship with Schumann was both personally warm and professionally significant. A year Mendelssohn's junior, Schumann recalled their first meeting, just after Mendelssohn's arrival in town: 'The first impression was of an unforgettable human being'.[7] Though he lionised the conductor personally, Schumann's criticism of Mendelssohn's work was candid, often insightful, and by no means altogether positive (there is a persistent undercurrent of concern for Mendelssohn's dependence on past models). Mendelssohn, on his part, described Schumann as 'rather quiet and turned-in upon himself, but a friendly, extremely talented and very good man at heart'. It was Schumann who discovered Schubert's Great C-major Symphony among the late composer's papers in Schubert's brother's house; Mendelssohn conducted the première of the work on 21 March 1839. In 1841, the Gewandhaus programmes included the premières of two of Schumann's symphonies, the First (whose brass opening, like that of Mendelssohn's own 1840 Lobgesang, may owe a debt to Schubert's symphony) and the Fourth.

Others are conspicuously absent. The score of a C-major Symphony by the twenty-three-year-old Richard Wagner evidently disappeared while in Mendelssohn's possession (Wagner suspected, rather improbably, foul play motivated by artistic envy). Berlioz, too, makes no appearance in the course of the thirties; we have had occasion already to observe his basic antipathy to Berlioz's music. To his credit, Mendelssohn would turn the Gewandhaus over to the older composer for an 1843 all-Berlioz programme, and was energetically involved in rehearsals and preparations.

Under Mendelssohn's directorship, the Gewandhaus also played host to some of Europe's most celebrated virtuosi. Clara Wieck, who would later marry Robert Schumann, was Leipzig's own leader at the keyboard (with the possible exception of Mendelssohn himself), and performed frequently at the Gewandhaus. William Sterndale Bennett, whom Mendelssohn had heard as a seventeen-year-old in London in 1833, was the talk of Leipzig's 1836–7 season. During the same London visit, Mendelssohn had heard for the first time 'the pure silvery ring'[8] of the fifteen-year-old soprano, Clara Novello, who took Leipzig by storm in the winter of 1837–8. Pianists Dreyschock and Thalberg – the latter was Mendelssohn's favourite among contemporary virtuosi – were there the following winter.

The mightiest of them all, Franz Liszt, arrived in 1840, fresh from victories in Vienna and Prague. Mendelssohn had passed happy hours with Liszt and Hiller in Paris eight years before, where Liszt had astounded Mendelssohn by sight-reading his new G-minor Concerto. Amazed as they were at Liszt's artistry, the Leipzig public objected to the ticket prices set by his opportunistic manager. Mendelssohn took it upon himself to see to the success of this 'amiable, warm-hearted' man, whom he liked and genuinely admired as a pianist (though he found his compositions 'inferior to his playing, and . . . only calculated for virtuosos'). The conductor organised a 'private' soirée in the Gewandhaus to which several hundred people were invited, offering Schubert's C-major Symphony, his own Calm Sea, Prosperous Voyage overture, his Psalm 42, and Bach's Triple Concerto, performed by Liszt, Hiller and Mendelssohn. For Schumann, the event represented 'three joyous hours of music such as one does not experience otherwise for years at a time'. Liszt and the Leipzigers were reconciled at a stroke.

By now one of Europe's most sought-after conductors, Mendelssohn continued to dedicate himself tirelessly to the choral festival circuit. The 1836 Lower Rhein Music Festival saw the première of his long-awaited first oratorio, St Paul, to which we shall turn in a moment, along with Beethoven's Ninth Symphony. St Paul formed a centre-piece of the four-day Birmingham Festival the following summer, where it shared top billing with Handel's Solomon. Mendelssohn performed at the organ – mostly Bach – on the first and last days of this festival, which he looked back on as one of the greatest popular successes of his career. Handel's Joshua kicked off the 1838 Lower Rhein Music Festival in Cologne, whose programming committee Mendelssohn had at last succeeded in persuading to include a work of J. S. Bach's, the Himmelfahrtskantate. Bach's work appeared on the second day, along with Beethoven's Preis der Tonkunst, a resetting of the occasional cantata, Glorreicher Augenblick, composed for the Congress of Vienna. Posterity has not proven sensible to the 'splendid things' Mendelssohn claimed to perceive in this work.

Mendelssohn was back in Düsseldorf in May of 1839 for his fifth

Lower Rhein Music Festival, which featured Handel's *Messiah* and Beethoven's *Eroica* Symphony, though his plans to dedicate the third day of this festival to Gluck's *Alceste* had fallen through. The following September he conducted a three-day festival at Brunswick (again, St Paul); a year later, another Birmingham Festival, which included the première of his recently completed symphony-cantata, *Lobgesang*. He would take the same work with him to the Lower Rhein Music Festival in 1842.

By the end of his first half-decade in Leipzig, the thirty-one-year-old Mendelssohn would have been described by many as the most influential German musician alive, and one of its most celebrated composers. If his professional life charted a rapid, unchecked escalation to this pinnacle, his personal life during the same period was a good deal more turbulent. In the first days of 1835, in the process of deciding whether to accept the Leipzig offer, Mendelssohn had suggested to his father that it might be better to 'remain free for the next few years, which I can still count among my youthful years, and make the art trip I had planned'.[9] If these are the words of a young man clinging to the last days of a happy, blessed childhood, the events – both tragic and joyful – of the eighteen months that followed swept him fully to life as an adult.

*

In the middle of October 1835, Rebecka and her husband passed through Leipzig on their return from a brief tour through Belgium and Ostend. Moscheles was visiting Mendelssohn at the time, and the two pianists were persuaded to return to Berlin with the Dirichlets. After a three-day visit, much of it spent at the keyboard, Felix left once more for Leipzig, promising to return at Christmas. According to Hensel, his father met this promise with the words, 'Well, humanly speaking, we may hope to be spared till then'.

At the age of fifty-nine, Abraham was an old man. His own father was two years in his grave by the time he reached the same age. Cataracts had almost completely taken Abraham's eyesight; he had begun dictating his letters to Rebecka and Fanny a year before, and found any form of society outside of the family – one daughter or the other was with him every evening – increasingly difficult.

On 18 November, a month after Felix's departure, Abraham complained of a slight cough. His condition had worsened sufficiently during the night that physicians were called the following morning. They were quick to assure the family that there was no immediate danger, and discouraged the anxious company from contacting Felix. Around ten o'clock in the morning, Abraham decided to take a nap. He was dead within half an hour. Though the physicians could not name his malady, it was almost certainly a stroke. Fanny's account was philosophical and lovely: 'It was the end of the righteous, a beautiful, enviable end, and I pray to God for a similar death'. Leaving Abraham's children to console his widow, Wilhelm Hensel set off for Leipzig to break the news.

Felix was shattered. During his ten-day visit to Berlin, he evidently cried little, but vanished into an interior mourning whose intensity even the family found disconcerting. Felix and his father had grown closer than ever over the three years since his first Düsseldorf festival in 1833; he had invited Abraham to the 1835 festival in Cologne with words whose sincerity we can scarcely doubt: 'one word of praise from you is more truly precious to me, and makes me happier, than all the publics in the world applauding me in concert'. These feelings only intensified with his death. 'I shall never cease to endeavour to gain his approval as I formerly did', he wrote in early December, 'though I can no longer enjoy it'.

Mendelssohn found a creative outlet for his grief in the oratorio he had been working on for almost two years. Abraham had eagerly anticipated the première of St Paul, giving vent to his impatience in his last letter to his son. Work moved steadily ahead through the winter – 'I must exert all my energies to finish it', the composer wrote to his collaborator, Schubring, 'and make it as good as possible, and then think that he takes an interest in it'. As Schelble's illness had made impossible the planned Caecilienverein première, St Paul was at last brought before the world at the Lower Rhein Music Festival in Düsseldorf on 22 May 1836.

St Paul's success was immediate and, for a time, sustained. Within a few years, it had received performances in dozens of German cities, rapidly making its way, too, to England, Switzerland, Holland, Denmark, Poland, Russia and the United States. The *Düsseldorf Zeitung* hailed it at once as 'a classic musical work of our time'. Chorley, writing in the *Athenaeum*, greeted the 1837 English première with similar strains:

> For his oratorio it would be difficult for us to say too much in its praise – simple, massive – every note of it full of expression: written in the spirit of the great ancients, but not according to their letter. We should be disposed, unhesitatingly, to rank it next to the immortal works of Handel.[10]

If the piece's popular success was unequivocal – in terms of its public impact, this was far and away Mendelssohn's most important composition to date – there were nay-sayers among its critics. Schumann was suspicious of the oratorio's 'transparent and popular nature', allowing that its pitch to general appeal might pass this time, but 'could in future compositions detract from his music something of its strength and spirit'. Others focused on the stylistically hybrid nature of the work. Though the Handel oratorio clearly played the 'host genre', there were strong strains of Bach, as well – particularly in the much-discussed inclusion of chorales – and more than occasional intimations of Italian seventeenth-century vocal polyphony. Thus the *Allgemeiner musikalischer Anzeiger* recognised the work, after its Vienna première, as 'more a skilful mosaic-work than a real whole, broken out from the towering heights'. Heinrich Heine's 1842 assessment of the work encapsulates a critical kernel that has echoed through Mendelssohn's reception right to the present day. With his trademark twist of the tail, Heine observes that Mendelssohn's work is

> characterised by a great, strict, very serious seriousness, a determined, almost importunate tendency to follow classical models, the finest, cleverest calculation, sharp intelligence, and finally complete lack of naïveté. But is there in art any originality of genius without naïveté?'[11]

Given the rigour with which Mendelssohn screened potential opera libretti for dramatic persuasiveness – its absence was a habitual excuse in his rejection of project after project – St Paul's manifest dramatic failings are difficult to comprehend. The first part sets off at a high emotional pitch, with the sentencing and stoning of St Stephen. Mendelssohn's setting is sure-footed and effective. Paul's interview with the transfigured Christ on the road to Damascus sustains this level. In one of the most novel strokes of the work, Mendelssohn uses four female voices to depict the transfigured Christ; 'so beautiful, so surprising, so touching', wrote Fanny, who sang among the altos at the première, 'that I know little in music to equal it'. The aria of the blind Saul, 'Gott, sei mir gnädig', is the emotional heart of his character. We may well discern here a glimpse of Mendelssohn's feelings towards his father, another converted Jew facing the prospect of life in darkness (the aria was completed months before his father's death). But the second part moves through the preaching of Paul and Barnabas with little clear dramatic impulse. Though much of the choral writing throughout is powerful, the tendency towards sheer monumentality does not always feel sufficiently motivated by the material at hand. The sturdy simplicity of many of the arias verges, at times, on sentimentality, elsewhere, on the sublime – the soprano aria, 'Jerusalem', speaks from a height of melodic inspiration Mendelssohn would rarely equal in his vocal writing.

By the time of St Paul's première, it had become clear that Johann Schelble's illness might well be his last; he spent much of his time now at his home at Hüfingen, near Baden, and had abandoned all but the slightest hope of resuming his duties as director of the Caecilienverein. The Mendelssohns' memory of Karl Friedrich Zelter had been poisoned by the 1833–4 publication of the old musician's correspondence with Goethe; the strong anti-Semitic overtones of Zelter's remarks on the Mendelssohn family would, by all accounts, better have been left private (a typical remark on Abraham: 'He treats me very favourably and I can dip into his cash, for he's become rich during the general wretchedness without, however, damaging his soul'). In light of this, Schelble had emerged as the closest thing to a father figure in Mendelssohn's professional life, and this impending loss hit Mendelssohn hard. Given the lamentable fact that Mendelssohn could not conduct all choirs at all times, a worthy successor would have to be found. Mendelssohn had received the offer in February, and declined, but took an active role in the search.

His immediate contribution was to give up a well-deserved vacation to take over the directorship of the organisation in the summer of 1836. He took up residence in Schelble's own spacious house at the corner of Frankfurt's 'Schöne Aussicht', overlooking the river. Ferdinand Hiller was there, and for a time Rossini, with whom Mendelssohn struck up an extremely cordial relationship based on genuine mutual respect, artistic and personal.

During Mendelssohn's days in Berlin following the death of his father, the question arose of just how long Felix planned on remaining a bachelor. Fanny had broached the subject, which was doubtless a strong subtext in Mendelssohn's remark to Schubring that 'a new life must now begin for me, or all must be at an end: the old life is now severed'. In a 13 July letter to his mother, Mendelssohn indicates that he may have found in Frankfurt what he had not in Leipzig, in the form of 'an especially beautiful girl whom I should love to see again'.[12] The girl turned out to be the nineteen-year-old Cécile Jeanrenaud, to whose house Mendelssohn had begun paying regular and frequent visits. His fall was rapid and irreversible. 'I have not an idea whether she likes me or not', he wrote to Rebecka on 24 July. 'But one thing is certain, that to her I owe the first real happiness I have enjoyed this year, and now for the first time I feel fresh and hopeful again.'

All but persuaded that his heart had made its choice, Mendelssohn exercised admirable self-restraint in his next move: he headed to Scheveningen, in Holland, where he spent the first weeks of August taking 'what they call the small cure' of twenty-one baths. There, in the company of Wilhelm Schadow and his son, Mendelssohn reached his decision. On 9 August, he wrote to his mother requesting her consent – to which he was bound by respect, not law – to an engagement. Soon after his return to Frankfurt, the matter was formalised. The news came to his mother in a letter of 9 September: 'I have just been accepted by Cécile Jeanrenaud. My head is quite giddy from the events of the day . . . I feel so rich and happy.'

Cécile's parents were prominent members of Frankfurt's Huguenot aristocracy. Her father had been the pastor of the French Reformed Church. Upon his death in 1819, Cécile's mother had moved, with her three young children, back into her mother's house; it was thus among the Souchays – 'people of much distinction in town' – that Cécile was raised. Though her education hardly rivalled Mendelssohn's own, she was a person of refinement and poise, an excellent painter, and a figure of stunning beauty. Elise Polko describes this '*beau idéal* of womanly fascination and loveliness':

> Her figure was slight, of middle height, and rather drooping, like a flower heavy with dew, her luxuriant golden-brown hair fell in rich curls on her shoulders, her complexion was of transparent delicacy, her smile charming, and she had the most bewitching deep blue eyes I ever beheld, with dark eyelashes and eyebrows.[13]

Contemporary descriptions of Cécile are not all so charitable. Sebastian Hensel, writing in tones qualified by the rather stiff relationships that would develop between his mother, Fanny, and her sister-in-law, reports, 'She was not a striking person in any way, neither extraordinarily clever, brilliantly witty, nor exceptionally accomplished'. Many Leipzigers reportedly found her cold and distant in her social life. But she and Felix seemed, by every account, extraordinarily well suited to one another and happy in their union.

In the months following their engagement, Cécile and Felix took every opportunity to see each other. He was in Frankfurt for some ten days in December, during which visit etiquette demanded of the couple some 163 calls on family and friends in town (how many were actually executed history does not record). Cécile and her mother came to Leipzig for a stay of several weeks in February and March; though not an accomplished singer, Cécile joined in the Leipzig première of St Paul on 16 March. Immediately after this event, they set off for Frankfurt to finalise preparations. The marriage took place on 28

March in the French Reform Church. Felix's family was represented at the event only by his Aunt Dorothea Schlegel, then residing in Frankfurt, to whom he had grown deeply attached; the Berlin Mendelssohns' attitude towards the Souchays never moved beyond benign ambivalence.

The honeymoon, of which the couple kept a detailed, richly illustrated diary, took them south through the Rhine Valley, passing through Worms and Straßburg into the Black Forest, returning from Freiburg up through Heidelberg and Darmstadt. After a brief sojourn in Frankfurt in the middle of May, they set off once more, this time tending northwards through Oberad, Bingen and, by early August, Coblenz. They arrived on 10 August in Düsseldorf, where Cécile – now some three months pregnant – would remain while Felix set off to England for the Birmingham Festival. These first months of intense, unbroken companionship were not, of course, without their rough spots; the diary makes mention of at least one incident concerning a 'very pretty flower girl', and the glances Felix casually cast her way, whose emotional shadow seemed to loom large for the young couple. But the candid recording of such incidents only makes more believable the pervasive tone of idyllic joy. Cécile captured eloquently the pleasures of one July evening, which will stand for many:

> The weather this evening was glorious, and objects in the furthest distance lay free of haze before us. We rested beneath the young trees which surround the church, lay for a long time on the dried grass, counted the many islands in the Rhine, observed the Feldberg and the Main valley, the Donnersberg, and all the fertile country around us here, and enjoyed ourselves greatly.

Cécile's view of her own marital bliss is as richly steeped in a Romantic rhetorical tradition as her view of the Rhine is in a pictorial one. But the prospect was, we can scarcely doubt, a magnificent one.

★

One lesson Cécile had learned well by the end of these happy summer days was that her marriage to Felix had not compromised his

13 Cécile Mendelssohn Bartholdy: oil painting by Eduard Magnus

commitment to his work. The five months between their wedding and Mendelssohn's August departure for London comprise one of the most productive creative periods of his entire life. As striking as the sheer ambitiousness of his compositional programme through these months is its curiously systematic nature. If his wedding signified a new step into adulthood, Mendelssohn seized the occasion to take stock of his broad compositional domains, producing a piece of choral music (Psalm 42, op. 42), an orchestral piece (the D-minor Piano Concerto, op. 40), a piece of chamber music (the E-minor String Quartet, op. 44/2), a piano piece (the *Song Without Words*, Duetto, op. 38/6), and a number of the organ preludes that would appear among his *Three Preludes and Fugues*, op. 37.

In hand with a pervasive move towards a more lyrical language came, if intermittently, some of the most engaging melodies he would ever produce: Mozart would have been proud of certain melodic turns in the second movement of the concerto, Schubert, of the haunting opening subject of the quartet; the first movement of the psalm is built around a melodic kernel, at once graceful and stately, that must have been at the heart of the work's immediate popularity; the Duetto – one of the few *Songs Without Words* for which Mendelssohn authorised a title – is a model of the genre, built around exchanges between soprano and tenor, each with its own fetching, clean-lined melody. Given the pace of his work, however, it is perhaps not surprising that little of this – with the possible exception of the Duetto – feels like the finest of which he was capable.

Though the D-minor Concerto would become Mendelssohn's standard show-piece in the late thirties, Schumann recognised here the work of the craftsman:

> This concerto belongs to his most casual products. If I am not mistaken, he must have written it in a few days, perhaps in a few hours . . . So let us enjoy this bright, unpretentious gift; it is like one of those works we know from the old masters done when they are resting from their more important labours.

The piece presents itself as a sequel to the G-minor Concerto, reacquainting us at once with the familiar characters. As in the earlier work, the piano enters almost immediately, in a reflective mood, oblivious to the orderly thematic exposition the orchestra suggests, and finally insists upon. The piano's second subject is dulcet enough, but cut from a cloth Mendelssohn had used a dozen times before; it feels this time as though it is being sold by the yard. The same could justifiably be said of the brilliant, Weberesque finale.

Schumann's backhanded compliment concerning the pace at which Mendelssohn could have composed a piece of this kind points to what would, in fact, become a point of pride for Felix. The following spring, he took obvious delight in describing the forty-eight-hour gestation of his next work for piano and orchestra, the rightly forgotten *Serenade and Allegro giojoso*, op. 48. More impressive, given the calibre of the product, was the composition of the *Ruy Blas* overture in the first week of March 1839. When the Theatrical Pension Fund first contacted Mendelssohn with the proposal to write an overture for an upcoming performance of Hugo's play, he read the work and found it so despicable that he declined the invitation (though he did agree to provide a Romance). The Pension Fund's representatives responded that they 'were perfectly aware that time was indispensable for such a work', and that they would give him longer notice in the future. With the performance now some six days away, Mendelssohn took this as a challenge. He presented the copyist with the completed score three days later. Though hardly a peer of its three celebrated predecessors, the overture is impressively fresh in melody, particularly in a delightful subject introduced – in a classic Mozartian move – at the very end of the exposition, after the principal material of the movement had been laid out.

The E-minor Quartet of the honeymoon days was the first of a series of chamber works that represent, in the balance, a more substantial component of Mendelssohn's work than the orchestral pieces. Two more string quartets, in D and E♭, were complete by the summer of 1838, all three of them published as op. 44. Polished and often beautiful as these are, and weightier than the Cello Sonata (for Paul) that soon followed, most impressive is the D-minor Piano Trio, op. 49, completed in the summer of 1839, which approaches the level of the Octet.

Despite the lyrical beauty of much of this music, Mendelssohn's increasing fascination with song in his instrumental output (of which the *Songs Without Words* are only a most obvious manifestation) posed problems from a compositional standpoint. Lyrical melody, though appealing enough in itself, tends towards periodic self-sufficiency, towards a sense of immediate closure. Extended sonata-form movements in Beethoven's wake depended, by contrast, on teleological development and growth from thematic premises pregnant with possibility, but incomplete in themselves. Greg Vitercik laments of the E-minor Quartet's first movement, and similar later works: 'Form and content, rather than generating one another as they do in the early works, seem stiffly irrelevant to each other in this movement'.[14]

Mendelssohn frequently sought to answer this difficulty with a strategy that encapsulates, in compositional terms, the concern that had moved to the centre of his entire professional life: charting a course between an elevated, formally sophisticated musical language on the one hand and popular comprehensibility and appeal on the other. The first movement of his 1826 String Quintet, op. 18, maps out the essentials of the strategy in its remarkable development section. Though Mendelssohn professed nothing but scorn for brilliant variations as a popular genre, variation technique is precisely what he calls on to solve the problem of 'developing' the self-contained, lyrical opening subject of this movement. In the course of the development section, the principal melody appears first with a pervasive accompaniment of crotchets, then against staccato quavers, then against quaver triplets, finally against a *con fuoco* wash of semiquaver runs.

Though rarely so obvious or systematic, the idea of forward motion through a variation-like succession of accompaniments is an enabling force at the heart of the lyrical chamber works of the thirties. The first movement of the E-minor Quartet amounted to a study in the technique. The piece lays its opening subject first over a steady, syncopated chordal accompaniment that establishes itself, as the piano accompaniment of a vocal Lied might, a bar before the melody enters (this particular syncopated idea doubtless owes a debt to Mozart's D-minor Piano Concerto, which Mendelssohn admired and performed). In the closing bars of the exposition, the theme returns accompanied by new quaver arpeggios. In the course of the development section, a fragmentary version of the subject appears over a semiquaver accompaniment. The process culminates in the flashy, two-octave-spanning quaver arpeggios (each arpeggio shared by two instruments playing the roles, as it were, of the pianist's left and right hands in turn) that arrive with the theme at the outset of the recapitulation. Wilder by far is the climbing semiquaver arabesque woven by the first violin around the first subject's recapitulation in the first movement of the E♭-major Quartet, op. 44/3. The D-minor Trio's first movement makes use of the same device.

Psalm 42, completed (in a first draft) on the honeymoon, set the tone for a series of similar works: a setting of Psalm 95 was completed in 1838; Psalm 114 premièred on New Year's Day 1840. Where Mendelssohn's achievements at fugal polyphony were pushed almost polemically to the fore in the earlier Psalm 115 (completed in Italy), contrapuntal finish is pressed, in the post-St Paul works, into the service of a warm, even sentimental, lushness. There is little remaining trace of the archaising tendencies common to much of his earlier vocal polyphony.

Ever conscious of the need for effect – these were concert works, after all, intended to sit cheek-by-jowl with symphonies and overtures – Mendelssohn insisted on the big finish, whether the Psalm at hand called for one or not. In keeping with the *Gloria Patri* of the Catholic Psalmodic tradition, Mendelssohn added to Psalm 42 a magisterial 'Praised be the Lord' conclusion; Psalm 114 (which employs eight-part chorus throughout, without the solo parts of the other two) ends just as mightily, with an added 'Hallelujah! Sing to the Lord

Forevermore!' This impulse reached its height in one of the most substantial works of these years, the *Lobgesang*, op. 52 ('Hymn of Praise'), composed for the 25 June 1840, Leipzig celebration of the four hundredth anniversary of the invention of the printing press.

This 'symphony-cantata' (a designation suggested by Klingemann) consisted of three symphonic movements followed by nine numbers for chorus and soloists clustered around the general theme of high thanksgiving. Despite the effectiveness and power of the opening and closing choral numbers, and a duet for two sopranos with chorus ('I Waited for the Lord') that ranks among Mendelssohn's best choral music, the *Lobgesang*'s length feels fatally unmotivated in the absence of any narrative propulsion. Schumann's assurances, and similar ones by countless contemporaries, that it is 'one of his freshest and most charming creations' have not saved the work from oblivion. Housed in a conventional symphony, the three opening instrumental movements would doubtless have navigated a happier course through posterity; the first is well crafted and – notwithstanding a pompous opening motto whose innate interest Mendelssohn rather over-estimates – light on its feet. The $^6_8$ Allegretto that follows is among his most haunting scherzos, into which a chorale subject insinuates itself to striking effect (the chorale melody is original to this work, though its descending final phrase is a version of the stock conclusion shared by *Ein' feste Burg* and *Vom Himmel hoch*).

Where *Wachet auf* had served as the thematic chorale in *St Paul*, that distinction goes, in the *Lobgesang*, to *Nun danket*. This chorale appeared not only as the eighth number of the *Lobgesang*, but as one of the four items in the *Festgesang* for men's chorus and brass band which Mendelssohn also composed for the 1840 celebration. Ironically, this *Festgesang* – an odd, pseudo-religious hymn of praise to Johannes Gutenberg the relevance of which had dwindled to nothing the day after the festivities – would outlive the *Lobgesang*. It included the melody to which William Cummings would later attach the words, 'Hark, the Herald Angels Sing'.

★

Married life suited Felix well. Cécile and Felix took up residence on the second floor of a large building near the town gates called Lurgensteins Garten. Hiller recalled of his visit in the winter of 1839–40:

> Mendelssohn's house was pleasantly situated, with a nice open look-out from the front upon the Leipzig boulevard, and the St Thomas's school and church, once the sphere of the great Bach's labours. The arrangement of the rooms was as follows: first, a sort of hall, with the dining table and a few chairs; to the right of this a large sitting-room and some bed-rooms; to the left my friend's study with his piano. Opening out of this was a fine large drawing-room.

It was to Hiller that Mendelssohn offered what appear to have been heartfelt musings on the joy he took in his new domestic surroundings in the early months of his new life:

> I am living as a married man in a pretty, new, comfortable house, with a fine view over gardens and fields, and the towers of the city, and feel so comfortable and happy, so glad and so peaceful, as I have never done since I quitted the parental roof . . .

On 7 February 1838 – four days after Felix's twenty-ninth birthday – Cécile gave birth to her first child. With Felix's brother, Paul, and his wife, Albertine, standing as godparents, the child was baptised Carl Wolfgang Paul. Amid the joy of the event, there was not a little trepidation, as Cécile took to her bed with a fever that lasted four days; agonising ones for Felix. Cécile's fever was not sufficiently harrowing to prevent her setting down the same path four more times; a daughter, Marie Pauline Hélène, arrived in the autumn of 1839; Paul Felix Abraham in January 1841; Felix followed in 1843; Lili in 1845. Their third son, Felix, was granted a life of only eight years; the rest survived to adulthood.

Felix was, to all appearances, an involved and happy father, who seems to have had a way with children. During his last extended stay in Berlin, in 1832–3, he had grown very close to Fanny's son, Sebastian. 'He remembers you quite well and mentions you every day',[15] Fanny wrote some months after his departure. 'He often says without any special reason, "When is my dear Uncle Felix coming back?" We catch a telling glimpse of the avuncular Felix on the beach with Schadow's son during the summer of 1836, just before his engagement to Cécile: 'I had to coax him into the water, because he always screamed so with his father and was so frightened'. About the five-month-old Carl, he wrote with obvious, and characteristic, pride that the boy 'takes after his mother both in looks and disposition, which is an inexpressible delight to me, because it is the best thing he can do'.

Cécile never grew especially close to Felix's family in Berlin. Lea was stand-offish when it came to the elder, snobbish (as she saw them) Souchays, and a bit mystified as to the younger Souchay's appeal for her son; Fanny saw in Cécile – whom she did not meet until almost a year after the wedding – little of the intellectual or musical acumen on which her own intense relationship with Felix was founded. She was more than civil to the well-coiffed young stranger, twelve years her junior, her brother had brought into the family, but the relationship never became a close one. Rebecka's joy in her Felix's married life appears to have been, among the Berlin Mendelssohns, the most unalloyed. 'I will not say there are no husbands who love their wives as much as Felix loves you', she wrote to Cécile after Felix's brief Berlin visit in the summer of 1840, 'but I have never seen one so much in love before. However, I can understand it, for . . . I am a little in love with you myself.'

The bliss of the Mendelssohns' domestic life in Leipzig was registered by contemporaries – and most biographers – as a utopian model of Biedermeier *Gemüthlichkeit*. 'Everyone knows how happy Mendelssohn was at home', Hiller reflected. 'His beautiful, gentle, sensible wife spread a charm over the whole household, and reminded one of a Rafael Madonna'. Biographer Eric Werner's chapter title, 'The Tranquil Years', encapsulates his take on the first years of their marriage. But Mendelssohn's interior life appears, in fact, to have been far from tranquil. His peculiar breed of suffering was not, it is true, the suffering around which Romantic myths crystallised:

Mozart's (generally overstated) poverty, Beethoven's deafness, Chopin's consumption, or Schumann's mental illness. But Mendelssohn quickly came to realise that the very wealth of opportunities placed before him as a father, a husband, a conductor, a composer and an administrator brought with them responsibilities that a single lifetime was not sufficient to meet.

In a letter to his brother penned shortly after returning to Leipzig with his new bride, fresh from the dazzling successes of the Birmingham Festival, Mendelssohn sounds a tone that would resonate through dozens of letters in the years that followed. Already it becomes clear that he is having trouble explaining, even to himself, the purpose of a life so torn among manifold obligations:

> So few traces remain of performances and musical festivals, and all that is personal; the people indeed shout and applaud, but that quickly passes away, without leaving a vestige behind, and yet it absorbs as much of one's life and strength as better things, or perhaps even more; and the evil of this is, that it is impracticable to come half out, when you are once in; you must either go on the whole way, or not at all. I dare not even attempt to withdraw, or the cause which I have undertaken will suffer . . . I long for a less busy life, in order to be able to devote myself to my peculiar province, composition of music, and to leave the execution of it to others. It seems, however, that this is not to be; and I should be ungrateful were I dissatisfied with my life as it is.

A few weeks before, Fanny had already begun commiserating with her new sister-in-law on the subject (perhaps sparking Felix's own confessional lines): 'If only I could once hear about Felix that he gets away from this eternal unrest; this eternal mad rush in which he lives year in and year out . . .'

Though Felix seeks to fix the motivation behind his hectic public life squarely in his artistic 'cause', much of the blame should probably be placed on the continued effort – conscious or otherwise – to please his late father. The turning point in their relationship, as we saw, was the 1833 Düsseldorf Festival. Never had Abraham been so proud of his son as on seeing him, as a conductor, in a position of palpable power and respect. Mendelssohn's compositions had never had this effect. Abraham's response to the brilliant early trios and the C-minor Symphony – perhaps the greatest achievements of any musical child prodigy in history – had been cautious ambivalence: it took the mighty Cherubini to convince him that a career in music might be worth considering. Throughout his adult life, despite repeated protestations that 'to have no fixed situation would be best, after all', we find Mendelssohn re-enacting, year after year, the moment at which his father's acceptance of his calling became absolute.

The paradox was that Abraham, through his own early retirement from public life, had afforded a model utterly incommensurate with the life of the busy conductor. Thus Felix often articulates a strong desire to replicate the conditions of his own childhood, venting sentiments evocative of his parents' self-imposed seclusion from Berlin's life:

> I daily rejoice afresh in the peaceful monotony of my life. At the beginning of the winter, however, I had some difficulty in avoiding the social gatherings which bloom and thrive here, and which would cause both a sad loss of time and of pleasure if you were to accept them, but now I have pretty well succeeded in getting rid of them.

The strains of this fragmented existence had begun to take a physical and psychological toll. In the last week of December he began complaining of 'occasional pains in the head and neck', and of deafness in one ear (a symptom he had experienced before, and which alarmed him extremely). He was seriously ill for several weeks again in the spring of 1840, and was weak enough that his doctors even discouraged him from undertaking the Birmingham Festival that September; he went anyway. Throughout, his wife and friends witnessed the intermittent symptoms of depression which had already been evident – 'black days', as he called them – in Berlin. 'In the midst of the manifold occupations and social meetings in which he gladly took part', Hiller recalled of the winter of 1839–40, 'there would come days of exhaustion, even of depression'. Cécile remarked to Hiller, as if by way of reassurance, that he would often spend two days at a stretch doing nothing but sleeping on the sofa.

Cécile had watched her own mother struggle, with her three young children, through the untimely loss of her husband. Felix was already beginning to show signs of the infirmity, coupled with a relentless refusal to be governed by it, that would finally leave Cécile, in her thirty-first year, in much the same position.

7 More frustrations in Berlin

Suppose that when you wanted something terribly
A man should neither grant it you nor give
Sympathy even; but later when you were glutted
With all your heart's desire, should give it then,
When charity was no charity at all?
Would you not think the kindness somewhat hollow?
                    Sophocles, *Oedipus at Colonus*[1]

In June of 1840, Friedrich Wilhelm IV was crowned King of Prussia. 'After a long series of dark, disappointing years', Ernst Dronke wrote of the occasion at mid-decade, 'a breathtaking movement arose from the heart of Prussia'.[2] The reactionary policies that clouded the oppressive final years of the reign of Friedrich Wilhelm III had held at bay the liberal impulse that had taken root decades before elsewhere in Europe. There was widespread hope that the new king would prove an intelligent, forward-looking leader through whom the whole character of the Prussian government might be transformed, indeed, that northern Germany might at last be guided into the era of constitutional, participatory politics.

That Friedrich Wilhelm sought to be a benign, genuinely enlightened ruler seemed clear enough from the start. Most encouragingly, he at once set forth plans for making Berlin a cultural and intellectual capital of unprecedented vigour, with his own court at the epicentre.

Those summoned to Berlin to this end included the writer and translator Ludwig Tieck, the Grimm brothers, and the painter Peter Cornelius. But the king did not, as it turns out, have much interest in the progressive political ideals many had hoped he would address. Though he made gestures towards reviving the spirit of reform that had been pushed underground by 1819 – perhaps most importantly through an initial scaling back of governmental censorship – the notion of a constitution interested him not in the least. Friedrich Wilhelm's view proved more or less feudal in outlook, rooted in a disconcertingly medieval conception of royal power in which the idea of contractual interaction with his subjects was meaningless.

At the same time, Friedrich Wilhelm displayed a much greater capacity for ambition than for genuine vision. Though Berlin was to be a cultural Mecca, he seemed to have little idea what he actually expected the celebrities he gathered there to produce. Indeed, his rule soon distinguished itself by vacillation and uncertainty, traits Heine captured mercilessly in his satiric poem, 'The New Alexander': 'And if I moved forward yesterday, Today I move backwards'. David Friedrich Strauss's parodistic 'Ein Romantiker auf dem Throne der Caesaren' ('A Romantic on Caesar's Throne') – an essay ostensibly aimed at Julian the Apostate – formalised the increasing popular perception of the king as a political incompetent, lost in Romantic musings. At the same time, liberal factions wasted no time in making clear what they had expected of the king. In February of 1841, Johann Jacoby published his 'Vier Fragen', demanding for citizens 'lawful participation in the affairs of the state' through the establishment of a parliament, the dismantling of monarchic power, and a loosening of restrictions on freedom of activity and thought. Discouragingly, the work was banned, and Jacoby was ultimately arrested and sentenced to two and a half years in prison (amid popular outcry, an appeals court acquitted him). Bettina von Arnim proved another articulate advocate of reform, her call for a republican people's monarchy, *Dies Jahr gehört dem Konig* (*This Year Belongs to the King*), appearing in 1843.

Among the king's closest advisors in the optimistic first months of his reign were Christian Karl Josias von Bunsen, the diplomat and scholar who had served the Prussian embassy in Rome and London, and Wilhelm von Humboldt, who, as we have seen, masterminded the educational reforms of the war years. Given the close personal contact both of these men had enjoyed with Felix Mendelssohn in former times – Bunsen during Felix's Roman sojourn and, later, in England; Humboldt at 3 Leipzigerstrasse – the gist of their plans for musical reform is hardly surprising. In October of 1840, Bunsen drafted a proposal for 'reintroducing the most beautiful and noble music into life' through the establishment of an educational institution, the reform of liturgical music, and oratorio performances. His conclusion is unambiguous and unsurprising: 'I rather think it would be too much for anyone but Felix Mendelssohn'.3

The Under-Secretary for the Royal Household, Ludwig von Massow, made his first overtures to Mendelssohn the following month, communicating initially through Mendelssohn's brother, Paul. The plans – at once vague and massively ambitious – that had reached Mendelssohn by mid-December 1840 called for the division of the Academy of Arts into four classes: painting, sculpture, architecture and music. Mendelssohn was to be appointed director of the musical class, with a salary of 3,000 Thaler. At the centre of his position was to be a conservatory which would draw, both in the classroom and in performances, on the energies of members of the city's existing musical institutions. Precisely how this was to take place, and how many concerts were to be given, was not specified. Nor had the plan been drafted with the participation of anyone currently conducting, teaching or playing music in Berlin, those ranks at whose head the king sought, at a stroke, to place the thirty-one-year-old conductor who had never succeeded in establishing himself in the city. And as vague as the plan was, just as vague was the schedule for its execution. The first matter of business, and the only one firmly fixed in these first communications, was to get Mendelssohn to come to Berlin and begin drawing his salary.

In light of the manifold benefits of his position in Leipzig, we may well understand why Mendelssohn hesitates to express anything more than cautious interest. On 7 December 1840, he begs, as he would time and again in the months ahead, for clarification and firmer commitment: 'Without a definite sphere of work . . . I should hesitate much to accept the proposal'. Particularly worrisome was the vagueness surrounding the performance life of the institution he would direct; '[L]ittle good', he wrote to Paul on 20 December, 'could accrue from merely occasional performances, even by royal command'. In the tortuous series of exchanges that follows, genuine enthusiasm for the plans never emerges as a serious possibility for Mendelssohn. The only real issue is whether he can turn down the opportunity to return to the family fold, to bring his own growing family into the circle that surrounded and supported his mother in her advanced years.

In May 1841, Massow arrived at last at a compromise to which Mendelssohn seemed poised to agree. The composer, Massow stipulated, would reside in Berlin for a year at the king's disposal while plans for the school developed. Mendelssohn was to be named Kapellmeister, a position Fanny described – not without a touch of irony – as 'the highest human office next to Privy Councillor and Pope'.[4] Uncharacteristically, Mendelssohn himself had insisted on the title, thinking it essential to establishing his credibility among the resident musicians. At the same time, as Massow described the proposal in a 20 May communication to the king, Mendelssohn 'is neither to hold any office, nor to undertake any definite duties, unless in the course of this period Herr Eichhorn [the Minister under whom Massow worked] should furnish him with the long-wished-for details, and he should declare himself satisfied with them'. During this year he would draw a salary of 3,000 Thaler.

Mendelssohn expressed tentative satisfaction with all of this, and began making preparations to move his family to Berlin. Appalled as he was to receive a July communication from Eichhorn retracting much of what had been agreed upon – particularly the assurance of the

'Kapellmeister' title – Mendelssohn went ahead with the move. By the 1st of August, he and his family had arrived once more in the city of his childhood. Even at this point, he was far from certain that anything productive would come of the king's schemes, writing to his concert-master – and deputy Gewandhaus director – David, 'The affair is on the most extensive scale, if it be actually on any scale at all, and not merely in the air'. To Klingemann he described the move as 'one of the sourest apples a man can eat, and yet eaten it must be'. A month into his stay, Mendelssohn – still without salary or title – remained cheer-less about the situation:

> it is nicest when we are alone with our family in the evenings, and those are really the only moments in which I am entirely happy about being in Berlin . . . The less I see of Berlin and Berliners, the happier I am. The few musicians with whom I am on close terms are either long gone or dead.[5]

Though he willingly played into his mother's cautious optimism concerning the move, Mendelssohn's communications with his most intimate friends make no secret of the fact that he had one foot out the door from the moment of his arrival. Nevertheless, a succession of plans, promises and negotiations would keep Mendelssohn tied to Berlin for the next three years. Though Concertmaster David proved a more than competent deputy in the direction of the Gewandhaus orchestra during Mendelssohn's first winter in Berlin, Ferdinand Hiller serving the same duty with more mixed results during the second, Mendelssohn at no point considered cutting ties with Leipzig. He was to become well acquainted with the rail line between the two cities, which opened for operation a month after his arrival in Berlin.

By the end of September 1841, agreements concerning salary and title were at last formalised. As Kapellmeister, Mendelssohn was authorised to present a number of concerts in the course of the winter and spring. By Leipzig's standards, these did not add up to much, though they were generally well received by the public. St Paul was given twice, once in the royal theatre and once at the Singakademie. An April concert featured the Lobgesang and some of his own piano works.

Much more intriguing was the unique artistic challenge he found himself facing almost at once upon his arrival. The king had recently stumbled on to J. J. Donner's translation of Sophocles' Antigone. In conversation with the royal 'Vorleser' ('lecture-reader'), Ludwig Tieck, Friedrich Wilhelm arrived at the idea of seeing the play revived on the stage. Tieck was to direct the production, Mendelssohn to create suitable music for the chorus. When it became clear to Mendelssohn that the plans were in danger of slipping away unrealised, it fell to the composer himself to take the initiative: 'the noble old style of the piece fascinated me so much', Mendelssohn wrote to David, 'I got hold of old Tieck, and said "Now or never!" and he was amiable, and said "Now!"'

Mendelssohn composed the work in characteristic haste, completing the score on 10 October. The première took place at the king's Neuer Palais in Potsdam eighteen days later before an audience of court officials and university professors. The production was hailed as a revelation, its first audience persuaded that a new era in the revivification of Attic drama was at hand. The general public saw the work for the first time on 13 April 1842 at the Berlin Schauspielhaus. It soon found its way to stages across Europe (in 1845, Antigone played for forty-five nights in London).

Mendelssohn's part in the project was, by all accounts, critical to its popular success. Though keenly responsive to issues of scansion and poetic structure, Mendelssohn had no interest whatever in creating music akin to what Sophocles' first audience might actually have heard. He set out, instead, to create a score whose very comprehensibility and immediacy of appeal might serve as a dramatic anchor for an audience which might otherwise have felt altogether alienated from the ancient spectacle. As Fanny wrote, 'if Felix had tried to make his music antique also, the spectacle and the spectators would never have met'. Like Fanny, Felix's friend and former tutor, Gustav Droysen, immediately perceived the wisdom of Mendelssohn's decision to adorn the tragedy with thoroughly modern music:

> Insofar as what is old belongs only to ancient times, one *cannot* revive it. But it has something that is great and important at all times, something immortal, and that should come to us in fresh and lively fashion today.[6]

Rooted as this composition was in the specific needs of its original audience, its slide into obscurity is almost certainly permanent. Indeed, in setting the incidental music to *Antigone* alongside those works of Mendelssohn whose relevance today is well established, it is difficult to weigh the achievements of this work except in negative terms. Impressive it is, but principally as a demonstration of what Mendelssohn could do, as it were, with one hand tied behind his back. In keeping with the aim of poetic clarity, he abandoned altogether the imitative counterpoint that animated the great bulk of his choral music, opting for the restraints of a homophonic, declamatory style. At the same time, though music for male chorus and orchestra might have been rich with cultural resonance at the time (witness Mendelssohn's own 'Gutenberg' *Festgesang* of the previous year and the proliferation of convivial societies dedicated to the performance of songs for male chorus) the music for Sophocles' on-stage Chorus feels texturally colourless today. Similarly unrecoverable is the dramatic effectiveness of the extended melodrama – that is, a passage of orchestral accompaniment to words spoken, not sung, on stage – at the play's climax. This passage proved sufficiently moving to Mendelssohn's contemporaries to merit concert performances of the melodrama as an abstracted, self-contained number, a practice unthinkable today. In general, even at its most dramatic moments, the music for *Antigone* tends to make us aware of the tightly circumscribed rhetorical limits within which Mendelssohn was composing. And rarely in Mendelssohn's music are we made more conscious of his own favourite harmonic and melodic turns, which stick out as clichés in this uncluttered musical landscape.

Antigone was the first of four stage productions for which Mendelssohn would provide music. In 1843 followed *A Midsummer Night's Dream*, to which we shall return. In 1845, after Mendelssohn had abandoned Berlin as a residence once and for all, he continued to complete royal commissions for incidental music, providing scores for Sophocles' *Oedipus at Colonus* and for Racine's *Athalie*. The king's proposal for a third Greek drama, Aeschylus' *Oresteia*, Mendelssohn tactfully but forcefully declined. Insisting that he was not equal to the dramatic difficulties the play posed, the composer bowed out with a diplomatic reference to 'the refined artistic feeling of the king – to whom it is impossible to offer indiscriminately failures and successes...'

One of the greatest achievements of Mendelssohn's first months in Berlin was the completion, on 20 January, of the 'Scottish' Symphony (a designation he used in correspondence, not as a published title), premièred at the Gewandhaus on 3 March. Initial ideas for the symphony dated from his 1829 visit to Scotland, its first movement invoking the same misty landscape as the *Hebrides* overture which was begun at about the same time. Indeed, the opening gambits of the overture and the symphony's first-movement Allegro are united both in their dark-hued scoring and their broad harmonic outlines. The symphony's second movement revisits the simple, lyrical grace of the 'Reformation' and 'Italian' Symphonies' slow movements. In this case, the song-like idea brackets an imposing pronouncement from a brass choir whose tone of vaguely ritualistic solemnity must have been more effective still on pre-Wagnerian ears. From an altogether different realm comes the fleet-footed scherzo whose opening subject, taken first by clarinet, invokes the pentatonic scale of much Scottish folk melody.

We have meditated already on the distinctly public nature of the music that closes the *Calm Sea, Prosperous Voyage* overture, a trumpet fanfare evidently welcoming the ship, at journey's end, to a port crowded with celebrants. The tendency to locate musical culmination in a scene of public spectacle comes to fruition in the coda of the 'Scottish' Symphony's finale. After the fiery Allegro guerriero that forms the main body of the movement, the coda greets us with a stately, lyrical new subject marked Finale maestoso. Not only do the disposition and range of the voices call to mind an accompanied men's chorus, but the new melody itself bears a striking resemblance to the second number of Mendelssohn's 'Gutenberg' *Festgesang*, the tune that has since become familiar as 'Hark, the Herald Angels Sing'. If the dark opening of the symphony feels steeped, like the *Hebrides* overture, in the aura of Ossianic legend, this closing invocation of *Festgesang* – the musical genre through which the German public habitually celebrated great deeds of the past – affirms this historical gaze.

*

As the concert activities of spring 1842 drew to a close, Mendelssohn was less convinced than ever that his move to Berlin would prove a permanent one. Plans for the reorganisation of the Academy had made no discernible progress towards realisation, and he felt as full an investment as ever in the continuing progress of the orchestra in Leipzig. At the same time, the daily mingling of Felix and his family with his siblings and theirs had hardly proven an unambiguously happy arrangement. Cécile and Felix's sisters had developed a mutual fondness in their correspondence before the Felicians' (as Fanny called them) move to Berlin, but their temperaments were far from complementary in person, and fissures in the family were fast becoming apparent. Felix's frequent absences for the sake of his Leipzig duties only exacerbated these difficulties.

May 1842 brought with it a much-needed break from this routine, though not an immediate opportunity for relaxation. Mendelssohn and Julius Rietz shared the direction of the Lower Rhein Music Festival in Düsseldorf, a three-day event whose programme included *Israel in Egypt*, Beethoven's 'Emperor' Concerto, and Mendelssohn's

Lobgesang. After a brief sojourn in Frankfurt, Felix and Cécile journeyed to London for a stay of several weeks. Cécile soon endeared herself to Felix's closest friends in England – Karl Klingemann, Ignaz and Charlotte Moscheles, and the Horsley family – and Felix once again received a hero's welcome from the city's musical public. The 'Scottish' Symphony was played to terrific acclaim at a Philharmonic Society concert of 13 June. After Mendelssohn's 20 June performance of his D-minor Concerto, the audience – according to the composer's own testimony – 'clapped their hands and stamped their feet for at least ten minutes'; at the same concert, the *Hebrides* overture had to be repeated. In a letter of 21 June, Mendelssohn recalls to his mother an emblematic episode from these heady days:

> Lately I went to a concert in Exeter Hall where I had nothing whatever to do, and was sauntering in quite coolly with Klingemann – it was already the middle of the first part and there was an audience of about three thousand present – and no sooner had I come in the door, than such a clamour, and clapping and shouting, and standing-up ensued that at first I had no idea that it concerned me; but I discovered it did when on reaching my place, I found Sir Robert Peel and Lord Wharncliffe close to me, and they continued to applaud with the rest till I made my bow and thanked them . . . When I left the concert they gave me another hurrah.

Less spectacular, but much more personally meaningful, than such public outbursts were Mendelssohn's two interviews, of 20 June and 9 July, with Queen Victoria and Albert. 'He is very pleasing & modest', wrote Victoria in her diary after their first meeting, '& is greatly protected by the King of Prussia'[7] (Mendelssohn had come equipped with a letter of introduction in Friedrich Wilhelm IV's own hand). The composer's report on the second meeting bears citation at length:

> I found him [Prince Albert] alone; and as we were talking away, the queen came in, also quite alone, in a house dress. She said she was obliged to leave for Claremont in an hour; 'But goodness! how it

looks in here', she added, when she saw that the wind had littered the
whole room, and even the pedals of the organ (which, by the way,
made a very pretty feature in the room), with leaves of music from a
large portfolio that lay open. As she spoke, she knelt down and began
picking up the music; Prince Albert helped, and I too was not idle . . . I
began [at the organ] my chorus from St Paul: 'How lovely are the
Messengers!' Before I got to the end of the first verse, they both began
to sing the chorus very well, and all the time Prince Albert managed
the stops for me so expertly – first a flute, then full at the *forte*, the
whole register at the D-major part, then he made such an excellent
diminuendo with the stops, and so on to the end of the piece, and all
by ear – that I was heartily pleased.

In the course of Mendelssohn's visit, Albert, too, offered a performance at the organ, performing a chorale 'so charmingly and clearly
and correctly', Mendelssohn wrote, 'that many an organist could have
learned something'. When Mendelssohn's first volume of songs
(published around 1827) was discovered in the queen's music collection, the composer requested a performance of one of these from the
queen herself. Victoria settled on 'Schöner und schöner', which she
rendered, in Mendelssohn's estimation, more than competently: 'it
was really very charming, and the last long G I have never heard better
or purer or more natural from any amateur'. Only at the end of her performance did he reveal that the song, like two others in the collection
of twelve, was actually composed by Fanny. The queen was soon
cajoled into performing one of Mendelssohn's own. The composer
received, by way of souvenirs of the visit, a ring engraved 'V. R., 1842',
and a favourable reply to his request to dedicate the 'Scottish'
Symphony to Victoria.

Soon after their mid-July return to Frankfurt – and to their children,
who had been in the care of Cécile's mother over the previous weeks –
Felix and Cécile were off again for a holiday in Switzerland, during
which Felix had succeeded in breaking altogether free of professional
commitments. In an 18 August letter to his mother from Interlaken,
Mendelssohn gives touching testimony to the mellowing process he

14 Prince Albert playing the organ before Queen Victoria and Mendelssohn at Buckingham Palace

perceives in his own personality, a longing for a simpler, slower existence that he only desires now that it has become a virtual impossibility: 'I have a completely different impression than last time, as I see
everything with Cécile; before I wanted to go running off to every
jagged mountain and green pasture I saw, but this time I want to stay
put and remain everywhere for months'.[8] This strain would become
more and more distinct in his correspondence through to the end of
his life.

By the end of September, the Mendelssohns were back in Leipzig,
with Felix gearing up for the beginning of the concert season. On 2
October, he conducted the first concert in the Gewandhaus, and
departed soon afterwards for Berlin. If his arrival in the Prussian
capital fourteen months earlier had been fraught with uncertainty, he
now came with a perfectly clear sense of his duty. The trial year
Mendelssohn deemed a failed experiment, and he prepared to
announce his resignation to the king and to quit Berlin once and for
all. In a note of 23 October to Under-Secretary Massow, in which he
requests a royal audience, Mendelssohn pronounces the matter
settled, remarking gravely, 'there is no opportunity on my side for a
practical, influential, musical efficiency in Berlin'. The meeting with
the king was set for 26 October.

According to Mendelssohn's nephew, Sebastian Hensel, it was
only on the evening of the 25th that Felix could bring himself to break
to his mother the news of his decision. Her response was complete
emotional collapse; 'He too was affected, even to tears', Hensel tells
us, 'by his mother's distress'. In the event, she might have been spared
much of her distress had the conversation been put off for twenty-four
hours further, for the meeting with the king did not unfold as
Mendelssohn had planned.

Despite Massow's grim assurances that Mendelssohn should
prepare himself for the full weight of royal wrath, the king appeared
not in the least perturbed by the composer's assessment of the situation. 'I never saw him so amiable and so really confidential',
Mendelssohn reported to Klingemann. Rather than releasing him

once and for all, however, Friedrich Wilhelm suggested a reconfiguration of Mendelssohn's duties along more realistic lines. With plans for the Academy in disarray, the king now proposed to place Mendelssohn in charge of a new ensemble which would provide music for the cathedral, a small, select choir to be accompanied by members of the royal orchestra. Attracted to such a possibility, but wary of an extended stay in Berlin that might again prove fruitless, Mendelssohn diplomatically agreed to take charge of this 'Music Institute of the Court and Cathedral Church' (as the ensemble was to be known) as soon as it actually came into existence. Until that time, he insisted that he be free to live and work where he chose. The organisation of the Music Institute was to be undertaken in his absence under the supervision of Massow and the Intendant-General of Court Music, Count Wilhelm von Redern. Mendelssohn insisted, too, on surrendering half of his salary until there was actually work for him to do. The new agreement was formalised in a Supreme Cabinet order of 22 November, naming Mendelssohn Generalmusikdirektor for church music. 'This is another new title and a new honour', a bemused Mendelssohn wrote to his mother, 'whereas I really do not know how to do enough to deserve the old ones'.

After his 26 October interview with Friedrich Wilhelm, Mendelssohn journeyed straightaway to Dresden for an audience with the King of Saxony. As ambiguous as the future of the Berlin projects seemed, Mendelssohn's conversation with Friedrich August II placed before him an immediate and welcome task in Leipzig. In February 1839, the wealthy lawyer Heinrich Blümner had died, leaving 20,000 Thaler for the establishment of an institution advancing the arts or sciences. This sum was to be disbursed at the king's discretion. In April of the following year, Mendelssohn had petitioned the king 'to dispose of the sum . . . in favour of the erection and maintenance of a fundamental music academy in Leipzig'. Mendelssohn took the opportunity of this October 1842 meeting to restate the request, which Friedrich August now granted, the formal announcement coming on 21 November 1842. As it happened, Mendelssohn would not have long to bask in the glow of this major victory for his 'cause', for it was soon eclipsed by an even greater personal tragedy.

On the evening of Sunday 11 December, in the course of a small dinner party, Felix's mother fell ill and was seen to her bed. After a brief struggle, she died the next morning at around 9:30. The obituary carried in the *Vossische Zeitung* bid farewell to one of Berlin's 'most eminent inhabitants. Lea Salomon, the widow of Town-councillor Mendelssohn Bartholdy, and mother of the king's Kapellmeister, Felix Mendelssohn-Bartholdy.'

Felix had come at once on receiving word of Lea's illness, but still hoped to find his mother alive when he boarded a train on Tuesday morning. Though the discovery of this loss was not as palpably shattering as the death of his father had been – Felix had matured immeasurably in the intervening years – he spoke for all of Lea's children in his sad assessment of this new chapter in their lives: 'the point of union is now gone, where even as children we could always meet, and though we were no longer so in years, we felt that we were still so in feeling . . . we are children no longer'. In the course of Lea's last evening, Sebastian Hensel tells us, she exacted from the Woringen sisters a promise to celebrate Christmas with her for the next ten years. Christmas 1842 was not celebrated at all in the Mendelssohn household.

Upon returning to Leipzig, Mendelssohn ventured out little in the weeks after his mother's death, receiving few guests besides Schumann and David. Conducting was an odious task, and at times a painful one; in one instance, he was so moved at a rehearsal of his Psalm 42 that he was forced to leave the room to cry. The chief source of solace through this period was complete immersion in the revision of his secular cantata, *Die erste Walpurgisnacht*, whose first draft had been completed in Rome a decade earlier. On 17 January, he wrote to Klingemann of the role these revisions played in the grieving process:

I feel more vividly than ever what a heavenly calling art is. For this too I have to thank my parents! At a time when everything else which ought to interest the mind appears repugnant, empty and vapid, the smallest real service to art takes hold of one's innermost being, leading one away from town and country, and the earth itself, and seems a blessing sent by God.

In its new form – 'altogether a different thing now, and a hundred times better',[9] as Mendelssohn described it to Hiller – Die erste Walpurgisnacht was performed at the Gewandhaus on 2 February, 1843.

This month brought another distraction, in the form of a visit from Hector Berlioz. As we have seen, Mendelssohn had never worked up much enthusiasm for Berlioz's music, in which he perceived an utter lack of the hard-won technical rigours he valued so highly. Nonetheless Mendelssohn had magnanimously agreed to turn the Gewandhaus over to Berlioz for two concerts. The preparations turned out to demand more of Mendelssohn's diplomatic gifts than of his musical ones. Fanny, who visited Leipzig for a week in February, recalled in her diary: 'Berlioz's . . . odd manners gave so much offence that Felix was continually being called upon to smooth somebody's ruffled feathers'. The affair concluded in a ceremonial exchange of batons (or rather, 'tomahawks', as Berlioz described them in a comical note addressed 'To Big Chief Mendelssohn').

A composer in whom Mendelssohn ultimately took a much keener personal and artistic interest was the young Dane, Niels Gade, whose First Symphony Mendelssohn conducted on 3 March 1842. Rarely had Mendelssohn sounded so enthusiastic about a new work – or its composer – as in his early communications with Gade on this occasion: 'Not in a long time has any piece made a more vivid, beautiful impression on me', he wrote to the composer the day after the first rehearsal of the work. This enthusiasm soon expressed itself in the form of an invitation to Leipzig. Within three years, Gade was sharing Mendelssohn's conducting responsibilities at the Gewandhaus, and had been placed on the faculty of the Leipzig Conservatory. His final service to Mendelssohn would be as pallbearer.

The bulk of Mendelssohn's energies through the early months of 1843 went, of course, into the organisation of the new Leipzig Conservatory, whose ceremonial opening came on 2 April. The conservatory was housed in a two-storey building which the town council had newly constructed in the courtyard of the Gewandhaus. By the summer, operations were in full swing, with thirty-three male and eleven female students and an impressive roster of instructors. Schumann taught piano and composition, David violin. Instruction in theory and counterpoint was entrusted to the theorist Moritz Hauptmann, also the Cantor of the Thomaskirche. Mendelssohn himself taught piano and ensemble, and would shortly take up composition as well.

Mendelssohn undertook his teaching obligations dutifully enough, but never seems to have developed much fondness for them: 'I shall have to go to the Gewandhaus three or four times a week', he wrote to Hiller in the midst of preparations for the opening, 'and talk about 6–4 chords in the small hall there. I am quite willing to do this for love of the cause, because I believe it to be a good cause'. Mendelssohn's composition students were compelled, as he had been, to learn their trade through exercises modelled closely after the style of the old masters. He sought to maintain – hardly through the gentlest means imaginable – the highest standards among his piano students, as well. William Rockstro, who attended Mendelssohn's classes between 1845 and 1846, recalls:

> He never gave a learner the chance of mistaking his meaning; and though the vehemence with which he sometimes expressed it made timid pupils desperately afraid of him, he was so perfectly just, so sternly impartial in awarding praise, on the one hand, and blame on the other, that consternation soon gave place to confidence, and confidence to boundless affection. Carelessness infuriated him. Irreverence for the composer he could never forgive.[10]

Another powerful expression of Mendelssohn's reverence for his predecessors came at around the time of the conservatory's opening with the unveiling of the monument to Johann Sebastian Bach, a project for which Mendelssohn had, as we have seen, raised a good deal of money. The unveiling itself was the occasion for a giant musical celebration that included performances of the *Ratswahl Cantata*, the D-minor Harpsichord Concerto, and the *Sanctus* from the B-minor Mass.

As full a head of steam as Leipzig's musical life had worked up in the course of this spring, events were unfolding in Berlin which would soon necessitate Mendelssohn's grudging return to make good his promises. The new cathedral choir officially came into existence on 1 May 1843 – and performed the following Sunday – though Mendelssohn was not expected to take charge of the organisation until the winter. Even with the choir in place, Mendelssohn's precise relationship to the royal orchestra remained a thorny matter, and negotiations on this point dragged on for much of the summer. Kapellmeisters Carl Henning and Wilhelm Taubert had begun their own series of subscription concerts not long before. Mendelssohn perceived (evidently more clearly than the king himself) the inappropriateness of a relative outsider like himself being placed over them at a stroke. By mid-July, it was agreed that Mendelssohn would, in the course of the winter season, conduct a series of orchestral concerts as well as two oratorio performances, and that thirty-six members of the orchestra would be placed at his disposal in the cathedral on high holy days. All of this was ratified in a cabinet order of 2 September.

Before Mendelssohn set about discharging these duties, however, the king offered him a much more welcome – and, as it turns out, more historically consequential – artistic challenge. If the completion of the 'Scottish' Symphony and the overhaul of *Die erste Walpurgisnacht* had brought Mendelssohn into engagement with the musical artefacts of his youth, a new royal proposal afforded the composer the opportunity to delve even further back, to one of his first masterpieces. As the next item in the series of stage productions with incidental music, the king proposed Shakespeare's *A Midsummer Night's Dream*. The score that Mendelssohn provided for the 14 October production at the Neue Palais constitutes one of his greatest achievements, altogether worthy of the seventeen-year-old overture that stands at its head. The Nocturne and the Scherzo rank among the finest gems of his instrumental output, shining no less brightly for their miniature scale and their persistent playfulness; the Wedding March is, of all of Mendelssohn's creations, the piece which truly needs no introduction. Never had Mendelssohn achieved more finely nuanced orchestration than in this incidental music, and rarely such melodic freshness.

Ludwig Tieck – who had collaborated with, then superseded, Friedrich Schlegel in generating the famous series of Shakespeare translations through which Mendelssohn himself first came to know this play and others – directed the production. Fanny, Paul, and their great aunt Sara Levy were all present at opening night, as were Hiller, Gade, David, and the teen-aged violinist Joachim, whose career Mendelssohn had lately been doing everything in his power to advance. Eleven full rehearsals had ensured a production of exceptional polish, though marred, in the event, by the king's decision to serve refreshments to members of the court during an intermission. Indeed, as onlookers readily perceived, Mendelssohn's mood was spoiled for the evening by the talk and the clatter of teaspoons that accompanied the introduction of the third act. The work made its impact nonetheless, and Fanny was altogether accurate in the prediction she intimated to Rebecka four days later: 'Is it not just the luck of this fortunate man that this first work of his youth which established his fame, should again be brought forward in a form which will certainly cause it to find its way through the whole of Germany?'

After some weeks of dashing back and forth between Leipzig and Berlin, Mendelssohn at last moved to the Prussian capital, with his family, on 24 November. His interest in such a move seemed to have dwindled to an all-time low in the months following his mother's death: 'What made me specially cling to Berlin . . . no longer exists now'.[11] Nonetheless, Fanny sensed that the move agreed with him, or at least she portrayed the situation thus to Rebecka: 'Felix is as amiable, in as good spirits, and as delightful as you know he can be in his best days'. She continued this strain two weeks later: 'He never gives way to temper now as he used to, and, if he remains like this, we cannot be thankful enough for having him here'. Mendelssohn's appearance of contentment in all likelihood stemmed, at least in part, from his certainty that the move would not be a permanent one. On 23 December, two days before the Christmas celebration that would constitute his first performance with the choir, Felix wrote to Rebecka: 'I must say between ourselves that so far I do not expect much from it, but do not tell anybody!'

The king's devout hope was that Mendelssohn's work in this chapel would spark – as if by royal decree – a kingdom-wide revitalisation of sacred music that had first been envisioned by Friedrich Wilhelm III. In 1817, the king had called for the unification of Prussia's two chief Protestant strands, the Lutheran and the Reformed (Calvinist) Churches. Together these were to become the Evangelical Church of the Union, an arrangement formalised in the 1829 *Agende für die evangelische Kirche in den Königlich-Preussischen Landen*. Karl Friedrich Zelter had been called upon to generate a musical supplement to the *Agende*, a project of compilation, arrangement and composition geared principally towards the chordal, devotional style favoured by the king. In 1843, three years into Friedrich Wilhelm IV's reign, the Cathedral Ministerium drafted a revised version of the liturgy set forth in the *Agende*. The new version was musically more ambitious than its predecessor, new musical numbers including an Introit psalm at the beginning and the singing of the Verse that precedes the Alleluia. Who better than Felix Mendelssohn to set the tone, and the standard, for musical composition within this new mould?

Mendelssohn would ultimately provide pieces for only four services – Christmas, New Year's Day, Passion Sunday and Good Friday – but this impressive assortment of chorale arrangements and psalm settings set the bar high. Though fully imbued with the dignity and textural clarity of the sixteenth-century masters, the services for

Christmas and New Year's Day make lavish use of orchestra and organ (an important exception being the Christmas verse, 'Frohlocket, ihr Völker', for double chorus *a cappella*). Amid the turbulence of manifold personality conflicts between Mendelssohn and the clerics with whom he worked – Friedrich Adolph Strauss in particular – Mendelssohn's use of the orchestra fast emerged as a particular bone of contention. The harp in the New Year's setting of Psalm 98 proved especially irksome, though such specific caveats almost certainly stood in for more general concerns about the sheer opulence of Mendelssohn's artistry in a liturgical environment. It is true that Mendelssohn settled on a much simpler musical language in his music for Passion Sunday and Good Friday (including settings of Psalms 43 and 22), abandoning orchestral accompaniment altogether and turning more often towards recitative and a simple declamatory style. But even in these pieces artistic concerns tend to outweigh liturgical ones, and we sense that Mendelssohn had not fully overcome a basic conceptual stumbling block he had articulated in an oft-quoted 1835 letter to Belzig Pastor Albert Bauer:

> Real church music, that is, for the evangelical Divine Service, which could have its place within the ecclesiastical ceremony, seems to me impossible, not merely because I am not at all able to see where music is to be introduced during the service, but because I am unable to conceive of this place ... As yet ... I have been unable to understand how for us music may be made to become an integrated part of the service and not merely a concert which, to a greater or lesser degree, stimulates piety.[12]

(Some bewilderment on this point is hardly surprising, of course, in an artist who did as much as any other to move the work of J. S. Bach from the church into the concert hall.) When Mendelssohn received the catalogue of introits for services between Good Friday and the Fifth Sunday after Pentecost, he took the occasion to initiate his withdrawal from the whole affair, suggesting to Redern that other composers should perhaps be sought to share in this work.

In the course of the winter, Mendelssohn also conducted seven of

15 A Philharmonic Society concert in the Hanover Square Rooms, London, from the *Illustrated London News*, 24 June 1843

the ten concerts offered by the royal orchestra, prevailingly conservative programmes that culminated, in March, in a revelatory performance of Beethoven's Ninth Symphony. '[N]ever did I understand and appreciate the gigantic work as I did this time', Fanny wrote to Rebecka of this final work. 'But you should have seen how Felix conducts it, and the way he has made the orchestra understand it'. Mendelssohn's own hopes for the future of orchestral music in Berlin were far from sanguine. 'There is much to be praised in these concerts but there are also a few things to be criticised', he wrote to David. '[M]oreover there is one small item which they lack and which is generally overlooked here, but which I prefer not to do without, namely an innate vigour and hearty enthusiasm . . . real joy is lacking. If our people dream of an Orchestre du Conservatoire, they will have to dream on for all eternity.'

These months represent, too, the high-water mark for Fanny's Sunday gatherings. Hummel, Joachim, David, Fanny, Felix, and many other celebrities made appearances in the course of the winter, attracting an audience as distinguished as ever. One noteworthy Sunday in mid-March saw 'twenty-two carriages in the court, and Liszt and eight princesses in the room'. This must rank among the happiest periods of Fanny's life, though the last that she and her famous brother would spend in such close proximity.

★

Mendelssohn left Berlin at the beginning of April. After stays in Leipzig and Frankfurt, he turned once more towards England, where he had been entrusted with the direction of six Philharmonic concerts. The Society had been losing money for the last several years, but succeeded, with Mendelssohn at its helm, in turning a generous profit in this season. Mendelssohn met once more with Victoria and Albert, and also made the acquaintance of Charles Dickens. 'As an artist', Klingemann wrote with his traditional reverence of tone, 'no stranger ever held the position here that Felix does; his strong, calm disposition elevates him far above all the smoke and hubbub, and even the Philistines feel this and respect and appreciate, each in his own way, the power all acknowledge'.

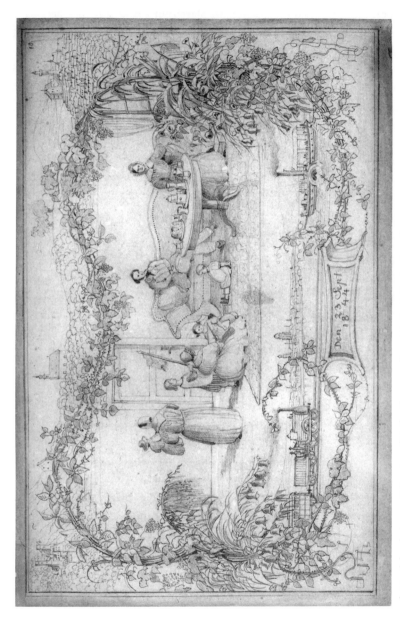

16 Mendelssohn's pencil drawing of his family on vacation at Soden in September 1844

Mendelssohn left England in mid-July for a hard-earned vacation with his family in Soden, a spa near Frankfurt. These were glorious weeks, given over – apart from a music festival at Zweibrücken at the end of July – to a breed of relaxation whose appeal was becoming clearer and clearer to Mendelssohn. 'What is not done today is done tomorrow, and there is leisure for everything'. These words, penned by a thirty-five-year-old worn well beyond his years, would have been unthinkable ten years before.

Relaxation in Mendelssohn's case hardly meant complete inactivity, and the weeks in Soden witnessed the completion of his final unqualified masterpiece, the Violin Concerto. The orchestral textures of this work are as inspired and crisply detailed as those of the *Midsummer Night's Dream* music. Its haunting opening sonority may well form a homage to the first bar of Mozart's G-minor Symphony, which fascinated Mendelssohn (when he heard of Liszt's claim that any orchestral sonority could be reproduced on the piano, Mendelssohn cited the beginning of this symphony – its violas in particular – as a likely counter-example). The main subject of the first movement is cut from the rhetorical cloth he had used to good effect in the first movement of the E-minor String Quartet, op. 44/2, though the concerto's melody is less pathos-laden, more poised, infinitely more memorable. This movement boasts, too, one of Mendelssohn's most effective dramatic climaxes, as the rapid arpeggiations that conclude the soloist's cadenza (which appears at the end of the development section rather than the end of the recapitulation, as in the traditional scheme) are made to accompany the first subject's return, indescribably light in the orchestra's hands. The idea is lifted straight from the remarkable first-movement coda of Beethoven's E♭ Quartet, op. 74, a piece whose fascination for Mendelssohn had been evident from his own earliest quartets. It is true that the concerto offers occasional glimpses of Mendelssohn's tendency – remarked on even by contemporaries – to repeat himself in his later works; the second subject of the finale, for instance, is rhythmically identical to the second subject of the 'Italian' Symphony's first movement. But at a tempo like this, who has time to grouse?

In the course of his English visit, Mendelssohn had begun negotiations, through Bunsen, for his final release from his Berlin obligations. His withdrawal from operations at the cathedral was formalised soon after his return to Berlin, on 30 September, though he remained until November to perform several concerts in the city. Thereafter Mendelssohn would serve the king only through the fulfilment of individual commissions. His time – what little was left of it – was once more his own.

8 Endings

Make sweet melody,
Sing many songs,
That you may be remembered.
                                                   Isaiah 23:16

Little of our story remains to be told. In Mendelssohn's three final
years, his drive to ceaseless activity had not disappeared, but he no
longer trusted it with command of his life. Fewer and fewer regions of
public activity seemed worthy of his energies, and he talked ever more
frequently of retiring to a private existence dedicated to composition
and the raising of his family. More frequent, too, were headaches and
episodes of acute fatigue, symptoms of a downward physical spiral he
would not survive.

In November 1844, after his final Berlin concert, Mendelssohn at
once dashed to Frankfurt to join Cécile in the care of their youngest
child, Felix, who had been seriously ill with a case of the measles
(though the boy recovered, his constitution was never strong, and he
would not long outlive his father). The Mendelssohns remained in
Frankfurt through the winter and spring. The Gewandhaus Orchestra
was in Gade's more than capable hands – even for the 13 March première of Mendelssohn's Violin Concerto – and Mendelssohn seemed
content to let the situation remain thus. 'I have for some time', he
wrote to Rebecka on 10 January, 'felt the necessity for complete rest –

not travelling, *not* conducting, *not* performing – so keenly that I am
compelled to yield to it, and hope to be able to order my life accordingly for the whole year for repose . . . I do believe that I was intended
for a quiet, uneventful life'.[1]

Something more fundamental than exhaustion is at work here;
Mendelssohn's whole attitude towards the business of musical per-
formance – the whole 'programme' of reform he had undertaken in
Leipzig – was undergoing a discernible shift. As he wrote to
Moscheles in March:

> So little benefit is derived even by the public itself from all this
> directing and these musical performances – a little better, a little
> worse, what does it matter? How quickly it is forgotten! . . . one book
> of your studies has had more influence on the public and on Art than I
> do not know how many morning and evening concerts during how
> many years.

The chief compositional project of these months was the completion
of his six 'Organ Sonatas', more a compendium of movements for
organ than tightly argued sonatas *per se*. No less lively for their contrapuntal challenges – fugue, as one might expect, holds a position of no
small importance in these works – these pieces well deserve their continued popularity, and the pride with which their composer first set
them before his publisher: 'I attach much importance to these
sonatas (if I may say so of any work of mine)'. In the course of the
summer, which was once more spent in Soden, Mendelssohn also
completed his second String Quintet in B♭ major, a work more polished than inspired, which pales beside the A-major Quintet of nine-
teen years before.

Mendelssohn was also in the midst of an edition of Handel's *Israel
in Egypt*, commissioned by London's Handel Society. The Society was
baffled to discover that the editorship of the great Mendelssohn
amounted to almost no editorship at all, for Mendelssohn's ideal publication appeared to be one which would contain no markings of any
kind but Handel's own. Stepping well outside the editorial customs of

the mid-nineteenth century, Mendelssohn insisted that, even if new tempo and dynamic markings were deemed an absolute necessity to ensure comprehensibility to a contemporary audience, 'on no account whatever would I interpolate marks of expression, tempi, etc., or anything else, in a score of Handel's if there is to be any doubt whether they are mine or his'. Following editorial principles still fully in force today, Mendelssohn's *Israel in Egypt* finally came out with his own suggestions for tempo, expression and dynamic markings in brackets, and a preface carefully explaining the meaning of this notation. The following year, Mendelssohn would bring the same critical eye to a series of editions of Bach's organ compositions.

In response to gentle pressure from Saxon minister Falkenstein, Mendelssohn rather grudgingly consented to take up his duties once more in Leipzig. On 13 August 1845 the Mendelssohns returned to that city, taking up residence at 3 Königstrasse. But Mendelssohn brought with him dreams of a permanent return to Frankfurt, as he indicates in a letter to his Frankfurt friend, Senator Bernus:

> I have considered in all seriousness giving you a commission
> (according to your promise) to buy me a house with a garden, or have
> one built, and then I would return permanently to that glorious
> country with its gay, easy life. But for the time being, of course, such
> good fortune cannot be mine. A few years will have to pass and the
> work I have begun here must have produced concrete results and be
> considerably further advanced (at least I must have tried to
> accomplish this), before I can think of such a thing . . . The sooner
> that occurs, the happier I shall be. I have always followed all my
> external musical pursuits, such as conducting, etc., purely from a
> sense of duty, never from inclination, so I hope, before many years
> are over, to turn up as a house builder.

Indeed, neither conducting nor teaching seemed to bring Mendelssohn much pleasure, and friends often find him ill-tempered and irritable. This work no longer brought out Mendelssohn's best side, and he was no longer convinced that it ever had. By mid-winter, Mendelssohn's physicians also persuaded him to retire from keyboard performance; he appeared in Leipzig thereafter only as a conductor.

For Mendelssohn, the high point of the 1845–6 season, musically and personally, was the arrival of Jenny Lind, the 'Swedish Nightingale' whose crystalline voice and utterly unaffected manner (or brilliantly cultivated simulation of such a manner) were fast winning the musical heart of Europe. Though vague tales of moody and capricious behaviour sprouted up like weeds around her reputation, to the public at large she was a breath of fresh air in an operatic world governed by personalities of a more – to express it gently – assertive bent. Lind and Mendelssohn had met in October 1844 at the house of their mutual friend, the sculptor, Professor Wichmann. The attraction was mutual, immediate and extremely powerful. Lind accepted Mendelssohn's invitation to Leipzig, and appeared there for the first time on 4 December 1845. Whatever bad feelings were raised by the dramatic increase in ticket prices for this event were put to rest by Lind's second concert, whose proceeds went to Mendelssohn's pension fund for members of the Gewandhaus Orchestra. She appeared in Leipzig again in a concert of 12 April 1846.

If Cécile looked askance at her husband's keen, and much noted, attentions to Lind – and there are signs that she did – there is no evidence whatever that the relationship developed into a romantic one, though it soon grew into a degree of intimacy exceptional, at the time, between a man and a woman under any other circumstances. In the days surrounding the 1846 Lower Rhein Music Festival at Aachen, where they both appeared, Mendelssohn and Lind set off – in the company of her chaperone, Louisa Johanson – for lengthy excursions on the Rhine. Though an affair seems genuinely unlikely, it is perhaps safest to acknowledge, in this of all situations, that absence of evidence does not necessarily constitute evidence of absence. After Mendelssohn's death, Lind would describe him as 'the only person who brought fulfilment to my spirit'.[2]

What cannot be questioned is the impulse that Lind's artistry gave to Mendelssohn's in his last years: 'I consider her without hesitation as the absolutely first singer of the day and perhaps of many days to come', he wrote to the manager of the 1846 Birmingham Music Festival in January. Mendelssohn's Elijah would be premièred at the Birmingham Festival that year, and though Lind was not there to sing it, the soprano part had been composed expressly for her, Mendelssohn drawing at every turn on his intimate familiarity with her instrument. It was Lind's voice, too, that drove him to look more seriously than he had in years at the possibility of an opera. In October 1846 he wrote to her, 'if I do not attain to the composition of a fairly good opera now, and for you, I shall never accomplish it at all'.[3] By the end of the year, he had entered into negotiations with Benjamin Lumley, the financially imperilled manager of Her Majesty's Theatre in London, concerning an opera on The Tempest (Lumley, in desperation, even went so far as to advertise this as a forthcoming attraction, attaching Lind's name, too, to the anticipated première). Mendelssohn had, we may recall, been considering an opera on this subject sixteen years before. Nonetheless, when the libretto – which was undertaken by the well-seasoned Scribe – arrived in mid-January, the composer voiced his usual dissatisfaction with its dramatic shape and negotiations on the project soon broke down. More promising still was a second project on the Rhine legend of the Loreley. Poet Emanuel Geibel had drafted a libretto, which the more theatrically experienced Eduard Devrient undertook to revise, a final product reaching Mendelssohn in February 1847. At the time of his death, Mendelssohn had drafted the finale of the first act and a single chorus of this work.

Though the August première of Elijah was obviously the main event of Mendelssohn's summer, the weeks beforehand were far from uneventful. As we have seen, Mendelssohn directed his last Lower Rhein Music Festival in Aachen, which ran from 31 May to 2 June. Dominated by Lind's electrifying performances, the programme included Haydn's Creation and Handel's Alexander's Feast, as well as

Beethoven's Fifth Symphony. After his final Rhine tour with Lind, Mendelssohn travelled via Düsseldorf to Liège, for the city's sexcentenary celebration, on 11 June, of the feast of Corpus Christi. Mendelssohn had composed an imposing setting of *Lauda Sion salvatorem* for the occasion, a work that hearkens back to the ambitious Catholic works of his youth, the *Tu es Petrus*, the *Te Deum*, and the sixteen-voice *Hora est*. Arriving only very shortly before the performance, and struck by the inadequacy of the preparations, Mendelssohn declined to conduct the work himself.

Three days later he was in Cologne, taking part in the German-Flemish Choral Festival, for which he had set Schiller's 'An die Künstler' (op. 68). Though its significance scarcely extended beyond this occasion, the song proved highly effective in the rendition it received here. Obviously moved, the composer reported to Fanny: 'when the greater part of the two thousand singers sang my "Volkslied" *by heart*, I was not only immensely pleased but quite overcome'. After a brief return to Leipzig, Mendelssohn set off for Birmingham, where he would have occasion to be more pleased still.

*

In 1837, with the thunderous applause of the *St Paul* première still ringing in his ears, Mendelssohn had taken up with Klingemann the question of a second oratorio. The composer soon settled on Elijah as a suitable subject – St Peter was another serious contender – but Klingemann found himself unable to warm to the project, and had produced only preliminary sketches before he asked Mendelssohn to seek another librettist. With the *St Paul* libretto under his belt, Julius Schubring was an obvious second choice, and set to work at once.

By 1839, after a series of exchanges on the subject, Schubring had made only minimal headway on the project, and Mendelssohn was himself involved in so many other enterprises that he elected to drop the whole matter for the time being. But it was to Elijah, and to Schubring, that Mendelssohn returned in the summer of 1845, when Joseph Moore invited him to provide a new oratorio for the 1846 Birmingham Festival. After Mendelssohn's first meeting with

Schubring on the subject in January 1846, the composer undertook one of the most sustained creative pushes of his compositional career to complete the whole in time for the festival. The première took place under his direction on 26 August 1846.

The victory was total. A euphoric Mendelssohn wrote to his brother of the première, 'No work of mine ever went so admirably at its first performance, nor was received with such enthusiasm by both the musicians and the audience. I was able to sway at will the enormous mass of orchestra and choir and organ . . . No less than four choruses and four arias were encored.' The only source of dissatisfaction for Mendelssohn was the soprano, Madame Caradori-Allan, whose voice – elegant, pleasing and pretty, as he allowed, but vacuously 'amiable' – proved a sorry substitute indeed for the voice his imagination had provided over the previous months (Caradori-Allan's early suggestion that her aria, 'Hear ye, Israel', might be taken down a tone was countered curtly by the composer with the suggestion that the committee might find him another soprano).

The report of the première that appeared in The Times suggests that Mendelssohn was not flattering himself in his own account: 'Never was there a more complete triumph – never a more thorough and speedy recognition of a great work of art'. Moscheles – who conducted most of the remainder of the festival – responded to the event with sentiments that would echo broadly through the work's early critical reception: 'God has endowed you with rare gifts, that permit you to approach Him in the true spirit of devotion and reverence'.[4]

Though Mendelssohn would not complete a mature opera, Elijah was situated much closer to staged drama than St Paul had been. Bent on doing away with 'the eternal "he said" etc'.,[5] Mendelssohn insisted on a libretto without a narrator, one in which the narrative unfolds entirely through the words of its characters. Mendelssohn's close friend, Charles Edward Horsley, perceived in Elijah the opera Mendelssohn never composed: 'Were it to English habits seemly, the whole oratorio without any material alteration might be placed on the stage with the greatest propriety, with scenery, costume and dramatic

17 Mendelssohn conducting *Elijah* in Birmingham, from the *Illustrated London News*, 29 August 1846

action. There is not a scene in the work which is not capable of the highest stage effect . . .'.[6] Otto Jahn – whose later biography of Mozart would form a landmark in the emergence of musical biography – warns against just such thinking in his critical essay on *Elijah*, which appeared the year after Mendelssohn's death: 'the epic element [i.e., the narrator] is peculiar to the essence of the oratorio, and . . . in abandoning it, one relinquishes a true advantage in the creation of the artistic form, for the sake of an imaginary one. The oratorio is incapable of truly dramatic form.'[7]

Few would argue with Jahn's discernment of 'a certain disjointedness, sometimes even indistinctness' that result from Mendelssohn's chosen mode of story-telling, but this is not to say that there are not moments of remarkable power here. Elijah's challenge to the followers of Baal to try the might of their god against the might of his, and the conflagration that his own prayers yield (nos. 10–16), constitute one of the most forceful sequences in all of Mendelssohn's vocal music. Similarly, the stirring 'Woe to Him!' (no. 24) makes a much more terrifying effect than the comparable 'Stone him to death!' (no. 8) of St Paul (made all the more powerful by occasional thematic recollections of the menacing overture). Indeed, *Elijah* generally maintains a higher level of inspiration than St Paul, and a much greater stylistic homogeneity; gone, for instance, are all but fleeting traces of the chorales that raised eyebrows in the earlier work. Several arias in Elijah – 'If with all your hearts' (no. 4) and the heart-rending (perhaps autobiographical) 'It is enough' (no. 26) at their head – stand worthily alongside the earlier oratorio's 'Jerusalem', which is saying a great deal.

With the première of this work, Mendelssohn had reached the absolute pinnacle of his fame. But the struggle to complete it in time, and the manifold activities of the summer, had left him utterly spent. Had he succeeded in his ardent desire to withdraw at once from the public sphere he might well have won himself more years of life, but naturally this proved impossible. The sentences that follow appeared in The Times as an account of the Elijah première, but they describe just as accurately the last fourteen months of Mendelssohn's life:

The last note of *Elijah* was drowned in a long-continued unanimous
volley of plaudits, vociferous and deafening ... Mendelssohn,
evidently overpowered, bowed his acknowledgement, and quickly
descended from his position in the conductor's rostrum; but he was
compelled to appear again, amidst renewed cheers and huzzas.

★

By late September, Mendelssohn was back in Leipzig. Soon after his
arrival, he wrote to Fanny:

So far I cannot make up my mind to a journey or anything else, but am
vegetating like a bunch of flowers after the exertions of the summer
and all the travelling back and forth. Ever since my arrival, when a
single glance told me that all were well and happy, I have done
nothing the whole day long but eat, take walks, and sleep, and yet I
never seem to get enough of the three.

Though the Gewandhaus concerts were nominally his once more, he
shared a large proportion of the conducting with Gade. His duties at
the Conservatory had become irksome, as well. Much to
Mendelssohn's delight, Ignaz Moscheles had accepted his offer of a
post at the Conservatory, and arrived from London in late October.
Though much of Mendelssohn's load was thus alleviated, he never
extricated himself fully from the daily life of the organisation.
Moscheles, for his part, was struck with the testy, difficult person that
his friend seemed to have become in much of his professional life.

Mendelssohn's almost total disenchantment with his position in
Leipzig is reflected in a letter to his brother of 31 October 1846, in
which he makes reference to his 'resolution not to continue in this
public official situation more than a few years'. He continues, 'just as
it formerly was my duty to fill such an office to the best of my ability,
it is now equally my duty to give it up'. By early December
Mendelssohn's dissatisfaction had grown more acute still:

Playing and conducting – in fact, any and every official appearance in
public – has grown intensely distasteful to me, so that each time I
only make up my mind to do it with the greatest reluctance and

unwillingness. I believe the time is approaching – or perhaps is already here – when I shall put all this kind of regular, public performance of music on the shelf, in order to make my own music at home, to compose and let this existence continue, as best it may, without me.

These tiresome months were made all the worse by the death of the Mendelssohns' servant and friend, Johann Krebs, in November, a loss which affected Felix deeply.

Mendelssohn had accepted a commission from Friedrich Wilhelm IV to provide a complete set of works for the German liturgy. These unostentatious, *a cappella* pieces for eight-voice chorus – pointing towards a simpler, purer style than the works he had composed in Berlin two years earlier – were completed on 28 October. Apart from his abortive operatic projects, the bulk of Mendelssohn's creative energies throughout the winter that followed were dedicated to the revision of *Elijah*, which would not be published until the summer. He had begun work, too, on a third oratorio, *Christus*, which would remain fragmentary at his death.

Mendelssohn's last birthday – 3 February 1847 – seemed one of the few bright spots in the gloom of this period. The celebration, which took place at Moscheles' house, began with a little prologue, in Frankfurt dialect, by Cécile and her sister. There followed a series of charades based on the syllables of the word 'Gewandhaus' ('Ge' took the form of an improvisation, by Joachim, on the G string, and so forth). At the conclusion of the whole, by way of a charade on the word 'orchestra', all the children in the Moscheles and Mendelssohn households were provided with toy instruments, Joachim with a toy violin, improvising a cacophonous finale with Felix – a man of thirty-eight who less and less often laughed this freely – at their head.

On 2 April 1847, Mendelssohn conducted *St Paul* at Leipzig's Paulinerkirche. This was the last time he would conduct in Germany. By 12 April he was in London once more, where he directed four performances of *Elijah* in the last two weeks of April, interspersed with single performances of the work in Manchester and Birmingham. He also took part, on 26 April, in a concert in the Hanover Square Rooms, conducting the 'Scottish' Symphony and *Midsummer Night's Dream* music, and appearing as soloist in Beethoven's G-major Piano Concerto. The concert was attended both by the queen and by Jenny Lind, who was then appearing in Meyerbeer's *Robert le Diable*. A 5 May organ concert in the Hanover Square Rooms was to be his last performance in England.

Victoria and Albert – who once more welcomed Mendelssohn at Buckingham Palace – were deeply impressed with *Elijah*, the queen reporting in her diary, 'The recitatives might be shortened, but the whole is a splendid work... [Mendelssohn] is a wonderful genius & is deservedly an amazing favourite here'.[8] After the 23 April performance, Albert inscribed a copy of the libretto:

> To the noble artist who, surrounded by the Baal-worship of false art, through genius and study has been able, like a second Elijah, to remain true to the service of true art; who has freed our ear from the chaos of mindless jingling of tones, to accustom it once more to the pure sounds of truly reflected emotion and regular harmony; to the Great Master, who, in a steady stream of ideas, unrolls before us the whole panorama of the elements from the gentlest rustlings to the mightiest storms; in grateful recollection,
>
> Albert

His labours had taken a visible toll on Mendelssohn; by the time of the composer's 8 May departure from London, Klingemann was sufficiently concerned about his friend's well-being to insist on accompanying him as far as Ostend across the Channel. Mendelssohn arrived in Frankfurt on 12 May a weary, ageing man; the news he received there left him a broken one.

★

The afternoon of Friday 14 May found Fanny at the piano directing a rehearsal of her brother's *Die erste Walpurgisnacht*, to be performed the following Sunday. Suddenly her hands refused to serve her. Leaving a colleague at the keyboard, she stepped into an adjacent room to soak her hands in warm vinegar. As the chorus continued, she remarked,

'How beautiful it sounds', and returned before too long to the piano. Her paralysis returned, though, now becoming general, and she fell almost at once into unconsciousness. She had suffered a stroke, and did not regain consciousness before her death, which came at eleven o'clock that night. When the news was broken – rather abruptly – to Felix in Frankfurt, he fell into a dead faint.

On 24 May, Mendelssohn wrote to a friend:

> what we, her brothers and sisters, have lost! And I in particular, to whom she was present every moment with her kindness and love; I, who could never experience any happiness without thinking how she would share it; I, who was spoiled, and made so proud, by all the riches of her sisterly love, and whom I thought nothing could ever harm because in everything hers was always the best and leading part. All this, I believe, we cannot yet estimate, just as I still instinctively believe that the mournful news will be suddenly denied. And then again I know that it is all true, but never in all the world will I become inured to it.

To Wilhelm Hensel – who was shattered by his wife's death, and never fully reassembled his personal or professional life – Mendelssohn was unable to offer any consolation whatever, but observed prophetically: 'This will be a changed world for us all now, but we must try and get accustomed to the change, though by the time we have got accustomed to it our lives may be over too'.

In early June, Felix and his family travelled to Baden-Baden; the season for the baths had not begun, and the town was quiet. Paul and his wife, Albertine, met them there. Amid the emotional trials of these weeks, long-standing tensions between Cécile and Albertine erupted into frequent squabbles. Deciding that a change of scene would be for the best, they travelled together, via Thun, to Interlaken, where they were joined by Wilhelm Hensel. Mendelssohn's friend Henry Chorley visited the composer at Interlaken, and observed that he looked 'aged and sad, and stooped more than I had ever before seen him do'.[9]

As always in times of mourning, Mendelssohn turned towards music for consolation – or, at least, distraction – undertaking what would turn out to be his last sustained creative effort. The String Quartet in F minor that resulted, intended as a requiem for Fanny, taps a vein of emotional intensity Mendelssohn had never located before. The opening subject of the quartet's first movement is one of the most viscerally hard-hitting musical ideas – 'ugly' is hardly too strong a word – he had ever committed to paper, emotionally moored less in sadness than in pain. If the second subject offers the possibility of consolation, the sense of reassurance is paper-thin, and soon proves unsustainable. The second-movement scherzo sets off with a syncopated, chromatic ascent in the cello that presses us forward with a feeling something like dread, hardly alleviated by a cheerless, dark-hued trio (the cello, viola and second violin spend nearly the entirety of the trio on their lowest strings). At the conclusion of the scherzo, the trio braves a fragmentary return, calling to mind a similar return in the scherzo of Beethoven's Seventh Symphony. But in Beethoven's work, the effect is comical, the entire orchestra blasting in to reject the idea of a third sounding of a trio which, in this case, we have already heard twice. In Mendelssohn's scherzo, the trio returns only tentatively, then simply gives up and lapses into silence; continuation is not forbidden so much as pointless. The elegiac third movement contains the only music in the quartet we might be moved to call 'beautiful', though the listener cannot revel even in this pleasant landscape without occasional nervous glances over the shoulder. A turbulent, relentless finale fulfils our worst fears.

The Mendelssohns returned to Leipzig on 17 September, where Felix's friends found him tired and distant. Before the Gewandhaus concert season commenced, Mendelssohn journeyed briefly to Berlin to make arrangements for a planned performance of *Elijah*. Upon seeing Fanny's room, unchanged since her death, he collapsed into an alarming state of emotional perturbation which left him, on his return to Leipzig, unable even to consider conducting. Felix had lost what little had remained of his interest in the city's affairs, and had already begun speaking of the possibility of moving soon to Berlin – 'abandoning all other considerations' – to spend his life with Paul and Rebecka.

On 9 October, while running through some new songs with the singer, Livia Frege, Mendelssohn's health began its final decline. Frege slipped out of the room briefly to fetch more light and returned to find Mendelssohn shivering, his hands cold, suffering from a violent headache. Insisting that exercise would do him good, he walked home, where Cécile found him on the sofa around seven o'clock that night with his symptoms unabated. In the course of the two weeks that followed, his situation seemed to improve. A 25 October letter to Paul, one of his last, even finds Felix optimistic about the possibility of conducting the Viennese première of Elijah the following month. 'But it is definitely settled', Mendelssohn writes, 'that after these concerts, which having once promised must now be fulfilled, I make no more engagements – even if I were not obliged to keep them! But one is!'

On 28 October, he was seated at lunch with Cécile when he suddenly started up, speaking with great excitement in English. He had suffered a mild stroke, and was taken at once to bed. On 3 November he suddenly became restless and, at length, uttered a single piercing scream before falling into a stupor. Charlotte and Ignaz Moscheles, Frege, David and Schleinitz were called for, and stayed at the house till around eleven that night; Felix's brother Paul was there, too, having arrived from Berlin a few days before. At 9:24 the following morning, Mendelssohn died.

Schumann, David, Gade, Hauptmann, Rietz and Moscheles bore Mendelssohn's casket to the Paulinerkirche on 6 November. That night, it was put on a special train for Berlin, where Mendelssohn was buried the following day near his sister in the Trinity Cemetery. In the weeks that followed, mourning services were held in Leipzig, Berlin, Vienna, Paris, London and New York.

Those who had known Mendelssohn – and the thousands more who had longed to – at once erected around his life a towering image polished, in retrospect, to a saintly glow, captured elegantly in Charles Edward Horsley's moving recollection of his friend and teacher: 'In all relations of life, as a son, a husband and a father, he was humanly speaking perfect. I never met a man who came up more to the standard of a Christian, a scholar and a gentleman.'[10] There is a veneer of mythology here, to be sure, but it is a myth for which the events of Mendelssohn's brief, remarkable life indeed provided abundant raw material.

We may discern a gentle irony in Horsley's choice of words. Mendelssohn's whole artistic and human persona had taken shape in the shadow of his grandfather, Moses, whose brilliant life was a sustained counter-argument to the age-old assumption that Christians held monopolies on virtue and intellectual excellence. Yet Horsley, in grasping for the term that most fully encompasses the human virtues of Moses' grandson, Felix, chooses 'Christian'.

Importantly, Horsley's remarks – penned in 1872 – come from within an ongoing conversation whose battle lines had been drawn by one a good deal less attuned to the late composer's virtues, Richard Wagner. Three years after Mendelssohn's death, under the pseudonym 'K. Freigedank' ('Free-thought'), the *Neue Zeitschrift für Musik* had published Wagner's article, 'Über das Judentum in der Musik' ('On Judaism in Music'). In Wagner's formulation, it is finally to Mendelssohn's Jewish heritage that we must ascribe the fact that 'he was not able, even one single time, to call forth in us that deep, that heart-searching effect which we await from art...' Thus began a tradition of anti-Semitic criticism in Germany that culminated, under the Nazis, in Mendelssohn's total erasure from the history of his country's music. In 1937, the statue of Mendelssohn that stood before the Gewandhaus was taken down and sold as scrap iron. Notwithstanding the continued popularity of his Violin Concerto and *Midsummer Night's Dream* overture, his works were expunged from concert programmes, his name from the standard historical narrative.

Anti-Semitism has hardly been the only force at work, of course, in the troubled reception history of Mendlessohn's music over the last century and a half. By the mid-1870s, English critics, too, had embarked on a general notching-down of the rhetoric that had, since Mendelssohn's death, placed him among the very first ranks of musical geniuses. This process came most sharply into focus towards the end of the century in the criticism of George Bernard Shaw.

The years since the end of the Second World War have witnessed a recrudescence in Mendelssohn's fortunes. Scholarly interest in his work is at an all-time high, and growing. Not only do his half-dozen most popular works appear as frequently as ever in concert programmes and compact disc catalogues, but formerly obscure recesses of his output – string *sinfonie*, the chorale cantatas, the early concertos – are coming before the public for the first time, a development that probably would have baffled, and perhaps amused, their composer. It is under such circumstances that a just evaluation of Mendelssohn's work at last becomes possible, and is, indeed, well underway. Here, too, there is irony, as this broad-based re-evaluation of Mendelssohn's music is made possible, in part, by a general disintegration of the idea of a musical canon, an idea whose development was itself the most significant legacy of Mendelssohn's life as a conductor, pianist and scholar.

★

After Felix's death, Cécile and her children lived for a time in Berlin, then in Baden, returning finally to Frankfurt, where Cécile spent her own last days – sad and withdrawn – in the company of her family. At an even younger age than her husband, she died on 25 September 1853. Ferdinand Hiller recalled meeting with Cécile and her children some years after Felix's death, and being overwhelmed by this glimpse of the simple life his friend so ardently longed for in his last years:

> I was one day dining with Mendelssohn's widow, surrounded by her charming children, and could not help feeling deeply affected; the ingenuous bantering prattle of the children, the graceful, gentle way in which Cécile tried to check their high spirits, nearly overcame me. How much happiness was lost to him who had been taken from us – how much happiness those who were left behind had been robbed of![11]

18 Mendelssohn on his deathbed, drawn by his friend Eduard Bendemann

Felix's grandfather, Moses, had offered at least the possibility of a happier vision. In his early masterpiece, *Phaedon, or on the Immortality of the Soul*, Moses had placed in the mouth of Socrates these comforting words:

> He who has taken care of his soul on earth by pursuing wisdom and cultivating both virtue and a sense of true beauty has surely every hope of proceeding on the same path after death. Step by step, he will draw nearer to the sublime Being, the source of all wisdom and epitome of all perfection, and to its pre-eminent manifestation, beauty itself.[12]

By Moses' logic, there was good reason to take heart at the passing of his grandson, who had himself once described the afterlife in simpler terms, as a place 'where it is to be hoped there is still music, but no more sorrow or partings'.[13]

1 Beginnings

1 Hannah Arendt, *Rahel Varnhagen: The Life of a Jewess*, ed. Liliane Weissberg, trans. Richard and Clara Winston (Baltimore: Johns Hopkins University Press, 1997), p. 85.

2 Hans I. Bach, *The German Jew: A Synthesis of Judaism and Western Civilization* (New York: Oxford University Press, 1984), p. 81.

3 Eva Jospe, ed. and trans., *Moses Mendelssohn: Selections from His Writings* (New York: The Viking Press, 1975), p. 52. From a letter to Johann Jacob Spiess, a Bavarian pastor and librarian.

4 Quoted in Herbert Kupferberg, *The Mendelssohns: Three Generations of Genius* (New York: Charles Scribner's Sons, 1972), p. 6.

5 Alexander Altmann, *Moses Mendelssohn: A Biographical Study* (University, Alabama: The University of Alabama Press, 1973), p. 18. My whole discussion of Moses' life is heavily indebted to this exhaustive study.

6 Quoted in Françoise Tillard, *Fanny Mendelssohn*, trans. Camille Naish (Portland, Oregon: Amadeus Press, 1992), p. 24.

7 Letter of 27 February to Gotthold Ephraim Lessing. Jospe, ed. and trans., *Writings*, p. 53.

8 Sebastian Hensel, *The Mendelssohn Family (1729–1847), from Letters and Journals*, 2nd rev. edn, trans. Karl Klingemann, *et al.*, vol. 1 (1882; rpt. edn, New York: Greenwood Press, 1968), p. 23.

9 Quoted in Kupferberg, *Mendelssohns*, p. 36. The following quote from Kant appears in Bach, *German Jew*, p. 70.

10 Quoted in Arendt, *Varnhagen*, p. 88. From this volume (p. 104) comes, too, the following quotation from Moses' *Jerusalem*.

11 Hensel, *Family*, vol. 1, pp. 43–4. The two quotations that follow appear on pp. 59 and 60. The following letter from Lea appears on p. 69.

12 Quoted in Arendt, *Varnhagen*, pp. 299–300.

2 The prodigy

1 Trans. Minetta Altgelt Goyne, in Herman Glaser, ed., *The German Mind of the 19th Century: A Literary & Historical Anthology* (New York: Continuum, 1981), p. 41.

2 My immediate source is Françoise Tillard, *Fanny Mendelssohn*, p. 39. The following quote from Clemens Brentano appears on p. 40; that from Goethe, on p. 114; that from Eduard Devrient, on p. 117. My own discussion of the situation of Berlin Jews at this time is indebted to Tillard's.

3 James Sheehan, *German History: 1770–1866* (Oxford: Clarendon Press, 1989), p. 790.

4 Sara Rothenberg, '"Thus far, but no farther": Fanny Mendelssohn-Hensel's Unfinished Journey', *The Musical Quarterly* 77/4 (1993), p. 698.

5 Julius Schubring, 'Reminiscences of Felix Mendelssohn-Bartholdy', in *Mendelssohn and his World*, ed. R. Larry Todd (Princeton: Princeton University Press, 1991), p. 222. Originally 'Reminiscences of Felix Mendelssohn-Bartholdy. On his 57th Birthday, February 3rd, 1866', *Musical World* 31 (12 and 19 May 1866). Subsequent quotations from Schubring appear on p. 223.

6 Hensel, *Family*, vol. 1, p. 75. This is the source of numerous subsequent letters cited in this chapter. Several others appear in Rudolf Elvers, ed., *Felix Mendelssohn: A Life in Letters*, trans. Craig Tomlinson (New York: Fromm International Publishing Corporation, 1986); others in G. Selden-Goth, ed., *Felix Mendelssohn: Letters* (New York: Vienna House, 1973). Many translations throughout this book are lightly emended.

7 Marcia J. Citron, ed. and trans., *The Letters of Fanny Hensel to Felix Mendelssohn* (Stuyvesant, NY: Pendragon Press, 1987), p. 66. My account of Mendelssohn's use of the name 'Bartholdy' draws on Jeffrey S. Sposato, 'Creative Writing: The (Self-)Identification of Mendelssohn as a Jew', *The Musical Quarterly* 82/1 (1998), p. 196.

8 Ferdinand Hiller, *Mendelssohn: Letters and Recollections*, trans. M. E. von Glehn (1874; rpt. edn, New York: Vienna House, 1972), p. 4. The following quotation from Hiller appears on pp. 5–6.

9 The recipient of this letter, 'Herr Doctor', has not yet been

identified. The letter is quoted in R. Larry Todd, 'The Instrumental
Music of Felix Mendelssohn-Bartholdy: Selected Studies Based on
Primary Sources', Ph.D. thesis, Yale University (1979), p. 30. The
present account of Zelter's pedagogical pedigree draws heavily on
this thesis, pp. 6–24, and on Todd, *Mendelssohn's Musical Education: A
Study and Edition of his Exercises in Composition: Oxford Bodleian ms.
Margaret Deneke Mendelssohn C. 43* (Cambridge: Cambridge University
Press, 1983).

10 'From the Memoirs of Adolf Bernhard Marx', trans. Susan Gillespie,
in *Mendelssohn and his World*, ed. Todd, p. 207. Subsequent
quotations from Marx appear on p. 207.

11 This discussion draws on the insights of Greg Vitercik, *The Early
Works of Felix Mendelssohn: A Study in the Romantic Sonata Style*
(Philadelphia: Gordon and Breach, 1992), pp. 41–6.

12 This account is indebted to R. Larry Todd, *Mendelssohn: The Hebrides
and Other Overtures* (Cambridge: Cambridge University Press, 1993),
p. 4.

13 A. B. Marx, cited in 'From the Memoirs', trans. Gillespie, p. 208.

14 Letter of 30 September 1823, in Bruno Hake, 'Mendelssohn as
Teacher, with Previously Unpublished Letters from Mendelssohn to
Wilhelm v. Boguslawski', trans. Susan Gillespie, in *Mendelssohn and
his World*, ed. Todd, p. 315.

3 *First maturity*

1 Hensel, *Family*, vol. 1, p. 90. Many of the letters quoted in this
chapter appear in this volume. Others appear in Elvers, ed., *Felix
Mendelssohn: A Life in Letters*, trans. Tomlinson; others in Hiller,
Recollections.

2 Fanny Lewald, 'Recollections of the Year 1848', trans. David
Jacobson, in Glaser, ed., *German Mind*, p. 179.

3 Citron, ed. and trans., *The Letters of Fanny Hensel*, p. 54.

4 Eric Werner, *Mendelssohn: A New Image of the Composer and his Age*,
trans. Dika Newlin (London: The Free Press of Glencoe, 1963), p.
75.

5 Todd, 'The Instrumental Music of Felix Mendelssohn-Bartholdy', p.
257.

6 Johann Christian Lobe, 'Conversations with Felix Mendelssohn', in *Mendelssohn and his World*, ed. Todd, p. 199.

7 Todd, *Mendelssohn: The Hebrides and Other Overtures*, p. 19. The foregoing discussion of the *Midsummer Night's Dream* overture owes a considerable debt to this volume.

8 Paul Mendelssohn Bartholdy, ed., *Letters from Italy and Switzerland by Felix Mendelssohn Bartholdy*, trans. Lady Wallace, 3rd edn (1865; rpt. edn, Freeport, NY: Books for Libraries Press, 1970), p. 349.

9 Quoted in Todd, 'Instrumental Music', p. 255.

10 Lawrence Kramer, *Classical Music and Postmodern Knowledge* (Berkeley: University of California Press, 1995), p. 137.

11 Arthur Groos, 'Constructing Nuremberg: Typological and Proleptic Communities in *Die Meistersinger*', *19th Century Music* 16/1 (1992), p. 19.

4 The Grand Tour

1 Jean-Paul Friedrich Richter, *Walt and Wult, or The Twins* (a translation of *Flegeljahre*) (Boston: J. Monroe and Company, 1846), pp. 129–30.

2 Letter of 21 April 1829; Elvers, ed., *Life*, p. 59. This is the source for several other letters cited in this chapter, though most of the letters from Felix himself are found in Paul Mendelssohn, ed., *Italy and Switzerland*; others come from Hensel, *Family*, vol. 1.

3 Citron, ed. and trans., *The Letters of Fanny Hensel*, p. 402. The letter below, concerning Rose Behrend, appears on p. 117.

4 Quoted in Mozelle Moshansky, *Mendelssohn* (London: Omnibus Press, 1982), p. 58.

5 A full account of this event appears in John Warrack, *Carl Maria von Weber* (Cambridge: Cambridge University Press, 1968), p. 361.

6 R. Larry Todd, 'Mendelssohn's Ossianic Manner, with a New Source – On Lena's Gloomy Heath', in *Mendelssohn and Schumann: Essays on their Music and its Context*, ed. Jon W. Finson and R. Larry Todd (Durham, North Carolina: Duke University Press, 1984), pp. 137–60. The following quotation appears on p. 137. The quotation from Schumann that follows appears in Henry Pleasants, ed. and trans., *Schumann on Music: A Selection from the Writings* (New York: Dover Publications, Inc., 1965), p. 37.

7 This discussion is indebted to Judith Silber-Ballan, 'Mendelssohn and his Reformation Symphony', *Journal of the American Musicological Society* 40/2 (1987), pp. 310–36.

8 Wiesmann, 'Vienna: Bastion of Conservatism', in *The Early Romantic Era: Between Revolutions: 1789 and 1848* (Englewood Cliffs, New Jersey: Prentice Hall, 1990), p. 86. The Trollope quotation that follows appears on p. 99.

9 Letter of April 1834; Selden-Goth, ed., *Letters*, p. 230.

10 Eduard Devrient, *My Recollections of Felix Mendelssohn-Bartholdy and his Letters to Me*, trans. Natalia MacFarren (London: R. Bentley, 1869), pp. 109–10.

11 This discussion is indebted to Brian Pritchard, 'Mendelssohn's Chorale Cantatas: An Appraisal', *The Musical Quarterly* 62/1 (1976), pp. 1–24.

12 Elizabeth Gilmore Holt, ed., *The Triumph of Art for the Public: The Emerging Role of Exhibitions and Critics* (Garden City, NY: Anchor Press, 1979), p. 179.

13 Steven D. Lindeman, 'Structural Novelty and Tradition in the Early Romantic Piano Concerto', Ph.D. dissertation, Rutgers University (1995), p. 144.

14 10 August 1832. *Letters of Felix Mendelssohn to Ignaz and Charlotte Moscheles*, ed. and trans. Felix Moscheles (1888; rpt. edn, Freeport, NY: Books for Libraries Press, 1970), p. 30.

15 Philip Radcliffe, *Mendelssohn*, 3rd edn rev. Peter Ward Jones (London: Dent, 1990), p. 101.

16 Hiller, *Recollections*, 25–6. The following quotation concerning the French musicians' response to Mendelssohn's 'Reformation' Symphony appears on p. 21.

17 Quoted in James Johnson, 'Beethoven and the Birth of Romantic Musical Experience in France', *19th Century Music* 15/1 (1991), p. 24. I am indebted to Johnson for this whole discussion of Beethoven's reception in France.

5 *Frustrations in Berlin and Düsseldorf*

1 Ed. Eric A. Blackall (Princeton: Princeton University Press, 1995), p. 190.

2 Paul Mendelssohn Bartholdy and Carl Mendelssohn Bartholdy, *Letters of Felix Mendelssohn Bartholdy, from 1833 to 1847*, trans. Lady Wallace (1864; rpt. edn, Freeport, NY: Books for the Libraries Press, 1970), p. 355. Apart from this volume, from which many letters in this chapter are drawn, many appear in Citron, ed. and trans., *The Letters of Fanny Hensel*; Elvers, ed., *Life in Letters*; and Hensel, *Family*, vol. 2.

3 Karl Klingemann, Jr., ed., *Felix Mendelssohn-Bartholdys Briefwechsel mit Legationsrat Karl Klingemann in London* (Essen: G. D. Baedeker, 1909), p. 98.

4 Werner, *New Image*, p. 227.

5 William A. Little, 'Mendelssohn and the Berlin Singakademie: The Composer at the Crossroads', in *Mendelssohn and his World*, ed. Todd, p. 74. The present account of this episode in Mendelssohn's life is richly informed by Little's.

6 Quoted in Susanna Großmann-Vendry, *Felix Mendelssohn Bartholdy und die Musik der Vergangenheit* (Regensburg: Gustav Bosse Verlag, 1969), p. 52. This volume is the source for much of the information concerning the works Mendelssohn programmed in Düsseldorf, as well as for Mendelssohn's letter, quoted below, to William Horsley.

7 Selden-Goth, ed., *Letters*, p. 220.

8 Quoted in Werner, *New Image*, p. 233. *Harmonicon* (1833), p. 134.

9 Trans. Martha Humphrey, in Glaser, ed., *German Mind*, p. 144. Though Mendelssohn was quite critical of this book, as he was of Immermann's next novel, it is noteworthy that – busy as he was – he continued to stay abreast of Immermann's work.

10 Vitercik, *Early Works*, p. 2. The present discussion of the 'Biedermeier' in music is indebted to Kenneth DeLong, 'The Conventions of Musical Biedermeier', in *Convention in Eighteenth- and Nineteenth-Century Music: Essays in Honor of Leonard G. Ratner*, ed. Wye J. Allanbrook, Janet M. Levy and William P. Mahrt, Festschrift series no. 10 (Stuyvesant, NY: Pendragon Press, 1992), pp. 195–223. The quotation from Dahlhaus that follows appears in *Nineteenth-Century Music*, trans. J. Bradford Robinson (Berkeley: University of California Press, 1989), p. 171.

11 Elise Polko, *Reminiscences of Felix Mendelssohn-Bartholdy: A Social and Artistic Biography*, trans. Lady Wallace (1869; rpt. edn, Macomb,

Illinois: Glenbridge Publishing Ltd., 1987), p. 48. Robert
Schumann's remarks are quoted in R. Larry Todd, 'Piano Music
Reformed: The Case of Felix Mendelssohn Bartholdy', in *Nineteenth-
Century Piano Music*, ed. R. Larry Todd (New York: Schirmer Books,
1994), pp. 192–3.

6 Scaling the heights in Leipzig

1 Heinrich Heine, *Poetry and Prose*, trans. Aaron Kramer, The German
   Library, vol. 32 (New York: Continuum, 1982), p. 51.
2 Letter of 6 October 1835; Paul and Carl Mendelssohn Bartholdy,
   Letters, p. 82. This is the source of many letters in this chapter. Others
   come from Hensel, *Family*, vol. 2; and from Hiller, *Recollections*.
3 Robert Schumann, *Gesammelte Schriften über Musik und Musiker*, ed.
   Martin Kreisig, 5th edn, vol. 1 (Leipzig: Breitkopf & Härtel, 1914),
   p. 117. My immediate source is Leon Plantinga, 'Schumann's Critical
   Reaction to Mendelssohn', in *Mendelssohn and Schumann: Essays on
   their Music and its Context*, ed. Jon W. Finson and R. Larry Todd
   (Durham, North Carolina: Duke University Press, 1984), p. 11. This
   is my source, too, for Schumann's later remarks on St Paul (p. 17)
   and the D-minor Concerto (p. 13).
4 Quoted in Werner, *New Image*, p. 322.
5 Großman-Vendry, *Vergangenheit*, p. 141. This is the source (p. 86),
   too, of the later *Düsseldorf Zeitung* review of St Paul.
6 Moshansky, *Mendelssohn*, p. 95. The following quote appears in
   Polko, *Reminiscences*, p. 73.
7 Quoted in Werner, *New Image*, p. 265. Schumann's remarks on
   Liszt's soirée appear on p. 316 of this volume.
8 Polko, *Reminiscences*, p. 58.
9 Letter of 15 January 1835; Elvers, ed., *Life in Letters*, p. 205.
10 *Athenaeum* (1837), p. 708. My immediate source is Werner, *New
   Image*, pp. 293–4. Werner (p. 330) provides, too, the review, quoted
   below from the *Allgemeiner musikalischer Anzeiger* 11 (1839), p. 242.
11 'Lutetia, Reports on Politics, Art, and Popular Life; Part 2, Report
   no. 43', in *Mendelssohn and his World*, ed. Todd, p. 360. The following
   remarks from Karl Friedrich Zelter's correspondence are quoted in
   Tillard, *Fanny Mendelssohn*, p. 212.

12 Quoted in Werner, *New Image*, p. 299.
13 Polko, *Reminiscences*, p. 50. The passage from the Honeymoon Diary appears in Peter Ward Jones, ed. and trans., *The Mendelssohns on Honeymoon: The 1837 Diary of Felix and Cécile Mendelssohn Bartholdy Together with Letters to their Families* (Oxford: Clarendon Press, 1997), p. 62
14 Vitercik, 'Mendelssohn the Progressive', *The Journal of Musicological Research* 8/3–4 (March 1989), p. 371. Schumann's later remarks on the *Lobgesang* are quoted in Werner, *New Image*, p. 317.
15 Letter of 22 October 1833; Citron, ed. and trans., *The Letters of Fanny Hensel*, p. 112. The letter that follows appears on p. 119.

7 *More frustrations in Berlin*

1 Robert Fitzgerald, trans., *Sophocles I*, The Complete Greek Tragedies, ed. David Grene and Richmond Lattimore (Chicago: University of Chicago Press, 1954), p. 114.
2 Quoted in Sheehan, *German History*, p. 621. The following quote from Johann Jacoby's *Vier Fragen* also appears in Sheehan, *ibid.*, p. 624.
3 Quoted in David Brodbeck, 'A Winter of Discontent: Mendelssohn and the *Berliner Domchor*', in *Mendelssohn Studies*, ed. R. Larry Todd (Cambridge: Cambridge University Press, 1992), p. 2. The following letter from Mendelssohn, seeking clarification on the king's plans, appears in Paul and Carl Mendelssohn Bartholdy, *Letters*, p. 203. Many of the letters quoted in this chapter come from this volume; others are from Hensel, *Family*, vol. 2; and Selden-Goth, *Letters*.
4 Letter of 13 July 1841; Citron, ed. and trans., *The Letters of Fanny Hensel*, p. 308.
5 Letter to Woldemar Frege of 28 August 1841; Elvers, ed., *Life in Letters*, p. 255.
6 Quoted in Werner, *New Image*, p. 376.
7 Quoted in Wilfred Blunt, *On Wings of Song: A Biography of Felix Mendelssohn* (New York: Charles Scribner's Sons, 1974), p. 224.
8 Elvers, ed., *Life in Letters*, p. 257.
9 Letter of 3 March 1843; Hiller, *Recollections*, p. 205. The following letter to Gade appears in Elvers, ed., *Life in Letters*, p. 261.
10 Quoted in Blunt, *Wings*, p. 246.

11 Letter to Hiller of 19 January 1843; Hiller, *Recollections*, p. 200.
12 Letter of 12 January 1835; quoted in Brodbeck, 'A Winter', p. 4.

8 *Endings*

1 Hensel, *Family*, vol. 2, pp. 308–9. Many of the letters quoted in this chapter come from this volume. Others come from Paul and Carl Mendelssohn Bartholdy, *Letters*; others from Selden-Goth, ed., *Letters*.
2 Quoted in Moshansky, *Mendelssohn*, p. 126.
3 Letter of 31 October, quoted in Werner, *New Image*, p. 443. This is also the immediate source for the review of *Elijah* in *The Times* (p. 476).
4 Moscheles, ed. and trans., *Letters of Felix Mendelssohn*, p. 280.
5 Letter to Schubring of 16 December 1845; quoted in Werner, *New Image*, p. 459.
6 Horsley, 'Reminiscences of Mendelssohn by his English Pupil', in *Mendelssohn and his World*, ed. Todd, p. 245.
7 Otto Jahn, 'On F. Mendelssohn-Bartholdy's Oratorio *Elijah*', trans. Susan Gillespie, in *Mendelssohn and his World*, ed. Todd, p. 367.
8 Quoted in Moshansky, *Mendelssohn*, p. 131.
9 Quoted in Blunt, *Wings*, p. 266.
10 Horsley, 'Reminiscences', p. 248.
11 Hiller, *Recollections*, pp. 217–18.
12 In *Moses Mendelssohn: Selections from his Writings*, ed. and trans. Eva Jospe (New York: The Viking Press, 1975) p. 195.
13 Letter of 11 July 1846, to Herr Velten, a stranger to Mendelssohn, who had sent the composer a sampling of the compositions of his son, an aspiring composer who had died young; Paul and Carl Mendelssohn Bartholdy, *Letters*, p. 363.

What follows is a selection of readings in English. This list concludes with information on where to go for more.

Mendelssohn's letters form a creative oeuvre almost as impressive as his musical one – thoughtful, well crafted and almost unbelievably expansive. Fourteen years after Mendelssohn's death, his brother, Paul, edited the first collection of the composer's letters to appear in print, the *Letters from Italy and Switzerland* (trans. Lady Wallace, London, 1862), a volume which cuts a distinctive profile in the crowded field of nineteenth-century travel literature. There soon followed *Letters from the Years 1833–1847* (trans. Lady Wallace, London, 1863) and *Letters of Felix Mendelssohn to Ignaz and Charlotte Moscheles* (ed. and trans. Felix Moscheles, Boston, 1888), along with a cornucopia of memoirs and documentary histories: Eduard Devrient, *My Recollections of Felix Mendelssohn-Bartholdy and his Letters to Me* (trans. Natalia MacFarren, London, 1869), Ferdinand Hiller, *Mendelssohn: Letters and Recollections* (trans. M. E. von Glehn, London, 1872), Carl Mendelssohn-Bartholdy, *Goethe and Mendelssohn* (trans. M. E. von Glehn, London, 1872), and the magnum opus of Fanny's son, Sebastian Hensel, *The Mendelssohn Family (1729–1847), From Letters and Journals* (2nd rev. edn, trans. Karl Klingemann, et al., New York, 1882). Reprint editions have made most of this material widely available today. Important recent additions to this list include *The Letters of Fanny Hensel to Felix Mendelssohn* (ed. and trans. Marcia J. Citron, New York, 1987) and the delightful *The Mendelssohns on Honeymoon: The 1837 Diary of Felix and Cécile Mendelssohn Bartholdy Together with Letters to their Families* (ed. and trans. Peter Ward Jones, Oxford, 1997). G. Selden-Goth, ed., *Felix Mendelssohn: Letters* (New York, 1945) and Rudolph Elvers, ed., *Felix Mendelssohn: A Life in Letters* (New York, 1986) are both thoughtfully

assembled collections. Briefer memoirs from Mendelssohn's contemporaries Johann Christian Lobe, Adolf Bernhard Marx, Julius
Schubring, Charles Edward Horsley, and others appear in *Mendelssohn
and his World* (ed. R. Larry Todd, Princeton, 1991).

In documentary rigour, cultural awareness, and sheer depth of
psychological insight, Eric Werner's magisterial biography,
Mendelssohn: A New Image of the Composer and his Age (trans. Dika Newlin,
London, 1963) has yet to be surpassed, though Werner's musical commentary is perhaps overly analytical for the non-specialist. At the
same time, the book is seriously marred – not just politically but historically – by a female cast comprised almost entirely of gossips,
viragos and flighty socialites. Readable and well crafted are the more
recent biographies of George Marek (*Gentle Genius: The Story of Felix
Mendelssohn*, New York, 1972), Herbert Kupferberg (*Felix Mendelssohn:
His Life, his Family, his Music*, New York, 1972) and Wilfred Blunt (*On
Wings of Song: a Biography of Felix Mendelssohn*, New York, 1974). Though
Mozelle Moshansky's *Mendelssohn*, from the series Illustrated Lives of
the Composers (London, 1982), is not precisely scholarly, it gives
entertaining testimony to how singularly rich a visual legacy was left
by Mendelssohn and his international career. Karl-Heinz Köhler's
article on Mendelssohn in the *New Grove Dictionary of Music and
Musicians* offers a succinct biographical sketch and exhaustive lists –
compiled jointly with R. Larry Todd – of compositions and further
readings. Françoise Tillard's excellent biography, *Fanny Mendelssohn*
(trans. Camille Naish, New York, 1993), paints a portrait exceptionally rich in cultural and historical details. There is every reason to
expect that R. Larry Todd's forthcoming biography – working title:
The Prodigy's Voice: A Life of Felix Mendelssohn Bartholdy – will set a new
standard.

Among many existing studies of Mendelssohn's music, the most
interesting and approachable include Greg Vitercik, *The Early Works of
Felix Mendelssohn: A Study in the Romantic Sonata Style* (Philadelphia,
1992), R. Larry Todd, *Mendelssohn: The Hebrides and Other Overtures*, in the

series Cambridge Music Handbooks (Cambridge, 1993), and John Horner, *Mendelssohn's Chamber Music*, in the series BBC Music Guides (London, 1972). Though far afield of the standard concert repertory, R. Larry Todd's *Mendelssohn's Musical Education: A Study and Edition of his Exercises in Composition* (Cambridge, 1983) represents a thoughtful handling of a uniquely interesting manuscript.

Apart from the bibliography at the end of the *New Grove Dictionary* article named above, those seeking closer acquaintance with the enormous body of scholarship that has grown up around Mendelssohn and his work should consult John Michael Cooper, *Felix Mendelssohn: A Guide to Research* (New York, 1999).

Illustrations are indicated by an 'i' after the page number. The abbreviation 'M' refers to the surname Mendelssohn. The abbreviation 'FM' refers to Felix Mendelssohn. Basic information on FM may be found under the headings 'Mendelssohn, Felix' and 'Mendelssohn , Felix, as musician'. Additional information on FM may be found under the headings: 'art, FM and', 'Berlin, FM in, 1840–1844', 'composing', 'compositions', 'compositions, reception of', 'conducting', 'early life', 'health', 'performing', 'reception, of FM', 'travels' and 'views'.